THE MODERN ACTOR

MICHAEL BILLINGTON

The
Modern
Actor

HAMISH HAMILTON
LONDON

First published in Great Britain, 1973
by Hamish Hamilton Ltd
90 Great Russell Street London WC 1

Copyright © 1973 by Michael Billington

SBN 241 02094 8

PRINTED IN GREAT BRITAIN BY
T. & A. CONSTABLE LTD., EDINBURGH

Contents

List of Illustrations

Acknowledgements

I SHOULD like to thank a number of people but for whose advice, assistance and inspiration this book would have remained only an embryo.

Hugh Cruttwell who generously threw open the doors of the Royal Academy of Dramatic Art to me; Yat Malmgren and Christopher Fettes who showed a similar hospitality at the Drama Centre; Gillian Diamond, Miriam Brickman and Martin Case who explained the mysteries of casting to me; Hugh Jenkins, M.P., Peter Plouviez, Assistant General Secretary of Equity, and Cary Ellison of the *Spotlight* organisation who gave me a lot of insight into the industrial aspects of the acting profession; Anna Carteret, Susan Hampshire and Richard Jackson who generously submitted to interview and gave me a lot of ideas and information; Iain Mackintosh of Prospect Productions and Craig MacDonald at the National Theatre who gave me a good deal of help with the illustrations; Faber and Faber for permission to reproduce extracts from *Look Back In Anger* and Methuen for permission to reproduce passages from *The Caretaker* and *H*; the three Arts Editors who employed me while this book was being written, John Lawrence and John Higgins at *The Times* and Michael McNay at *The Guardian*, who have all shown much kindness; my friend Keith Roberts who encouraged me to write a book in the first place; Christopher Sinclair-Stevenson at Hamish Hamilton Ltd who has shown a patience and forbearance that would put Grizelda to shame; and Jeanine Bradlaugh who not only assisted with the compilation of the photographs but who helped in other ways too numerous to mention.

MICHAEL BILLINGTON

Preface

I HAVE written this book for a number of reasons. For a start because I feel the modern actor gets a raw deal in comparison with the writer or director: the excellence of his work is all too often taken for granted and given too little attention by critics in all media. This book is partly an attempt to redress a necessary balance and to pay tribute to an art in which I rejoice. A second reason for writing it is that I feel the acting profession to be in a state of crisis: waste, muddle and chaos characterise our entertainment industry and this book hopefully offers a few pointers to ways in which the actor's talents, at least, might be more sensibly nurtured. And a third reason for writing it is that, like all journalists, I occasionally want to escape from the pressures of the nightly deadline.

Writing a first book is, of course, like experiencing a first love affair: a sense of exhilaration is balanced by a feeling that one will be able to rectify some of one's more grievous mistakes on another occasion. But I offer this book as a sincere expression of an ungovernable concern about the acting profession; and I apologise in advance to anyone on whose feelings it unwittingly tramples. After all, some of my best friends are actors.

Three final points. I have ranged over theatre, cinema and television partly because I have written professionally about all three and, more importantly, because these days no actor is confined to any one medium. I have also not

restricted myself entirely to British actors, since movies and
television particularly cross national frontiers. And I have
said a good deal about the conditions facing the actor since
these inevitably impinge on his work. This cannot, of
course, be an exhaustive study of the modern actor: it is a
partial, but I hope provocative, despatch from one who
spends a good deal of his time up at the front line.

And now let battle commence. . . .

WILLINGLY TO SCHOOL

Hey diddle-de-dee
An actor's life for me
(*Old Music-Hall Song*)

EVERYONE wants to act. Despite all Equity's propaganda about the overcrowded state of the profession, despite any number of chilling statistics about the high rate of unemployment, people still yearn to become professional mummers. The trouble is, as William Archer pointed out nearly a century ago, 'we are all actors in rudiment, the tendency to imitation being part of the mechanism of animated nature'. And if, he went on, the stage is besieged with incompetent aspirants, it is because the general tendency is easily mistaken for the special aptitude.

Today, however, we face the additional problem that we live in a world where the actor has become part of the new aristocracy. If he is a success in films as well as theatre, he will find his opinion sought on a variety of topics ranging from politics to birth control; he will be endlessly interviewed in both the posh and the popular papers; he will find his income and his sex life becoming public property and an inflated value probably being set on both. No matter that 75 per cent of the acting profession is at any one time unemployed, that Equity may take as many as 2,300 new members in a year, that some drama schools receive as many as 1,000 applications a term from would-be students: the myth that acting is the surest road to fame and riches still endures.

Entry into this hopelessly disorganised, ludicrously over-crowded heartbreak profession can come in one of several ways: via drama school or University, through achieving fame in another branch of the entertainment industry or through joining a humble repertory company as a student ASM. For the majority, however, drama school provides the key to the door of this unweeded garden. One immedi-ately has to qualify this, though, by pointing out that while there are perhaps half a dozen schools with enough of a national reputation to attract agents and casting directors, there are countless small-scale local academies which offer homespun diplomas that carry absolutely no weight in the profession. There's many a disenchanted teenager who finds that an honours certificate from Mrs Bracegirdle's School of Speech and Deportment in a Midlands watering-town cuts no ice in the metropolis. Rightly, Equity has made such schools, offering promises but few prospects, one of its chief targets.

The importance of the established drama schools, how-ever, lies not simply in the help they may provide in getting a job. It resides in the fact that they are determining atti-tudes to the art of acting and influencing people's method of work for the rest of their lives. When one hears (as I have) repertory actors pouring scorn on words like 'motivation' and claiming that the people who can talk most seriously about acting are the ones who are least good at it, then one knows that some of this disinclination to take acting too seriously must have stemmed from their initial training. If, as Kenneth Tynan once argued, there is still something Olympic about the British attitude to acting ('If we were to win too many gold medals, we would somehow forfeit our amateur status'), then again the schools must carry a fair share of the responsibility. To be fair to them, however, they do face a serious dilemma. To put it starkly, should they prepare students for the acting profession as it imperfectly exists or should they prepare them for the acting profession as it ideally should be? In short, should training be vocational or inspirational?

At the Royal Academy of Dramatic Art the approach is clear-cut and pragmatic. 'We have no Bible here,' says its Principal, Hugh Cruttwell. 'Neither Stanislavski nor Brecht. We assume that Stanislavski has been absorbed into the mainstream of theatre and doesn't need to be specially taught. We supply vocational training for a profession although we don't sweep all theory to one side, philistinewise. But even if you wanted to instil a particular approach to acting, it would be impractical. One has got eight to twelve directors working here at a time. If you were to teach particular ways and means about the business of acting, you'd find your practice being undermined by the directors. As it is, no two students experience the same directors along the line. There may also be directors working here with whom I'm out of sympathy but whose approach I think the students should learn about. It's a catholic affair.'

His argument is also that, unless you've got a small-scale school, it's not possible to stick to any one theory. As soon as you get a place of any size, then you lose any homogeneity. It's a valid point but I feel he is a bit over-optimistic in his view that Stanislavski has percolated the profession to such an extent that he does not need to be specially taught. And when he says that RADA's new library will provide literature for the students to study acting, I also feel too much of a burden is being placed on their initiative. One has to admit that RADA students often look better-equipped than their contemporaries but, simply because there is no definable theory underpinning their work, one often gets the impression that their technique is stronger than their grasp of character. I would instance a production of *Richard III* I saw put on with third-year students in the late autumn of 1969. The Richard, Stuart Wilson, had an admirable manual expressiveness, physical agility and vocal control that augured well for his future. There was not, however, much indication that he had penetrated deeply behind the lines or worked out the relationship between the character's physical deformity and daemonic instincts.

Judging by the quality of its products (who in recent years include Albert Finney, Peter O'Toole, Alan Bates, Tom Courtenay, Ian Holm and David Warner) RADA's pragmatism certainly pays dividends. And to find out how the approach works in more detail, I spent what apparently was a fairly typical day going to the classes at the Gower Street headquarters. As an outsider the first thing to strike one is the broiler-house nature of the institution. There is a frantic amount of activity going on in a very confined space; classes are often conducted in dark, sunless rooms; and nearly everywhere one is conscious of the noise either of traffic, activity from other classrooms or building operations.

Arriving at ten, one finds work very much in progress and is ushered into a voice class already under way. Four distractingly pretty girls lie prone on the floor doing breathing exercises. 'Fill your lungs and let the air out on the consonant R', cries the gaily-trousered lady teacher. 'Breathe in and attack.' The girls emit a forceful R sound like an air-raid siren, eerily echoed by a male group doing exactly the same exercise next door. The quartet proceed with a vowel-extending exercise on the lines of 'Hoo-Hoo-Hoo, Ho-Ho-Ho, How-How-How, He-He-He'; improve their projection by building up a stage whisper to an imaginary front row into a roof-raising shout; and swing their arms from side to side and bawl what sounds like 'Manay-La-Meney' as if soldiers in some central European country marching towards the front. I am a touch disturbed, however, when they are asked to give a passionate rendition of a polysyllabic Greek word and only after some minutes does it occur to anyone to ask what it means. How, I wonder, can one give a passionate rendering of anything without understanding its meaning or its context? 'Think feeling. . . . Inject some feeling into it,' exhorts the teacher. Yes. But what feeling? I am suddenly reminded of Macready's remark to Lady Pollock that 'no man could teach feeling and to teach the rest without that would only be to engraft his own manner on another'. A girl then gets up and presents an extract from the *Agamemnon*. The sound is strong and powerful but the sense doesn't emerge clearly. I long to stop her and ask her to paraphrase the meaning of the speech. I notice also that when the others get the chance to criticise her they concentrate on the technical deficiencies rather than on any failure to communicate the sense.

I move on to other classes. Upstairs, in a room heavy with the smell of sweat, a lean, angular lady is conducting a Movement Class with drum and stick in hand. She's teaching the pupils how to move across a stage surface with the ease of young Astaires. 'Instead of making an impact on the floor, one's going to glide into the floor,' she explains. They do it as a group and in small units. The boys do it seriously: the girls tend to giggle. Afterwards the teacher tells me that at the time of the kitchen-sink plays there was something of a reaction against movement in the theatre but now people are beginning to realise the importance of bodily control. I recall a remark of Peggy Ashcroft's to me that drama students these days tend to be much more expressive physically than vocally. So when I slink into a Voice Class, I'm encouraged to find the teacher being briskly disparaging about the pupils' work. 'That's a rather cruddy voice,' he tells one student producing a sound heavily stained with nicotine. 'Work on it and go and repent in sackcloth and ashes for that voice you're producing.' There is one particularly memorable exchange with a recalcitrant American student.

'Voice Production,' says the teacher. 'Do you know what I mean?'

'Like Beerbohm Tree,' ventures the pupil insolently.

'No, I want something much more ridiculous than Beerbohm Tree,' replies the teacher.

Presented with a few lines of poetry, the students are also asked to indicate where the voice breaks occur. The interesting thing is that they mostly get them wrong. Since the lines are basically simple ('With eyes upraised as one inspired Pale Melancholy sat retired') I am left wondering if it is their ear or their intelligence that is defective.

In another wing of the building Keith Johnstone, attached to the Royal Court as a playwright and script-reader during the Devine era, is conducting Improvisation Classes. Everywhere else one has a feeling of unremitting Work: here there is a sense of Organised Play and the students correspondingly seem much more alive. They are playing a game in which a boy with his eyes shut has to go on a journey through a tunnel, over a swamp and across a river. The sensations are simulated by his colleagues and at the end, when water is poured over his head and a balloon is burst in his ear, I am reminded of the children's game in which a reference to Nelson's blind eye is accompanied by the finger of a blindfolded child being poked into a hollowed-out orange. The atmosphere is, in fact, very similar to that of a children's party except that afterwards everyone sits round and analyses what they've done. Mr Johnstone then talks about the theory of masks ('The mask is the most powerful

thing ever invented. It's like the H-bomb,' he says somewhat disputably), but what one notices is how the use of
masks has a different effect on everybody. One girl refuses
adamantly to take hers off as if it affords a protective
safety; one boy gets spiritedly over-enthusiastic and I spy
him slipping the mask on before he goes into the next class,
presumably in order to give one of his chums a mild heart-
attack. But, although Mr Johnstone's work may have a
certain intellectual vagueness, it does at least fulfil one
function of teaching: it leaves the students more alert than
when they went in.

Undeniably RADA's empirical approach, as the Macmillan Government used to say of Conservative Freedom,
works. But the question arises of whether a drama school
should be setting standards for the future rather than
following those of the present. Because English actors are,
on the whole, innately suspicious of theory and analysis
('I'm an instinctive actor' is the phrase often used to disguise a distaste for doing one's homework), does it follow
that the schools should be perpetuating this attitude?

One that does not accept this is the Drama Centre in
Chalk Farm. Housed in a rambling, draught-ridden, ingeni-
ously converted Methodist chapel, it was set up in the
autumn of 1963 when a row at the Central School of Speech
and Drama led to the exit of one of its teachers, Yat
Malmgren. A large number of pupils followed him and,
being blacklisted by other schools as a result, determined to
set up their own academy. Entry is restricted to twenty-
five students a year for the Acting Course; ten are taken on
the Student Directors' and Professional Instructors' Courses.
The emphasis is on system and organic development. Mr
Malmgren himself describes it as a very methodical school.
'People say it is a modern thing or a new approach. We are
really very traditional. We see everything we do as an

organic process. The student goes through three years' education. He starts from the simplest possible origins—he goes through an education as a human being.'

In the first term he has lectures on the relation of the theatre to the arts in general. In the next term he studies a specific text and tries 'to get back to the impulse behind the source of creation'. He then becomes involved in a Project (the presentation of the Platonic Dialogues as drama was quoted as an instance) which he then has to mount before his colleagues. In the second year he finds himself engaged in the study, practical and theoretical, of drama from Aristophanes and Roman Comedy through to the development of bourgeois theatre in the nineteenth century and the present day. Plays on which he might find himself working include *Macbeth*, Lope de Vega's *Fuenteovejuna*, Sternheim's *The Underpants*, Chapman's *The Widow's Tears*, Brecht's *The Good Woman of Setzuan* and Beaumarchais' *The Marriage of Figaro*. 'By the end of the second year,' explains Christopher Fettes, the Administrator, 'they understand the whole tradition from classical to modern. Instead of teaching history in the form of lectures, we try to do it in a practical way. We relate everything to the time in which it was created and the world in which it was written. We attempt to get them to re-evaluate a play—to study the conflict between duty and passion in heroic drama, for instance, and to relate it to their own personal problems. When I've taught in Sweden people have said to me, "We don't know how to get students interested in Marivaux or Aristophanes". We believe they have to learn how to find this interest for themselves.'

At the end of the second year the students' progress is examined with great care. Some of them are considered ready to go out into the profession: they have learned all they are likely to learn at drama school. Sixteen of the original twenty-five, however, go into the third year. They then present to the public, including agents and managements, two plays a term. Critics were originally invited but few of them bothered to come and those that did, I am assured, concentrated on niggling details. 'If a hatchet-man writes about a boy as if he were Olivier,' says Christopher Fettes, 'then it can damage him a good deal.' The Drama Centre's system, both methodical and idealistic, seems an admirable one and it has to date produced two particularly remarkable performers in Jack Shepherd (especially good at playing characters trembling on the brink of madness such as John Osborne's Bill Maitland and David Storey's Arnold Middleton) and Sheila Scott-Wilkinson (arguably the best black actress in Britain). What is disturbing, however, is the struggle it has so far had to survive. Drama Schools are not the responsibility of the Arts Council but of the Department of Education and Science and that department's attitude is that, from the educational point of view, they are not worthy of grants. The students are invariably subsidised by local authorities but the schools themselves receive little in the way of external aid. Thus the Drama Centre in its early days had to cope with such depressing obstacles as over-large, draughty class-rooms, inadequate dressing-room accommodation and one lavatory for thirty-five boys.

The gulf between a school like RADA and one like the Drama Centre is enormous. Because of its reputation the former inevitably attracts high-quality students and seems to have a built-in glamour (for instance, the two students who win the Ronson hundred guinea awards for the Academy's most promising actress and actor of the year are invariably photographed by the national dailies drinking celebratory champagne in Hyde Park). The Drama Centre, however, has a lesser quantity of applicants to choose from

(300 as opposed to RADA's 900 or 1,000) and struggles even more strenuously to make ends meet. Yet in both cases the same nagging questions arise.

Is enough done to prepare students for the world outside?

Are too many students being turned out each year in view of the limited opportunities that exist?

Does the potentially brilliant but conceivably awkward individual suffer because of the need to get through a crowded syllabus and because the teachers owe just as great an obligation to the subsidised, middling-talented student?

The problem of preparation for the acting profession is a complex one. Too obsessive a concern with vocational training leads to a battery-hen system; too minimal a concern puts the student at a commercial disadvantage. But what amazes me is the relative indifference of drama school teachers to some of the specialised demands of the profession—in particular, camera acting. A recent Equity survey suggested that the average actor spends seventeen weeks a year working in the theatre and nineteen days in front of a camera: sufficient, I should have thought, to lead to courses in television and cinema work. Yet at RADA Hugh Cruttwell told me they were forced to abandon television work because of the cost. 'We used to get the students into the studio as a career exercise. We would have a play directed for the stage and get a TV director in and convert it into a television production. We stopped doing this because the cost is prohibitive. A day at the Granville Studios in Fulham cost £300. We abandoned it for those reasons. It seemed a minimal gesture anyway. As it is, actors are thrown in at the deep end with a TV studio and have to digest things quickly. If an actor knows how to use his body properly, he'll be all right. Ideally more time would be devoted to television and films but this is only a marginal extension of the basic work.' At the Drama Centre Christopher Fettes said likewise that camera-acting was largely a matter of different scale and projection. 'In doing television, the Royal Court or films, it's chiefly a difference of scale. The illusion of acting and doing something to someone is the same wherever you are.' Ironically, it's the less august institutions that often seem to take television work more seriously. For instance, a drama course currently being run at the South Warwickshire College of Further Education in Stratford has allowed for a studio suitable for television work. Students preparing to be teachers thus have better facilities than students going into the theatre. Moreover the often rather low standard of acting to be found in television becomes explicable when one learns that the drama schools lack either the time or inclination to take it seriously.

The second question—as to whether drama schools are turning out too many students—is still more serious. It is also perennially topical. In 1924 Constantin Stanislavski wrote in *My Life in Art* 'Without talent or ability one must not go on the stage. In our organised schools of dramatic art today it is not so. What they need is a certain quantity of paying pupils. And not everyone who can pay has talent or can hope to become an artist.'

Much the same situation applies in Britain today. At RADA Hugh Cruttwell admitted that he's fighting the idea that the Academy is a wealthy institution; that in fact the staff have to subsidise the school by accepting low salaries; and that in every intake of twenty-seven people there are bound to be some who are there just to make up the numbers. ('There just aren't twenty-seven really first-rate actors every two terms. Olivier says there is plenty of talent about but not enough skill. I would say there is too much competence but not enough flair'.) And if RADA, with its 1,000 applicants a year, has to take in a certain number of students to help balance the books, one can well imagine what the situation is like in less distinguished academies. Not surprisingly, therefore, drama schools almost invariably oppose any restriction of entry into the acting profession in order to protect their own future. However Equity, the actors' trade union, wants severely to limit the number of people coming into acting every year; and simply on numerical grounds it has a very strong case. In 1969 alone some 2,300 new members joined the Union. Yet net membership went up by only 1,000 which means that 1,300 actors must have given up the profession. Public money is obviously being wasted on training people for work that simply does not exist. And talent is also being wasted in that nothing saps an actor's self-confidence more surely than long and futile periods of unemployment.

The interesting thing about the arguments for and against controlling entry into the acting profession is that they have become much more public over the years. In 1962, for instance, one can find a long correspondence about the pros and cons of restricted entry being conducted in the correspondence columns of *The Stage*, the profession's own weekly newspaper. 'Regulation implies that artistic talent can be grown and controlled in the way one grows turnips,' a letter-writer would state one week. Back would come the reply the next week: 'The plain fact of the matter is, of course, that regulated entry is not possible.' By 1970, however, the crisis had become so acute that it was being debated in the correspondence columns of *The Times* as well as those of *The Stage*. Indeed between April 4, 1970, and April 25 one can find a succession of *Times* letters that put the whole situation in a nutshell.

The arguments for some restriction on entry, advanced by the President and General Secretary of Equity and several members of the Union, were basically these: that there was

currently far too little work and far too many actors; that
the situation was getting worse rather than better; that as
long as the acting profession had such a large labour force
there would be low wages and appalling backstage conditions; that if everyone who wanted to act had the right
to pursue his chosen profession, then these islands would
soon be populated largely by actors whose only possible
audience would be unemployed actors. On the other side
Professor H. G. Johnson of the London School of Economics
argued that 'restriction of entry into the profession would
bolster the efforts of its members to raise their wages at the
expense of the theatregoing public, restrict the freedom of
opportunity of aspiring actors and actresses and give undue power to whoever controlled entry'. And Richard
O'Donoghue, Administrator-Registrar of RADA, put what
is basically the drama school case very clearly and cogently.
He claimed that the stage had now become 'respectable';
that the use of drama in education was officially advocated;
and that therefore there was a positive encouragement
during formative years of a mimetic impulse which in the
past might not have been allowed to survive. 'Has then,' he
enquired, 'the individual actor a right to pursue his art as a
means of livelihood? It has never been suggested that there
are too many writers or that those who do not belong to
the Society of Authors should not be allowed to write
books. Similarly no actor should be barred from drawing an
audience or finding employment if he can.'

The O'Donoghue line that actors should be allowed to
act just as writers should be allowed to write is full of logical
flaws. For one thing a writer does not undergo an expensive, three-year subsidised training programme before being
launched into his profession; for another no one could say,
with publishers still putting out upwards of 20,000 titles
a year, that the opportunities to get into print are as

severely limited as an actor's opportunities for appearing
on the boards or in front of a camera; and a writer can
practise his craft in isolation whereas an actor must necessarily be part of a group. Admittedly Professor Johnson's
thesis that a restriction in the number of actors would lead
to a raising of the minimum fees and a consequent rise in
ticket prices is economically accurate; but to argue from
this that you should have a large pool of unemployed actors
to keep prices and wages artificially low is to return to a
nineteenth-century cheap labour principle that surely went
out when children stopped sweeping chimneys and working
fourteen hours a day in blacking factories. I have also little
sympathy with the argument advanced by Sir Bernard
Miles (*Evening Standard*, January 15, 1970) that it does
actors no great harm to be out of work periodically because
it brings them into contact with other people. 'Everything
an actor touches is enriching to his work', claimed Sir
Bernard, be it office-work or domestic cleaning. Admittedly
nothing can be more destructive to an actor than mixing
only with other actors. At the same time, having myself
once been a temporary office-worker in London, I can
vouch for the fact that employers regard actors with a good
deal of suspicion (chiefly because they're likely to disappear
the second they find a job) and that actors often regard
anything that takes them away from their true craft with
a certain justifiable resentment.

If entry into the acting profession is to be operated
rationally and sensibly, the only possible solution is severely
to restrict the number of students accepted for formal
training; and that means rationing the number of drama
schools. At the moment the situation is appalling. Anyone
can set up a drama school provided the building has enough
lavatories and fire escapes to get planning permission.
There is no one to determine whether or not such a school

is necessary; no one to say whether standards are adequate; no one to determine whether or not the training is in any way related to the needs of the acting profession. There is even a terrifying shortage of facts about the number of schools in existence. In December 1969 the Equity Council invited representatives of a number of interested parties (including the Department of Education and Science, the Arts Council, the Council of Repertory Theatres) to their Harley Street headquarters to discuss the situation. It emerged that no one, including the Government, had any precise facts about the number of schools claiming to provide training or about the number of students pouring out every year.

In order to bring some kind of order out of the existing muddle and chaos, it seems to me the following steps should be taken:

(1) Establish a permanent, centralised body to exercise control over the drama school situation. Representatives of the Arts Council, Equity, the Department of Education and Science, the Council of Repertory Theatres, the Society of West End Theatre Managers, the BBC and Independent Television and film corporations such as MGM-EMI should form a committee with the power to grant a licence to drama schools—and to revoke the licence if the schools do not meet certain requirements.

(2) Licences should be granted to new drama schools only if they are attached to a specific theatre (as in the case of the Bristol Old Vic Drama School) or where it can be established there is no alternative acting academy within a reasonable distance; only if all members of the staff have a minimum of five years' experience in the professional theatre; only if they make provision for training in the art of camera-acting as well as that of stage-acting.

(3) Subject all drama schools to annual inspection by

the central authority to establish that their facilities are being adapted to suit the changing conditions of the profession.

(4) Oblige all schools to keep records of the careers of all their former pupils. If, over a period of years, it is shown that the degree of unemployment amongst their pupils is consistently and substantially higher than the national average, then their licence should be withdrawn.

(5) Make the provision of grants by local authorities to incipient students much tougher. This could be done through the local authority seeking the help of its nearest professional theatre before deciding to make a grant and putting the director of the theatre on its selection panel. Thus the potential student would have to convince not just the local butcher or baker but also the people working in the theatre that his training would not be wasted.

These suggestions may appear somewhat drastic but at a time when large amounts of public money are being spent on vocational courses that increasingly seem not to be followed by a vocation, they are a matter of urgent necessity.

Going back to my original questions—Is enough done to prepare students for the profession they are about to enter? Emphatically not. Are too many students turned out each year by the schools in view of the limited opportunities available? Emphatically yes. And my third query is whether the obligation to be fair to everybody (in terms, for instance, of casting for public productions) means that particularly talented individuals suffer. In fact, does the need to get a large number of students through a crowded syllabus mean that discipline becomes more important than talent? In a BBC 2 television interview Nicol Williamson made the point that there is discipline and self-discipline; that as a drama school student in Birmingham he was unpopular because he believed he knew best, because he wanted to apply the discipline to himself rather than have it imposed from outside. What response would such an attitude meet with today? At RADA Hugh Cruttwell says he would never turn down a Nicol Williamson because he was difficult to deal with. But he says his greatest problem is to dispel the idea the students have that they are competing with one another. 'They are not. But it's very hard to persuade them of this. At the moment it's too nerve-racking and worrying a process for the students. All one really wants to set up are the right conditions for acting.' The simple fact is, of course, that students are at the end of their course obliged to compete with one another for the attention of agents and casting directors; and that many of them feel aggrieved that they are signed up just because they happen to be well-cast on the particular night when someone of importance is out front. Acting, as everyone knows, is a group affair; but the brute truth is that in the slightly artificial atmosphere of an end-of-term shop-window production, a high degree of personal salesmanship is necessary.

Christopher Fettes at the Drama Centre was more adamant than Hugh Cruttwell about the need for group loyalty both in training and in actual performance. 'If a person had super-abundant talent and that person was undisciplinable, then that person would be asked to go. Early on people realise that discipline is an essential part of talent. Acting is not a business of doing a thing once beautifully. It is a case of repeating. An artist is privileged in that he knows there's an alternative to a repressive external discipline. In a drama school the discipline liberates you.' Does a conflict never arise, though, between the demands of the individual and the group? 'If the idea got abroad that the group was designed to break down the individuality of the pupils, it would be completely wrong. What constitutes a group is a common vision. But, within that common vision, the greatest possible individuality is still necessary.'

Thus a drama school confronts one with a basic paradox of the acting profession: that the structure of the whole entertainment industry forces the actor to be competitive, self-absorbed and even slightly ruthless in the pursuit of his own ends, but that the art of acting itself requires him to be alive to the feelings of others and capable of subordinating himself to the demands of an ensemble. It is only fair to say, however, that while student actors do often give self-advertising performances, they are also capable of putting the group first. Thus I have seen at RADA a stunning version of *Oedipus Rex* in which the actors were virtually unidentifiable as they were hidden behind huge, primitive masks; at the Central School of Speech and Drama an end-of-course production of *Guys and Dolls* in which the majority of the aspiring young actresses finished their student career as Hot Box Girls and Salvation Army banner-carriers; and a production of Gorki's *The Lower Depths* at the London Academy of Music and Dramatic Art in which nearly all the young cast had to play about three times their normal age. Ironically enough, if more of the agents and casting directors actually invited to drama school productions came (one school claims that only 10 per cent of the 250 regularly circularised ever turn up) there might be rather less group feeling than there is now.

Do the drama schools do a good job? Up to a point, yes. London's big five (RADA, Central, LAMDA, the Guildhall School of Music and Dramatic Art, the Webber-Douglas School) all have a character of their own, often mount very good productions and offer a reasonable after-care service— Central, for instance, holds an audition session in a West End theatre to which agents and managers are invited, and many principals and teachers write personally to provincial managers about particular students. In so far as their function is to provide a basic tuition in return for a fee, the main London schools give value for money. But if one looks to a drama school to instil a philosophy of theatre, to provide some kind of inspirational training, even to change the theatre by turning out a brand of student who will question the structure of the whole industry, then I would say they often fall alarmingly short. Obviously their work must be geared to the profession with which they are dealing; but the danger in turning out students capable of playing anything from Aeschylus to provincial panto-mime is that one loses all sense of missionary zeal. Pragma-tism has its place. However I would still like to see more schools that were built around a hard core of idealism and that had some vision of the kind of theatre they would hope, in the best of all possible worlds, to be serving.

2

THE MIDDLE MEN

Two ulcers were walking down Hollywood Boulevard. One said to the other: 'You're not looking well'. The other replied: 'Well would you, if you had an agent?'

(Antique showbiz joke)

'He looks as if he's stepped straight out of a Damon Runyon story. I would never be surprised to see him produce a machine gun from his violin case.'

(One agent of another)

THE actor just leaving drama school finds himself suddenly at large in an entertainment jungle in which strange beasts with a voracious appetite hungrily roam. These are popularly known as agents. Having netted one of these beasts for himself—or alternatively having been swallowed up by one —he will then find himself at the mercy of a little-known body of people whose hearts are not quite as big as their card-index systems and who may be crucial in determining whether he stays in the jungle or decides to look for greener and lusher pastures elsewhere. These are sometimes known as Casting Directors. Agents and Casting Directors both tend to shy away from the glare of publicity; but I decided it would be no bad thing to probe the secrets of their strange, twilit crafts.

The first question to be asked about agents is: Who needs them? They are seemingly an established part of the industry; indeed there are over 800 of them licensed with the Greater London Council alone. They act as intermediaries between actors and employers. They are to be found wherever one looks in the entertainment scene—at first nights and film premières, at television studios and showbiz soirées. Yet the Royal Court's very alert and intelligent Casting Director, Gillian Diamond, suggested to me that their function could be taken over by Equity, and by Spotlight (a multi-purpose organisation that publishes a twice-yearly actors' directory and also acts as a clearing-house for information about artists' whereabouts). This is a very attractive proposition on the surface since it would help to tidy up a chaotic and disorganised pro-fession. It would also eradicate the middle man grubbing after his 10 per cent. The trouble is that neither of the parties concerned greets the idea with overwhelming enthusiasm.

'We've tended to shy away', says Peter Plouviez, Assistant General Secretary of Equity, 'from that kind of job mainly because it's difficult for a Union when it finds itself in that kind of employer-agent capacity. We might be able to help in relation to the employment of people at the minimum rate: walk-ons, for instance, are paid at an accepted rate. The television companies could set up a casting department and we could become the agency supplying them. But when you're selling someone to an employer, you stress one client at the expense of another. How can you do this if you're a Union with an obligation to all your members?' Hugh Jenkins, Labour M.P. for Putney and Equity's repre-sentative in the House of Commons, put it even more strongly. 'It's a pernicious idea. Equity must never dis-tinguish between one actor and another. As far as they're concerned, Lord Olivier and a stripper are of equal value.' And although Cary Ellison of Spotlight thinks there are far too many agents and personal managers in the business ('If 200 agents disappeared overnight and 10,000 actors

B

went into the hotel business tomorrow, then the whole entertainment industry would be much refreshed'), he still doesn't wish to see Spotlight usurp the agents' function. 'We've built up a reputation,' he says, 'that is above money.' Which is a boast that not many people in the agency game would care to make.

Accepting for the moment that agents are a necessary evil in a mixed capitalist and socialist economy and that the more complex the entertainment industry becomes, the more value they have in negotiating for their clients, one still comes up against the appalling *quantity* of them: in fact, their profession is no less overcrowded than that of the actors. At the moment all you need to become an agent is a clean financial and criminal record, a fee of £1·05 and an office in a public building. You also have to place an advertisement in *The Stage* for three successive weeks announcing your intention of starting up in business. No qualifications for the job are required. No examination has to be passed. And, provided you don't get up to any financial hanky-panky, your licence will be renewed annually by the GLC. They have the right, in fact, to inspect your books at any time but one agent told me that, in practice, they come to see you shortly after you have set up in business, have a look at copies of your contract letters and accounts and follow through particular payments. Then, if they are satisfied, they leave you alone. But, not surprisingly, such a loosely-organised system leads to all kinds of breakdowns. Thus in September 1970 the Denton De Gray agency, which specialised in extra and walk-on engagements for television, went into voluntary liquidation leaving some £21,000 owing to its clients. The company's assets were insufficient to cover all the monies due and so the clients obtained only a percentage of what was owing to them. Other agents have been known to take commission on minimum-rate jobs and rehearsal money and even on National Insurance benefits. And, if agents are relieved of their licences in London, there is nothing to prevent them setting up shop again outside the GLC area; or even starting up in business under their wives' names in London.

Agents may be necessary. But can't anything be done to block the loopholes in the present law? Hugh Jenkins, in fact, drafted an Agency Bill in 1967 designed to do just this. But it was strenuously opposed by managerial consultants whose representatives in Parliament succeeded in talking it out. The Labour Government then promised to provide additional time for the Bill; but Jenkins was asked by Richard Crossman and John Silkin, the Chief Whip, whether he would allow the two Private Members Bills waiting in the queue behind his to take precedence. As one of them dealt with Abortion Law Reform, he readily agreed on condition that time was provided in the next session. But, as Jenkins rather acidly observes, the then Minister of Labour, Ray Gunter, ratted on the agreement. So his Bill languishes in a Parliamentary limbo: the malpractices of back-street abortionists are, after all, more important than those of Mayfair agents.

What, in fact, could be done to improve the actors' situation *vis-à-vis* agents? One solution (approved by Equity and Jenkins) is the negotiation of a standard agency agreement. At the moment, an actor can be bound to a single agent for an agreed period and can pay a fixed percentage of his earnings in commission. As Hugh Jenkins told me, there is nothing illegal in an agent signing up an actor for life at 40 per cent commission (though any actor who accepted such terms would have to be a born mug). He would like to see a standard contract with an escape clause for dissatisfied actors and a 10 per cent limit on all commission charged. When an agent himself had a financial interest in a show in which his client appeared, no commission would be charged.

I put this to one thriving, small-time agent whose answer was that the agent needed some protection as well as the actor. Protection from what? 'Poaching by bigger agents.' He outlined the case of a well-known film-star whom we shall call Mr X. This agent inherited him when he was young and unknown from an agency he had taken over. He carefully built up this young man's career, took him to see quality plays and films, got him good work. Mr X was then playing in the West End when he was seen by a big movie star, Mr Y. Mr Y liked him, asked him to be in his next picture, but made the condition that he must have the same agent as himself. Mr X agreed and asked to be released from his original contract with his own agent. The latter had no option but to agree and so saw someone else reap the benefit of all the work he had done. I sympathise with the agent concerned. But, in the words of the circus performer who saw his mother-in-law being eaten alive by one of the elephants, that's show business.

I think there is a strong case for a standard agreement to protect actors from the worst kind of middle man; but it is also worth noting that when it last came to a trial of strength between Equity and the agencies, the former won hands down. Thus in the summer of 1970 a number of agents started quietly to raise commission from 10 per cent to as much as 12½ or 15 per cent. Their argument was that their own expenses were drastically rising. One of them publicly calculated the cost of keeping in the theatrical swim over a three-day period: £2·50 to see *Oh, Calcutta*; £10 rail fare to see a new play in the provinces; and £5·50 for an hotel room afterwards, without breakfast. Equity countered by saying that, if expenses for the agent had risen, so had those for the artist, and that agents must try to meet rising costs by negotiating higher fees for their clients or obtaining more work. They also advised all members not to pay any increase in the standard rate of commission and to inform them if any increase was suggested to their clients. Nothing more was heard after that of a higher rate of commission: a heartening instance, in the Old Testament world of entertainment, of Goliath slaying Goliath.

Easily the most disturbing aspect of the present set-up, however, is the closeness of the relationship between certain producing managers and certain agencies. This is a situation to which the Arts Council drew attention in its admirably comprehensive 1970 Theatre Enquiry. Indeed it commissioned a full-scale, thirty-six page analysis by Peter Lowman of the ownership and control of theatres, producing managements and agencies, and of the links that exist between the separate branches of the entertainment industry. The result is a fascinating labyrinthine document that conclusively proves (*a*) that there are strong ties between the production and the agency business, and (*b*) that the three Grade Brothers—Sir Lew, Leslie Grade and Bernard Delfont—have a strong controlling interest in a large slice of the British entertainment industry.

To illustrate this latter point, let me simply mention some of the many pies in which the Grade Brothers have a finger or two. Thus Mr Bernard Delfont is either a director of or has a strong interest in EMI (which in 1970 went into partnership with MGM and the subsidiaries of which include the Associated British Picture Corporation, record companies, agencies and manufacturing concerns), several West End theatres (the Palace, the Prince of Wales, the Comedy), a flourishing restaurant-night-club (the Talk of the Town), and the presentation of summer shows. Meanwhile Sir Lew is Deputy Chairman and Joint Managing

Director of ATV which, since July 1968, has been programme contractor for the Midlands and which either owns
or part-owns eight West End theatres (the Apollo, Drury
Lane, the Globe, Her Majesty's, the Lyric, the Palladium,
the Queen's and the Victoria Palace), several major provincial theatres, record companies, bowling companies, the
franchise for Muzak and the theatrical costumiers, Monty
Bermans. And Leslie Grade runs the Grade Organisation
which, although a subsidiary of EMI since March 1967,
still operates as a separate entity. In fact, it functions both
as a theatrical agency and as a producing company and its
subsidiaries include cinemas, film companies, music and
record publishers.

Does it matter that the Brothers Grade have such a
strong influence on the entertainment scene? They themselves would argue not. 'I like to think,' said brother
Bernard on one occasion, 'that the only monopoly we
have is a monopoly of good will.' Others might think it
arguable whether such a large slice of Britain's theatre,
cinema, television and record industry should be controlled, however benevolently, by three brothers. But the
point at issue is the risk that arises from any connection
existing between a producer and an agent. Let me quote
at length from Section 149 of the Arts Council Report
which dealt with this precise point:

'Dangers at once arise if a producing manager has a
financial stake in an agency for this is plainly a situation
which could be exploited to the disadvantage of an artist.
An agent's duty and loyalty should always be to his client,
to advise him how to advance his career even if this could
lead to disappointment on the part of a management which
had different ideas on this matter. We do not know that
agents in this country transgress this vital principle but it is
possible for an agent linked to a producing management

to put his client's interest second and not first. Moreover, however impeccably the agency is conducted at its top level, a subordinate in the organisation could conceivably act in a detrimental way to the client because he believed it would please his employers even though they might be unaware of action he had taken to pressurise his client. Moreover, the fact that an agency was financed or controlled by a powerful theatre management would be likely to have a bad psychological effect on artists in search of employment for they might have reason to fear, justifiably or not, that they might become pawns in a power game. It is for this reason that we came to the unanimous conclusion that theatre managements should not enter into any kind of commercial association with agents and that agents should be precluded from investing money in theatres or in plays. In the United States this particular vertical association is now prohibited by law and we believe it would be a sound precaution to set up similar legislation in this country.'

Most objective observers would, I think, accept that; and the fact that The Grade Organisation has sold to outsiders many of its agency interests in the last few years would suggest that they agree.

Like most aspects of the theatre the agency game is, of course, a matter of wild extremes. At one end of the scale there is the London International Famous Agency which is situated in Hanover Street, approached via a smoothly operated lift and deep-piled carpet and which employs a large number of delicious-looking secretaries. At the other end lies the small agency where you ascend flights of stairs to reach a sunless room at the top of an inexpensive building. Visiting one of the directors of London International, I was impressed by the aura of good taste and elegance: books by Jerome K. Jerome, Richard Hillary and Compton Mackenzie on the shelves, pleasantly representational paintings on the walls, the tidy, well-arranged desk conveying an impression of order and calm. We talked of the problems of the over-crowded acting profession: he put the case against restricted entry and said that he thought the unemployment problem was somewhat exaggerated. 'I don't think you can look at this profession as if it were the Transport and General Workers Union. I don't know whether the problem is nearly as bad as people say; but if half the people who come into the business are girls, they'll probably leave to get married anyway. I think to dictate in art is very difficult. I'm against any form of dictation.' I quoted the standard actor's argument about organisations like the London International Famous Agency which is that they devote most of their time to the International and the Famous rather than the humbler clients on their books. He agreed there was no problem in looking after people who were well-established. 'For instance,' he said, 'a theatre producer would offer a part to Mick Jagger before an equally talented but unknown actor.' But he added that there was little jealousy amongst the clients even though there were always a dozen people whom one could recommend for any one job. A smaller agent readily confessed to me, however, that there was inevitable jealousy amongst actors competing for the same job. 'Obviously,' he said, 'if I send four people along for a job, that increases the likelihood of one of them getting it, but I would try not to let the others know they were all after one part. What I would try and do is get one an appointment for 2 p.m. and another one at 2.30 p.m. There's nothing worse than actors from the same agency meeting and discovering they've all been after the same part.'

The key question, of course, about any agent is whether or not he puts the need to make his 10 per cent above the interests of his client. He is obviously not in the business purely for his health or to run a philanthropic organisation: he usually has expensive overheads to meet in the form of a West End office and secretarial staff as well as a good deal of travelling and entertaining to do. Is it surprising, therefore, that actors often get pushed into films before they have had adequate stage training, that the possibility of a jack-in-the-box fame in the entertainment world is these days hungrily sought by agents? One top agent denied emphatically to me that agents manipulated actors like puppets or could make them do anything they did not really want to do. He argued that actors generally had control of their own destiny: if they decided, for instance, that for tax reasons they did not want to make any money during a particular year, one had to abide by that decision. This, however, is not the sort of decision that the bulk of Equity's 20,000 members are ever likely to be in a position to take. So I asked a smaller agent, himself earning about £1,500 a year in the way of clear profit, if he ever pushed actors before they were ready. He claimed that he considered only the interests of his client. 'In the long run,' he said, 'It will benefit him and me substantially. Take the case of —— I had to choose between sending him to do small parts at the National and playing a fair-sized part in a Granada serial, *Family At War*. I chose the former because I knew it would help his career much more even if there was less financial reward. The better the actor, the more cautious I am about what he does. I've got quite a few clients, though, who're suitable only for *Crossroads* or *Coronation Street*. But I've got about ten actors I wouldn't give just anything to.'

The main trouble with agents is not that they're unscrupulous or incompetent or wolves in Savile Row clothing (though a few of them are just that) but that there are far too many of them and that their own profession is somewhat disunited. There are three separate agents' organisations (the Agents' Association, the Guild of Independent Theatrical Representatives known to its friends as GOITRE and the Personal Managers Association) and many totally independent practitioners. It would make a lot of sense, it seems to me, if the three existing organisations were merged into one body, thus strengthening the negotiating power of the agents themselves and enabling their profession to speak with one voice on matters of crucial importance; if anti-trust legislation, comparable to that in America, made it legally impossible for anyone to act both as employer and agent in any branch of the entertainment industry; if no one was permitted to practise as an agent until he had worked for a minimum period of three years in some branch of the entertainment business whether as performer, manager or director; and if any agent found guilty of professional malpractice were debarred for life from practising again as an agent.

Of course, actors will always be emotionally dependent on their agent: as guide, philosopher and friend and as alibi, whipping-boy and enemy. On the one hand, there is the attitude summed up by the actor-hero of Michael Blakemore's superb theatrical novel, *The Season*. Depressed, hard-up and very much out of work, he decides that agents' lives consist of two things: 'making money out of the theatre and disguising even from themselves their essential redundancy to it'. On the other hand, there is the old story of the successful actor who comes home one day to find his wife in a state of visible distress.

'What's wrong?' he asks.

'Everything,' she says. 'The children had an accident on the way to school and broke their collar-bones; burglars got in while I was out shopping and stole all my furs, jewels and £5,000 in cash; a water-pipe burst, flooding the whole house; there was a telegram from your mother to say your father died last night of a heart attack; and then to cap it all, your agent burst in here this afternoon in a drunken frenzy and raped me three times on the sofa.'

'Ah hah,' says the actor, his eyes suddenly lighting up. 'Did he leave any messages?'

To move from agents to casting directors requires no great agility since the two professions are totally inter-dependent. As Cary Ellison observed to me, 'It's the casting directors who choose which agents are going to be success-ful'. But, first of all, what is a casting director? Quite simply, the person employed by a theatre, film or tele-vision company to advise on who shall play what, to cope with the flood of applicants from potential employees, to keep any eye open for emerging new talent. In England casting directors are still a relatively new breed. The BBC does not employ them although ITV companies have had them since their inception in 1955. The commercial theatre manages without them but they play a vital role in the work of the subsidised companies. In the cinema they are usually freelances employed by a specific company to deal with a specific film. There is no union or organisation of casting directors. Their names are totally unknown to the general public. Yet their influence is enormous. Someone described them to me as 'monstrous women with pitiful power' (the bulk of them are female), but in fact I found them far from monstrous and their power formidable.

The first myth to be dispelled is that the casting director simply fills in the small parts while the director deals with all the big parts. Gillian Diamond, who at the Royal Court casts for the main productions, the Sunday Night shows and the Theatre Upstairs, admits that she is surprised to find how many lead roles are cast from her suggestions. She sometimes even suggests people who are close friends of the director but who have not been thought of. An instance of her own power is provided by the fact that, when working for the Royal Shakespeare Company, she suggested Glenda Jackson for a role. Before that Miss Jackson had had a tough time spending long periods as a waitress, while out of work, and in the process getting varicose veins which had handicapped her chances of theatrical employment. The rest is common knowledge. Miss Jackson went from strength to strength with the RSC, was given a plum film role by Ken Russell in *Women In Love*, won an Oscar for her performance and is today one of the busiest actresses in Britain. Miriam Brickman, the top casting director in British cinema, confirms that her job carries with it a considerable power and responsibility. She instances *Far From The Madding Crowd*. It was designed, she says, for Julie Christie but the other principal parts were all cast as a result of discussions between herself, the director (John Schlesinger) and the producer (Joseph Janni): thus she had a strong say in the selection of Peter Finch, Alan Bates and Terence Stamp. She also mentions *If* in which all the parts were cast by herself and Lindsay Anderson.

Cary Ellison clinched the point about the power of the casting director when he analysed the crisis that has afflicted the acting profession for some time now: 'It got to the point a few years back when there were the right number of personal managers. They fed the talent to the casting agencies at just the right pace. These personal managers made a lot of money and the people who worked for them decided to branch out on their own. From sixty the number of personal managers grew to 280. Casting directors were absolutely overwhelmed with agents and actors. They put up barriers to keep all these people out—secretaries one couldn't penetrate, phones that were constantly engaged. They'd come to certain agents and say "Is Joe Bloggs free?" and the news was out that a certain part was being cast. In the end only those agents who were in the swim came to be used. In fact, it's the casting departments who really determine which agents are going to survive.' Now who can talk about pitiful power?

Having established that the power is genuine, let us look at casting arrangements in three separate institutions. First, the Royal Court. Situated in a cramped, paper-filled office, Gillian Diamond makes it clear that her job has to be done on a tight budget. Her own salary is undisclosed but she has no secretary and has to rely for help on a £5-a-week student. Every week she and the Court's assistant directors meet to decide who is going to see which productions: 'I used to go everywhere but I'm a little bit older and more choosey now. I prefer to send the assistants. It's partly because of time: if you go to a rep way out of London, it can mean either a whole day out of the office or coming back early in the morning on a milk-train.' Twenty letters a day come into her office from people wanting work—over 5,000 in a year. Once a week she tries to hold general auditions and sees as many people as possible but she admits that this is largely public relations and that very few people are actually cast this way. She says the whole system is ludicrous and that some kind of restricted entry is necessary. The only problem is—who operates it? Because of the overcrowding, she reckons two talents are now required: 'the talent of your talent and the talent of getting yourself on. If there's going to be an overhaul, it's got to be total.' But she is suspicious of the Scandinavian system whereby the only people who are taken on by the profession are the ones who are formally trained: she sees as many people who have not been to drama school as ones who have, and cannot always detect much difference between the two groups.

She makes one suggestion that I hear time and time again and that is endorsed by everyone but Equity: that the Union should churn out some of its dead wood, the people who have not acted for years but who still hold an Equity card. Equity's answer to this is that it's a misconception that their members keep paying their dues despite the fact that they never work. Without wishing to be uncharitable, though, it is not unfair to point out that Equity also has substantial overheads—the Union occupies resplendent premises in Harley Street—and that it needs the revenue that only a large membership can supply. And this is not just my view but also the opinion of Hugh Jenkins, a former Equity Deputy General Secretary.

Do actors regard the theatre (because of its rates of pay) as a poor third to working in films or television? 'Yes,' says Miss Diamond. 'If there is no film or television going, people will consider working here. One learns to accept this minor aggravation. Agents dictate it to actors because of money. There's no real necessity to have agents. If Equity were stronger, it could do the contractual work, and if Spotlight were super-organised, they could look after the availability side. In the last few years, the system's got twice as bad as ever in sheer numbers. People turn up without appointments and write in in ever greater numbers. And, however one chooses people, it's unfair: they either say they were badly directed or hopelessly off-form that night. I would like to see the whole profession sorted out by a body of such actors who'd decide what's going to happen. Their profession is in a mess at the moment and it should be left to them to sort it out. They should do a White Paper on the situation which Equity should organise but not control. Let the actors themselves try and work out what their own priorities are.'

I turned from Gillian Diamond to Miriam Brickman who, between casting sessions, gave me a snack lunch in her bulging Mayfair office-cum-flat. Files, scripts, books, records, the inevitable copies of *Spotlight* filled shelf after shelf and spilled over on to desks and tables as if to symbolise the mounting pressures on the solo casting director. As someone who wields enormous influence and who can determine the actual course of an actor's career, how much of the entertainment available does Miss Brickman manage to see? 'I see less television than anything, mainly because it doesn't give actors enough opportunity to develop in a role. Also the attitude to actors in television is often that they're pieces of machinery. The theatre, however, always makes demands on an actor and gives him a chance to develop a character. I do have periods of touring round the provinces—I'm off to Birmingham tomorrow—but I don't think I do it sufficiently. There comes a time, however, when you simply have to stop looking at plays and films because of saturation.'

Is the whole system, as Gillian Diamond averred, breaking down? 'It hadn't occurred to me but I'm sure it's all too true. Too many people are committed to being actors. But it's such an exciting profession and the people who come into it know the problems and iniquities before they arrive. I acted myself for a while: it's an obsessional business. It's disturbing for me when actors come in here wanting work because they're almost like lunatics and you are in a position to help cure their lunacy. It used to be awful auditioning when I worked at the Court: you'd often see people and think, "Should I tell them they ought not to be actors at all?" But how do you say such a thing? I know one actor who's convinced that the reason he doesn't get work is that he steals scenes from major actors. It isn't true. The real reason is that he's not very good. I tried to tell him this very gently, but it was no good: it made no impact at all because he had forced himself to believe this.'

The hardest age to cast? 'Men from forty-five to fifty-five. We've got a good group of thirtyish actors. We've got the Sirs. But between forty-five and fifty actors become a little set in their ways and it's difficult to get them to break out of their mould. Richard Wattis, for instance, has established a nice line for himself in Richard Wattis parts but I'm told that in the film *Tam Lin* he gets a chance to reveal aspects of his talent we've not seen before. My own system? I can't cope with letters so I don't attempt to. If actors phone me up, then I see them. And I may cast someone without having seen them work. Take a director like John Schlesinger, for instance, who loves improvising with an actor. If I find an actor has a vibration for me, then I can safely suggest him to John. But the whole process of selection is a weird one. Being a member of Equity—that's not a valid evaluation of an actor. And I'm also appalled that a casting director can be selected simply on the grounds that another isn't available. Even if it's a Hammer film, it's a work of art, not a business or an industry.' But what is it that makes people become casting directors in the first place? 'I'm not sure. In my case, it happened accidentally. I've worked in the box office, stage management, on the switchboard. When I was at the Court, the then manager, Pieter Rogers, thought all the actors should be channelled through one person and so I was made casting director. I did it without realising what I'd undertaken. Eventually all the Court's directors gravitated to film-making: Lindsay asked me to cast *This Sporting Life* and then Schlesinger asked me to do *A Kind of Loving*. I can't say I'm drawn to it. I think I was born to be an actress.'

Thirdly, Martin Case who is head of Casting at London Weekend Television. Unlike Miss Diamond and Miss Brickman, he doesn't have to work in an office cluttered with files and records, but there is no door to his working area and only a coloured partition separates him from secretaries and subordinates. It is all very democratic but it has the disadvantage of meaning that telephone conversations from the neighbouring cubicles impinge. Mr Case himself is a large, elegant man in his middle-forties with a long record of theatrical experience behind him, a spell in labour relations with Rediffusion and a fairly bland attitude towards the acting profession's current problems. 'Equity,' he says, 'produces a great many figures but there are a lot of people on their books who don't do much more than extra work. There are also plenty of married women who are part-time actresses. It's not a new situation—too many actors chasing too little work. Things are now only a degree worse than in the past, simply because it's easier for people to get grants, easier for people to get into schools. I can look back over thirty years in the business as an actor and a manager. In my early days there was less work because there was less TV. There was, of course, a flourishing touring theatre then but the growth of television has helped make up for this.'

Mr Case's genial optimism is certainly not shared by Equity. Indeed Ernest Clark, President of Equity, claimed in a letter to *The Times* (April 25, 1970) that 'Television alone provides, at most, half the amount of work which was available in the theatre it has supplanted'. Still, even if Mr Case's view of the state of the profession is a little bit rosy, he does what he can to see as many actors in work as possible. 'The company is very generous with theatre tickets and with the expense of getting to outlying theatres. We get to the local reps like Guildford and Leatherhead

and Greenwich but don't see much in places like Notting-
ham or Northampton. But I like to have a couple of weeks
off in the course of the year to do a tour of the reps. I also
have a strong dialogue with the agents. When you've been
in the business for a number of years, you get to know the
mainstream of actors and what they're like. Agents at
varying intervals send out an availability list which is very
useful. Films are also very helpful to television casting
people. The two-dimensional picture is what we're looking
for: whether an actor looks all right on the screen. *If*, for
instance, was a splendid source for young actors. But
something like *Oh, What a Lovely War* isn't very productive
because one knew all the actors to begin with.'

Like nearly everyone I spoke to connected with the
acting profession, Mr Case denied there was any need to
create a special school for television acting. He agrees that
'television acting is an art all its own' and that it's not
simply theatre acting on a smaller scale. Yet he thinks the
practical obstacles to studying television acting as a
separate art ('How do you decide which ones you're going
to train and which not?') make the idea non-viable. To
which all one can say is that if it is accepted that directors,
set designers and technicians need some specific training to
cope with the particular demands of television, why is it
that actors should be expected to adapt their technique
without any extra-rehearsal guidance?

The three casting directors I spoke to are undeniably
conscientious and proficient; but all admit that, because
of the time-factor, it's difficult to see much of what is
happening outside London. I find this sad. It also reinforces Cary Ellison's view that casting is done, in all media,
from a small pool of actors who are 'in the swim'. He
estimates that there are 15,000 trying hard to get into that
swim. If they have sufficient talent plus determination

plus energy, they will probably succeed. But it is sobering to reflect that casting is left to a group of, at the most, twenty people who cannot know every actor, who cannot be everywhere at once and who are bound to be more interested in the man who is easily available in London and at the end of a phone rather than the conceivably better actor doing a repertory stint in Lincoln or Liverpool. It seems to me another instance of the way the casting system has grown up haphazardly without forethought and is merely adding another element of confusion to an already confusing system. One agent pointed out to me that in certain television companies the casting department is in the hands of a glorified secretary. In one case the casting lady has not set foot inside her local rep in a year: in fact one actor who had been working no more than a mile away from her office for nearly twelve months was summoned for an interview, as soon as he had moved to London, because she had never seen him on the stage. In another instance, the head of casting had for years run his own agency. One is left reflecting that people like this could not even cast an aspersion.

One answer to the problem would be the increased payment of the casting director or even the division of the job into two halves: London and provincial. Just as every paper should have two dramatic critics (one for London, one for the road), just as every agency should have someone employed to tour the provinces, so casting should take cognisance of the revolution that has taken place in the English theatre in the last decade. Brief sallies to the provinces once a year or occasional nightly trips to Birmingham or Bristol scarcely do justice to the fact that acting standards are often just as high out of London as they are in and around the West End. The old days of what the French used to call the *tragédienne de province*, of the mummer good for a lifetime in the sticks, are now happily gone for ever. If the casting system were properly run, if the provinces were decently covered, then this division between mainstream and sidestream actors would probably not exist and much of the resentment and jealousy inside the profession would be lessened.

In the end, of course, what it all comes down to is whether or not we want a theatre that is haphazard, wasteful and fitfully brilliant or one that is sensibly planned. It is the point Matthew Arnold was making forcefully eighty years ago when he quoted a German professor's remark about the English to the effect that we have 'so much genius, so little method'. As Arnold pointed out, where the theatre is concerned, instead of devising a sensible plan of public organisation, 'we gladly took refuge in our favourite doctrines of the mischief of State interference, of the blessedness of leaving every man free to do as he likes, of the impertinence of presuming to check any man's natural taste for the bathos and pressing him to relish the sublime. We left the English theatre to take its chance. Its present impotence is the result.' Admittedly today we accept the necessity for 'State interference' but Arnold's final exhortatory cry is still as chillingly relevant as ever. 'The theatre is irresistible. *Organise the theatre!*'

3

THE ACTOR AS CIVIL SERVANT

'I feel there's something very un-English about the idea of companies.'

(*Young actor*)

THAT famous phrase of Matthew Arnold's about the need to organise the theatre occurs in an essay on 'The French Play in London'. And in the course of it he contrasts the benefits of the French belief in tradition and consistency with the disadvantages of the haphazard and chaotic English approach to the theatre. Then, in a remarkably prophetic passage, he imagines the French actors saying in an undertone as they leave our shores: 'Forget your claptrap and believe that the State, the nation in its collective and corporate character, does well to concern itself about an influence so important to national life and manners as the theatre. Form a company out of the materials ready to your hand in your many good actors or actors of promise. Give them a theatre at the West End. Let them have a grant from your Science and Art Department; let some intelligent and accomplished man, like our friend Mr Piggott, your present Examiner of Plays, be joined to them as Commissioner from the Department, to see that the conditions of the grant are observed.'

In other words, don't just organise the theatre: subsidise it as well. And one of the most heartening things one can say about the English theatre over the last twenty-five

years is that that principle has been accepted. We may have
far too many actors; our system of training may not be
ideal; there may be too many middle men coming between
the actor and his public. But at least the need for subsidy
is no longer a matter of violent public controversy. And
in the Royal Shakespeare Company and the National
Theatre we do have two giant ensembles confronting each
other like twin battleships.

One must not forget, however, the amount of blood,
sweat and prose that has gone into making such a situation possible. Matthew Arnold's essay appeared in 1879.
In 1911 Gordon Craig's *On the Art of the Theatre* drew
attention to the remarkable set of actors he had seen
working at the Moscow Art Theatre: 'Add to these', he
wrote, 'the hundred other actors and actresses who show
promise of forming a powerful and united dramatic force;
and let me tell you they are one and all intelligent, enthusi-
astic about their work, working continuously new plays
each day, new ideas each minute, and with this to go on
you can form for yourself whatever impression you wish.
If such a company could be conjured into existence in
England, Shakespeare again would become a force. As it is,
he is merely a stock-in-trade.' Nearly fifty years later
Kenneth Tynan sounded a similar note when describing the
difficulties confronting M. Julien, the organiser of Paris's
international drama festival. 'How shall he find a group fit
to compete with the French, German and Russian con-
tingents? Where, in the absence of a national playhouse, is
the best to be sought? Must we forever shrink from com-
mitting ourselves to a theatre which should enshrine our
drama, cradle and nourish it, presenting eight times a week
a performance of which we can say to our guests: This is
English acting. This is our style.'

Admittedly even before the formation of the RSC and

the National attempts had been made to create an ensemble in England but the companies concerned never had the necessary permanence or stability. Peggy Ashcroft once told me she felt that the RSC's forebear lay in the Gielgud seasons at the New, the Queen's and the Haymarket during the 1930s and 1940s but, for economic reasons, these could never be repertoire seasons and there was no sense of long-term planning. One also must not forget the pioneering work done by Joan Littlewood at Stratford East with Theatre Workshop in the 1950s. In the absence of any properly subsidised or officially recognised English ensemble, it was in fact Theatre Workshop that represented Britain at M. Julien's festival and scored a palpable hit with productions of *Arden of Feversham* and *Volpone*. During the 1950s Miss Littlewood also reared a remarkable team of actors: Frances Cuka, Dudley Foster, Roy Kinnear, Barbara Windsor, Brian Murphy, Glynn Edwards, Harry H. Corbett, Victor Spinetti amongst them. All boasted a remarkable freedom from that well-bred restraint which was the curse of post-Du Maurier English acting; all looked recognisably like people you might meet in a bus queue; all combined a vaudevillian ability to make contact with an audience with a Brechtian gift for *presenting* a character rather than identifying with it. A company was forged with a vigorous popular style of its own and we have Miss Littlewood to thank for it.

The decisive turning-point, however, in the formation of a large-scale ensemble came with Peter Hall's appointment to the post of director of the Royal Shakespeare Theatre (or Shakespeare Memorial Theatre as it was then known) in 1960. During the preceding decade the theatre had presented a series of glittering seasons in which star actors had played the star roles and companies of considerable merit had been gathered around them: we had seen

Olivier as Macbeth, Malvolio and Titus, Gielgud as Cassius, Angelo and Benedick, Tutin as Viola and Juliet, Ashcroft as Rosalind and Imogen. Rich years; starry seasons; but there was no continuing Stratford style. In any one season one might go from the Caroline gentleness of Mr Hall's own *Twelfth Night*, with its Van Dyck costumes and shimmering gauzes, to a comic-opera *Much Ado* complete with brass bands, frogged smoking-jackets and Napoleonic Dogberry. To some people this was the glory of Stratford; and I distinctly recall one actor, a rugged individualist if ever there was one, saying how enjoyable it was in any one season to work with five different directors on five wildly different productions. There, if ever, spoke the English actor's traditional mistrust of ensemble.

Peter Hall was much exercised by the absence of any tangible Shakespearean tradition when he took over at Stratford and both in print and on the air repeatedly hymned the virtues of an ensemble approach. 'Only a company', he wrote in the *Sunday Times*, 'can provide the necessary correctives against the modern methods which are of little use to Shakespeare. Young actors are taught to be "real", to improvise feelings on a given situation and character—a system which works for understated prose drama but which is confusing in a medium that is not "real" at all but highly artificial and literary. They then find to their horror that they have to act in blank verse and end up by playing Shakespeare like an opera singer giving a true impersonation of *Tosca* with a sublime disregard for the notes.' His declared aim was to produce a style of speaking that had more mind and less feeling, that was 'witty' in an eighteenth-century sense; to use highly selective visual effects that eschewed either total realism or chilly simplicity; to keep a permanent group of actors together; and to open a theatre in London so that actors had a chance to do other classical and modern work.

Inevitably it took time to form the nucleus of a company and to capture a feeling of ensemble rhythm. The first batch of productions, in fact, was as eclectic and starry as anything that had gone before. There was an opening *Two Gentlemen of Verona* that was mildly disastrous. As T. C. Worsley noted, the company was all over the place and contained both well-versed Shakespeareans like Eric Porter with an instinctive feeling for the pentameter and newcomers like Denholm Elliott and Frances Cuka who seemed conspicuously ill at ease both in period dress and period language. Stars also inevitably descended to give appropriately stellar performances: Peter O'Toole's Shylock in an eighteenth-century *Merchant of Venice* was a knockdown piece of heroic acting that might have come out of Stratford at any period. Given Shylock's instinctive racial and religious repugnance for the Christians, O'Toole allowed every step in his development to follow with inexorable logic, in particular establishing that his desire for revenge grew in direct proportion to his disgust at his daughter's behaviour. It was a performance commendably unafraid of the large gesture: at an emotional climax in the scene with Tubal, he took hold of a strand in his green watered-silk gown and, head thrown back in anguish, slowly rent it as if to externalise his erupting emotion. Inevitably the performance attracted superlatives and film companies and it was not long before O'Toole had signed a contract with Sam Spiegel to play Lawrence. In fact, during that first season at Stratford and the Aldwych it was hard to see much evidence of unified style. The one actor perhaps to emerge from that period as a pillar of the company was Eric Porter: as Malvolio, Ulysses, Leontes, Ferdinand in *The Duchess of Malfi*, Becket and Buckingham, he seemed to embody Hall's idea of a 'witty' approach to the verse. He was capable of disentangling the most complex lines of poetry to make the sense manifest; displayed a vocal precision that made many of his colleagues sound strangled or muffled; and exuded a gravitas that was always specific and unrhetorical. But, Porter aside, the company still seemed to be full of stars in their courses and satellites dutifully in attendance.

Hall's policy only really began to take effect in the 1962-3 season. One began to see actors like Ian Holm and Ian Richardson progressing from small parts to leads (Richardson played the Prince of Aragon in 1960, Oberon in 1962; Holm played Lorenzo in 1960 and Troilus in 1962). One noticed an elimination of painted scenery and an exploitation of new materials which reached its culmination in *The Wars of the Roses* with its steel and burnished copper. And the attention to meaning rather than word-music slowly began to pay dividends. Perhaps the precise turning-point came in 1962 when, because of Scofield's ill-health, the Peter Brook *Lear* had to be postponed. A production had to be arranged at short notice that would fill the gap and not take undue preparation: *The Comedy of Errors* was decided upon and the result was a miracle of ensemble work. At the beginning the actors, agile as greyhounds, bounded on to a steeply-raked stage clad in their black rehearsal gear. What followed was a spring-heeled and deft reworking of the play based not on scenic extravagance, funny noses or arch asides, but simply on adherence to the text and well-timed business. It has the sort of internal consistency and physical suppleness that no *ad hoc* group could have accomplished in three weeks: as Kenneth Tynan noted, almost for the first time in our theatrical history it was possible to talk of a company style.

The difficulty with any such style is knowing how to

keep it fresh and flexible enough to accommodate actors, directors and designers of varied temperaments and tastes. It must never be an end in itself, a Procrustean bed which every production must be made to fit. Nor must it be a straitjacket denying the possiblity of fresh exploration. Hall during the 1960s managed to keep the style fresh through allowing actors to work on both classic and modern plays, through the occasional importation of directors like John Schlesinger and William Gaskill who were totally new to the company, and through his own inspirational guidance. The problem that he did not solve was, however, a cardinal one. Having collected a company, how does one keep it together? Clearly one cannot yet do it in England through long-term contracts: at one stage Hall did suggest that five-year contracts might be issued but the actors, bred in a system of casual labour, were extremely nervous of anything so binding. So artists have been kept on a loose rein with a good many of the RSC's contracted players absenting themselves for long periods in order to pursue personally profitable careers in films. David Warner is a classic instance of a Hall-trained player more or less unknown until offered the part of Henry VI in *The Wars of the Roses* in 1963. From there he graduated to Richard II in 1964, Hamlet in 1965 and the inevitable film offers thereafter. Likewise, Diana Rigg left after playing Cordelia to go into the black leather world of *The Avengers*, was briefly tempted back to play Viola and is now a member of the National Theatre. Peter Hall turned the RSC into a marvellous talent-factory as well as a great company; but it is the movies that have benefited from many of the risks he took.

Allied to the problem of keeping a company together is that of ensuring that everyone in it is fully occupied. At Stratford the problem is especially acute since the actors are confined for nine months to a town that, whatever its charms for the casual visitor, offers precious few diversions for the metropolitan mummer. Peter Hall tried to solve the problem through the setting up of a studio under Michel St Denis but, when the finances grew meagre, this became a luxury the company could not afford. Theatregoround, the RSC's travelling unit taking portable productions to schools, colleges and institutions, has also done useful work in giving members of the RSC a sense of belonging. However, Trevor Nunn, who succeeded Peter Hall in 1969, has tackled the problem a different way: by slimming the company so that walk-ons, spear carriers and supers as such no longer exist. Everyone is a speaking member of the company; and lead actors in one production may turn up in minor roles in the next. Clearly this means a great financial saving at a time of general belt-tightening. It also rescues actors from the humiliating position of spending nine months by the Avon with nothing more than an occasional 'Aye, my lord' to utter from the stage. The snag of a slimline ensemble is that there are occasions when Shakespeare cries out for numbers, for sheer accumulation of bodies: witness the 1970 *Measure for Measure* in which Sebastian Shaw's Duke returned from supposed exile to be greeted not by a welcoming throng but by a scanty crowd which, like the Parliamentary Liberal Party, could have been comfortably accommodated in a couple of taxis.

Admitting that the RSC has done some astonishing work in the 1960s—Brook's *Lear* and *A Midsummer Night's Dream*, the Hall-Barton *Wars of the Roses*, Nunn's *Revenger's Tragedy*, Barton's *Troilus and Cressida* and *Twelfth Night*—one might ask what the limitations of the current style are. What are the excitements it does *not* give us? The most obvious, of course, is the excitement of the large-scale, grand-slam heroic performance: in a phrase, great acting.

'The business of great acting,' wrote Agate, 'is to raise the spectator above himself, to intoxicate him so that he is no longer himself but is raised to a power of appreciation undreamed of in his sober senses. In this way the ecstasy in the artist speaks to the ecstasy which is in all of us.' To be honest, this ecstasy has not been felt all that often at Stratford or the Aldwych since 1960. And significantly the two younger actors most capable of inducing that degree of ecstasy—Ian McKellen and Nicol Williamson— have preferred to remain outside the bastions of the big ensembles (although Williamson was seen in the RSC's experimental season at the Arts in 1962). This is not, I think, because either Peter Hall or Trevor Nunn has any distaste for great acting—indeed Nunn tried to persuade McKellen to join the RSC in 1969. It has more to do with the fact that there is an inevitable tension between the lone heroic performer and the demands of a company style. Get a great actor to play Hamlet with an *ad hoc* company and that production will take its tone from his temperamental bias: get a great actor to play Hamlet with a permanent company and he will inevitably have to relate his style to the existing manner of the company.

The most obvious instance of this tension between the individual and the ensemble is provided, I suppose, by Paul Scofield. Throughout the 1960s he did some excellent work with the RSC but there was a manifest and growing conflict between his idiosyncratic, mannered and riveting style of speech and the trend towards a greater simplicity and clarity in the company style. When he played Lear in 1962 this tension did not arise, partly because the RSC style was only just forming and partly because his own performance coincided perfectly with Brook's overall conception. The production was built around several logical, firmly anchored ideas. Firstly that, in Brook's words, 'Lear is not feeble but a strong old man, that he isn't pathetic and sentimental but hard, and obstinate, powerful and often wrong'. The assumption also was that Goneril and Regan were not a pair of evil Ugly Sisters but two brutally logical women who always managed to find some justification for the incidents building up to the final cruelties. And lastly Brook brought out the double-decker nature of the tragedy, the fact that the Gloucester-Edgar-Edmund sub-plot has immense tragic stature of its own. Some people thought Brook scaled down the play: in fact he provided an atmosphere of moral neutrality in which we had the chance to re-assess familiar actions. Scofield's Lear, arrogant, choleric and mercurial, fitted into this perfectly. In the early scenes he used a rough, gravelly voice throwing out words and phrases like the unexpected blows of a boxer; the first intimation of madness came in a beautifully poised scene with the Fool, presented simply as a conversation between two ageing figures seated side by side on a bench; the storm scene was not the usual unequal competition between the actors and the off-stage effects but a chilling assertion of human defiance; and the final scenes gained their pathos not from the fall of some Stonehenge pillar but from the fact that an errant, hot-tempered man had suffered excess punishment for his vices. 'He hates him that would upon the rack of this *tough* world stretch him out longer', seemed an accurate description of the bleak, godless universe in which this Lear suffered and repined.

Scofield's Stratford Timon in 1965 also harmonised perfectly with the production, conceivably because the director, John Schlesinger, was an RSC newcomer and made little attempt to relate the play to the prevailing Stratford style. The first half had the right riotous splendour and the great scenes of bogus conviviality came resound-ingly off; and Schlesinger took care to give every incident a precise social context. Thus, when Timon's servant came seeking money for his master in return for past favours, Ventidius was amorously engaged with his whore, Lucius was having a shampoo and manicure at the barber's and Lucullus made a very untentative pass at the suppliant boy. Scofield was excellent in the first half, declining from a sunny mellifluousness to an unhinged vengefulness with impeccable logic. But he came into his incomparable own in the second half with Timon's misanthropic tirades. With his broken phrasing and unresolved cadences he gave the hymns of hatred a skilfully varied intensity; when he forced Alcibiades' two whores to kiss there was not simply an instinctive physical disgust but also a ferocious logic about his demonstration to Apemantus that every beast is the prey of a stronger creature, and he confronted death ('Then, Timon, presently prepare thy grave') with a resigned, monastic simplicity. As Irving Wardle said, his way of handling verse often suggests a man struggling to lift a heavy weight or being carried along by its momentum: and here that alternation between intense pressure and sudden physical release was beautifully and exactly employed.

The first sign of a gulf between the star and the company only really became apparent the following year in *The Government Inspector* at the Aldwych. Deeply influenced by the Moscow Art Theatre's production of *Dead Souls*, Peter Hall directed the play as an outright comedy of humours peopled by thunderous grotesques. The caricatures were not as carefully individualised as in the Moscow Arts production but the production still had a rich comic texture: in particular the drunk scene, with hordes of people squeezed into a single room, and tripping endlessly over each other's feet, was extremely funny. In the midst of this

hurly-burly was Scofield's Khlestakov, the government
clerk from St Petersburg mistaken for an important official
and played here as a fantasticated poseur every bit as stupid
as his victims. His accent was incredible. Penelope Gilliatt,
slightly dazed, summed it up as a blend of Weybridge,
Birmingham, a lot of sermons and the girl who recorded
the speaking-clock on the telephone. Others detected crisp
Sandhurst tones, Parisian affectation and a wild parody of
American Method acting. And gesture was every bit as
extravagant as voice: Scofield was constantly essaying flut-
tering hand-movements briskly sawn off because of some
intrusive piece of furniture. The performance provided a
classic study of the affectations of pseudo-genteelism, oddly
reminiscent of Olivier's Malvolio, another social upstart
constantly betrayed by his Cockney barrow-boy vowel
sounds and his uncertainty as to whether you pronounced
'slough' as if it were 'sluff' or the name of a town in Bucks
county. The trouble with Scofield's performance, however,
was that it was at odds with the play—about an impostor
who is sharper-witted than the provincial townsfolk—and
that it stood out from the rest of the company like a
Gentile at a *barmitzvah*. The real rift, however, came in
Peter Hall's ill-fated *Macbeth* where the production was
angled towards a Christian interpretation of the play and
Scofield's vocally eccentric performance seemed to be
pulling in a different direction. The ideas governing Peter
Hall's production would probably have emerged more
cleanly with a lesser actor: Scofield's performance, however,
needed to have a production mounted round it to accommodate its idiosyncrasies. Not long after this Scofield
resigned from the artistic direction of the company apparently because of differences with Peter Hall over the production and a certain unease about the prospect of filming
it. And after a year working with the National as both

actor and Associate Director he is once more a freelance moving between screen and stage with his own uniquely haggard distinction.

But even if there is sometimes a tension between the style of an individual and that of the company as a whole, the RSC's ensemble precision had been developed by both Hall and Nunn to exquisite concert pitch. They have given the lie for a start to the old philistine heresy that English actors cannot really speak verse. W. H. Auden wrote in *The Dyer's Hand*: 'One can read Shakespeare to oneself without even mentally *hearing* the lines and be very moved: indeed, one may easily find a performance disappointing because almost anyone with an understanding of English verse can speak it better than the average actor or actress.' The RSC has shown that attitude up for the nonsense it is: at Stratford now you can hear the texts spoken with a regard for sense and sound that gives the plays a pristine freshness. One also gets a refreshing feeling of continuity from the company's work as if the virtues of one production were being carried over to the next. A classic instance occurred in the company's 1971-2 Aldwych season when the actors playing in Brook's *Midsummer Night's Dream* went straight on to do Gorki's *Enemies*, a compassionate, neo-Chekhovian study of a factory-owning family in pre-Revolutionary Russia. The energy and discipline achieved in *The Dream* fuelled *Enemies* so that one had the same sense of molten personal relationships and of minute attention to physical detail one might expect to find in, say, a Moscow Art Theatre *Cherry Orchard*. And it is a sure sign of the company's profound overall strength that it can even absorb a bad production into its repertoire without permanently damaging its identity: a good example was the 1969-70 *Bartholomew Fair* where the director misguidedly took a documentary drama set in a precise place at a

c

precise time and deposited it in some kind of fancy-dress limbo.

If one has any complaint about the RSC it is that, although it has the cohesion, unity and adaptability of a first-rate soccer team, it lacks any player with real strike-power, a histrionic George Best who can combine superb solo flair with the ability to play as a member of the team. At the moment there is one actor in the company who could develop along these lines: John Wood. He was a memorable Richard Rowan in Joyce's *Exiles*, lean, ascetic and as relentlessly inquisitive about his wife's emotions as an over-zealous private eye. He was even better as the drunken Yakov in *Enemies*, reminding me very much of Michael Redgrave in his ability to suggest a blend of intellectual refinement and bottled hysteria. He came unstuck, I thought, only as Brutus in Stratford's 1972 *Julius Caesar* in that his determination to mine the text for every single nuance of meaning slowed his scenes down to snail's pace and damaged the whole rhythm of the production. But he does at least have the qualities of intellect, emotional volatility and thoroughbred intensity that make for great acting. Individual artistry is, of course, far from being the theatre's only pleasure and it seems to me the Agate-style critic who goes to the theatre for the acting alone is missing a lot. 'To demand more from the theatre', wrote the old maestro, 'is to argue a lukewarmness about the art like that of the half-hearted gourmet who should demand a wit to listen to, music to be conscious of and a crowd of other diners to distract him.' I should have thought the highest theatrical pleasure, however, came from a blend of all the possible ingredients: fine acting in a great play beautifully directed and designed. Admittedly a production like Laurence Olivier's *Uncle Vanya* comes once in a generation but it is a worthy ideal to aim at. Meanwhile the Royal Shakespeare Company has shown, in a relatively short period of time, what can be achieved in terms of disciplined ensemble achievement. What one would like to see in the future is not only further proof that it can create its own stars (of the calibre of David Warner, Ian Holm, Ian Richardson, Diana Rigg and Janet Suzman) but that it can also call upon their services with a much greater frequency than at present occurs.

Britain's other major subsidised company, the National Theatre, faces a slightly different problem: how to achieve a strong corporate identity while putting on what is virtually a library of world classics and new plays. Asked on a BBC radio programme, *Options*, if he could identify a National production without knowing its origins in advance, Harold Hobson suggested there was a certain cheerfulness and gaiety about the National one did not always find with the RSC. On the same programme Robert Stephens claimed that the National did not have a style of its own and ought not to have a style of its own. This seems to be fully in accordance with the Company's original intentions. Kenneth Tynan, when appointed Literary Manager, was asked in *Encore* about this very question. His reply: 'I am not persuaded that, in the absence of an absolutely great director or father-figure like Stanislavski, that it is the function of a National Theatre to have a recognisable style. We shall be using a number of different directors. But to attempt to impose a National Theatre style on every production isn't, I think, part of our job. I think we have to be a little more anonymous than that.'

Looking back over the Company's nine years of existence, the most striking fact is that they have failed to retain the services of many of our most distinguished actors who have appeared with them once or twice, have only belatedly given consideration to allowing their younger actors to flex their muscles and have only recently regained their initial sense of headlong creative impetus. But firstly let us pursue the question of style. It is a vague word but it signifies a recognisable manner of presentation and a consistency of approach in acting, decor and production. I think it is fallacious to argue that because the National is not anchored to a house-dramatist (like Shakespeare, Chekhov or Brecht) and has to run through the whole dramatic spectrum from Sophocles to Stoppard that it therefore should not have an identifiable style: the RSC may range from Marlowe to Mercer but their productions are always linked by a rigorous attention to the text and, visually, by an emphasis on props and furniture rather than on elaborate scenic backgrounds. Moreover a style springs from the growth of a company spirit, the retention of a nucleus of actors and a shared attitude to life and work. That attitude, as with the Berliner Ensemble, may be political in origin. It may, as with Gielgud's Haymarket company in the '40s, spring from a love of the classics. It may, as with the American Group Theatre in the '30s, be a case of firm belief in the efficacy of radical protest. But in each case there was a style. The National, for all its isolated achievements, does not quite get the best of any world. It does not have the identifiable manner that comes from precise social conviction. But neither could one truthfully say that it is presenting us with the best casts working with the best directors on an *ad hoc* basis.

Its chief mistake perhaps has been the employment of rather too many guest directors and designers for single productions. In the first three years of its existence it had a strong directorate in Laurence Olivier, William Gaskill and John Dexter and there was a glimpse of a developing style. Gaskill's superlative production of *The Recruiting Officer*, for instance, adopted a precise, down-to-earth approach to a Restoration text. There was no dandy-mincing, no posturing with fans, no flutter and inter-polated cries of 'La'. Instead there was a strong, clear emphasis on the play's social content and on its unsparing criticism of recruiting techniques employed in the late seventeenth and early eighteenth centuries. Likewise Peter Wood's version of *Love For Love*, through such touches of selective naturalism as a boy lugging a desk across the stage on his back, reminded one that outside the charmed circle of Congreve's *dramatis personae* was an almost Dickensian workaday world. Classics were constantly being related to the society of their time without any sense of distortion and one began to see some developing artistic purpose. This was dissipated, however, by the split-up of the original directorate. William Gaskill left in 1965 to return to the Royal Court. John Dexter left in 1967 because of a dispute over his projected all-male *As You Like It* (finally directed by Clifford Williams) and did not return for another three years. Kenneth Tynan ceased to be sole Literary Manager in 1969, though in 1972 he again assumed total control. More and more directors were brought in to do single productions: thus out of five productions playing in the repertoire in the autumn of 1969, four were the work of guest directors whose sole production for the company that was. Attempts at international cross-fertilisation have also not always had the happiest consequences: in 1971 Manfred Wekwerth and Joachim Tenschert were brought in to re-create their famed Berliner Ensemble version of *Coriolanus*. Unfortunately, however, they arrived thinking they were going to present Brecht's version of the play while the National were expecting them to do Shake-speare's. That the result was an unhappy imposition of the Berliner Ensemble style on an English company need surprise no one.

It is, of course, possible to be over-critical of the National Theatre simply because it *is* the National Theatre, because (as Irving Wardle once pointed out) it began as a secure institution in search of an expressive need rather than an expressive need in search of an institution. And it would be foolish to overlook its many fine achievements: its dazzling restoration of seventeenth-century English comedy; its exhumation of neglected classics that no commercial management would ever dare present (*The Dance of Death*, for instance, or *Back To Methuselah*); its intelligent promotion of young writers like Tom Stoppard and Peter Nichols. It is also encouraging to record that the directorate has once again been enlarged and, in addition to Olivier, now includes Michael Blakemore, John Dexter and Frank Dunlop. If there is a lesson to be learned from the Royal Shakespeare Company's continued artistic success throughout the 1960s, it is that they have managed to ensure artistic continuity by keeping more or less the same team of directors together: the number of arrivals and departures at the National, however, has often been more consistent with the policy one expects from Waterloo Station than from a theatre in the Waterloo Road.

The same argument can be applied to actors. There has been a great deal of coming and going of star names but too little attempt to integrate the majestic visitors into the ensemble and too little development of the company's younger personnel. In the star field, one can understand the fairly hasty arrival and departure of guest performers like Peter O'Toole and Tom Courtenay: hired to play one part, they left to pursue flourishing careers in the cinema. But with Olivier's contemporaries, like Redgrave and Gielgud, it seems to me tragic that no permanent place was found for them in the ensemble. Redgrave joined Olivier at Chichester in 1962 to play Uncle Vanya and one remembers it as a stunning portrayal of a man bursting with sexual frustration and unchannelled, misdirected energy. The voice became shrill, hysterical and petulant as he attacked the Professor's academic vanity and success with women; the windmilling arms would fly defensively to his face whenever he was attacked; there was a feeling of unutterable spiritual desolation as he gazed at the bouquet ('Exquisite, mournful roses') that he bought for Yelena only to find her in Astrov's arms; and in the great scene at the end of the Third Act there was a brilliantly controlled acceleration of emotion so that the shooting became the logical culmination of his hysteria and a symptom of his lumbering ineffectualness. This was greatness; and to see Olivier and Redgrave sharing the stage with such total unselfishness and joyfully clasping their hands together in blessed union at the curtain call was an uplifting, hopeful experience. One was reminded of the singular fact that Britain's four or five greatest actors have always been on the friendliest personal terms and shown scarcely a glimmer of professional jealousy: a far cry from the often poisonous rivalries of great actors in the eighteenth and nineteenth centuries.

Alas, though, the Olivier-Redgrave union proved to be even more short-lived than that between Harold Wilson and George Brown, another pair of temperamental opposites seen sharing a platform with arms jubilantly linked in the early 1960s. Redgrave later came into the National company where he was a superb Claudius to O'Toole's lack-lustre Hamlet. He followed this with the eponymous North-country hero of *Hobson's Choice*. In many ways it was a bizarre piece of casting: an actor of aristocratic grace and refinement called upon to play a proletarian tyrant. Redgrave made Hobson an almost majestic figure: portly, booming and bearded like seventeen pards, this was a

Salford Lear with his feet planted firmly on the ground but his head aspiring towards the clouds. One could describe it as the kind of wrong-headed performance that only a great actor could give but one appreciated it all the more when Colin Blakely assumed the role later in the run. Short, stout and with a voice pickled in alcohol, Blakely brought out all the robust North-country comedy that was in the part but for me lacked the dimension of eloquent majesty imported by Redgrave. Redgrave gave the impression that in Salford he was lord of all he surveyed by some kind of latter-day divine right: Blakely was more of an earthy usurper asserting his own *de facto* authority.

A similarly instructive contrast came when Olivier succeeded Redgrave as Solness in *The Master Builder*. Redgrave played it, in Ronald Bryden's words, 'as a Nordic hero wrestling amid green and cloudy glooms with the primal guilt on his soul. His Solness was a giant neurotic obsessed like Brand with his offences against God and a sleep-walking wife whose happiness he had sacrificed to his ambition. He came into his own in the third act when social drama turns into something metaphysical and when Solness's residual guilt is manifested in bizarre and foolishly heroic action. Olivier's Solness was in a different, more earthly vein. To quote my own white-hot, instant reaction:

'His Solness is no crumbling giant harried merely by the thought that his day is done, that he is to be forever dislodged from eminence by the young and talented. Instead we are presented with a man at the peak of his public success and therefore most ripe for ruin, a man aware of his doom and yet rushing helplessly towards it. This Solness is disturbed less by the thought of being displaced than by the strength of his own will in influencing other human beings or large-scale events. It happened with Kaja, the drab little secretary whom he dominated and mesmerised; it happens when Hilde Wangel arrives on the scene; and it seemingly happened when his previous house was so disastrously, and yet so fortuitously, burnt to the ground. What other actors have seen merely as a typical Ibsenite undercurrent adding a mystical dimension to the main character is promoted by Olivier into a major theme. With this power lurking inside him, what may a man not do?

'To an original conception, Olivier adds a breathtakingly exciting execution. There is both a wealth of acute psychological detail and of stirring theatrical effect within his performance. From his first appearance—dapper, granite-grey and austerely dominant—we understand this man. The self-absorption is conveyed by his taking a cigarette for himself while forgetting to offer one to his guest; the natural impatience by the restlessly drumming fingers, the constantly roving eyes; and the domestic misery by the furtive, fretful looks at his watch while his wife, Aline, drones on about their past.

'It is a performance full of rage and pathos. "What has your success cost you?" he is asked. "My peace of mind!" Olivier blurts out, his back to us, with the staccato fury of a machine-gun. Yet there is a profound and almost unbearable regret (comparable to that in his famous Fifth Act of *Macbeth*) when he faces up to the desolation of his future life. "No home . . . no happy children . . . ever . . ." he cries, with the last syllable trailing away into infinity. As always Olivier finds concrete ways of demonstrating what is going on within his soul and mind and is not afraid even directly to illustrate a line. Of Ragnar Brovik, he tells us "he is youth [pause while his left foot beats twice on the floor] knocking at the door". Connoisseurs of those fruity Olivier cadences will also thrill to his re-enactment of the last occasion he hung a wreath from a tower's top, hurling defiance as he did so at the Almighty with the resonant cry, "I am the Master Builder". Truly, Olivier was.'

If the mind boggles at what Olivier and Redgrave might have achieved in tandem or alternating some of the major classic roles, it likewise yearns to imagine what he and Gielgud (the perfect combination of romantic and classical, burgundy and claret, Sublime and Beautiful) might not have achieved together. Hopes rose when it was announced in 1967 that Gielgud would join the National to play in Ibsen's *The Pretenders* (with Olivier) and Molière's *Tartuffe*. Alas, *The Pretenders* never even got into production. Instead Gielgud played in Peter Brook's production of Seneca's *Oedipus*. But the *Tartuffe*, directed by the late Sir Tyrone Guthrie, came first and received much criticism for turning the hypocritical, eponymous hero into a sly, devious rustic and for making Orgon, the duped bourgeois pater-familias, the central character. In fact, both devices were totally justified. By making Tartuffe a chip-on-the-shoulder countryman with a Ralph Wightman accent, Guthrie ensured that everyone in the house could plausibly see through him, yet also rendered it plausible that Orgon would feel sorry for the man and guilty about his own superior opportunities in life. Martin Esslin seized on a brilliant parallel when he mentioned Frisch's *The Fire Raisers*, another classic example of a man blithely welcoming into his house the cause of his own destruction: this explains why it is the gull rather than the guller who is the centre of attraction and why Gielgud was cast as Orgon. To see him smiling seraphically as the maid, Dorine, recounted tales of Tartuffe's gluttony and almost sanctifying him with his cries of 'Poor fellow' was to understand totally the character's guilt about his own affluence and security. Guthrie also gave Gielgud some superb bits of business: kneeling at one point before a Tartuffe adopting the posture of an El Greco Christ, Orgon glanced nervously at his hands to see if they did indeed show any trace of religious stigmata. Gielgud's stage persona has about it a sweetness and elegant grace that enabled him to play Molière's dignified, noble goose with an accuracy that was severely underrated. Next came Seneca's *Oedipus*, directed by Brook as a spare, electrifying ritual drama: as one entered the theatre, the actors were strapped to pillars like the captives of some vanished Sioux tribesmen; the centrepiece of the set was a revolving golden box that would spin dazzlingly round to disgorge another black-garbed actor; and at the climax of the drama a huge golden phallus was wheeled on stage and the cast roistered through the auditorium singing 'Yes, we have no bananas' presumably to remind us of the play's phallic earthy origins and of the emotional adaptability of the audiences for whom it was originally played. Gielgud has revealed in interviews how apprehensive he was and how nervous of such direct exposure to an audience; but in the end his poker-backed tautness, his vocal clarity and austere hierarchical authority lent Brook's production a needed gravitas and physical weight. But, alas, no sooner had Gielgud established the desirability of his presence at the National than he too departed to spend a year playing the not vastly rewarding role of the Headmaster in Alan Bennett's *Forty Years On*. What would one not have given to have seen him stay at the National and undertake, say, Shakespeare's Henry IV, perhaps a repeat of his John Worthing, Ibsen's Rosmer, Shaw's Shotover. If Redgrave and Gielgud had remained with the National, their mere presence would inevitably have influenced the repertoire, taught the younger members of the ensemble a good deal and made it a company more truly representative of the best in British acting.

Lord Olivier's answer to many of the criticisms of the

National is that it is his duty to see that the public in all circumstances gets the best possible choice of actors he can give them. One would accept that; but, as a corollary, one would say that the public also likes to see young talent being nurtured and slowly brought to the fore. But, with the important exceptions of Anthony Hopkins, Derek Jacobi and Ronald Pickup, it is hard to think of many actors or actresses comparatively little known when they joined who have since been entrusted with lead roles and who have given one the frisson that comes with recognising the blossoming of real talent.

Of these three, Hopkins promises to be the most remarkable. I first saw him in the winter of 1963—coincidentally it was the night of President Kennedy's assassination—playing Andrew Undershaft in *Major Barbara* in a Leicester repertory company. Inevitably memories of that night's tragedy have driven out clear recollections of what took place on the Phoenix Theatre's tiny stage. But I do still remember the dark, indelible imprint of this young actor. He was ridiculously young to be playing Shaw's munitions manufacturer, but he brought to the role a speech of fire that fain would blaze, a passionate *certainty* that lent credibility to the character's defence of his profession and that sense of animal danger that demands an actor be continually watched. Since then he has risen within the ranks of the National to the point where in 1971 he was playing three lead roles in three consecutive productions—*The Architect and the Emperor of Assyria*, *A Woman Killed With Kindness* and *Coriolanus*; and he has established himself firmly with the public in a number of movies. Strangely, of all his performances at the National the one that has impressed me most was his Frankford in Heywood's *A Woman Killed With Kindness*. I say strangely because the character of the solid Yorkshire dignitary who discovers his wife in bed with a treacherous friend and then packs her off to another house instead of killing her, is not one that would seem to offer much for a bravura actor like Hopkins. In fact Hopkins brilliantly suggested a man of volcanic temperament camouflaging his emotions under a mild façade. With his bulging breeches, clay pipe and uncontoured features, he looked the epitome of bourgeois placidity. But to see him recoiling from the lovers' bedroom in tears because he could not bring himself to kill the sleeping pair and later encasing his adulterous chum in a cloak to protect his naked body from the cold, was to comprehend completely the character's conflicting emotions and desires. It was Caryl Brahms who put her finger most accurately on Hopkins's special quality when, in the course of a *Times* profile, she applied to him Max Beerbohm's words on Herbert Campbell: 'He always seemed to be the offspring of some mystic union between Beef and Thunder'.

As I write, in the summer of 1972, the National Theatre company as a whole appears to be in a state of flux. It lacks that feeling of solidity and weight it acquired in its early years from actors as versatile and dependable as Frank Finlay, Colin Blakely, Robert Stephens and Robert Lang. Meanwhile it is only just coming to realise that you can achieve infinitely more satisfactory results from promotion within the company than from the constant importation of star actors. One suspects that had the company tackled a play like *The School for Scandal* five years ago they would have given it a sumptuous, lavishly-cast Haymarket-style production. Yet as Agate wisely, but somewhat surprisingly, pointed out thirty years ago, 'It is possible for a piece to be so brilliantly acted that it makes no sense, as anybody must realise who has seen an all-star performance of *The School for Scandal*'. Jonathan Miller's superlative production, rooted in the raw, tangy, eighteenth-century world of

Hogarth, Smollett and Fielding, triumphed partly because it assumed Sheridan to have been writing about a real world of men and women and not about a society of fan-fluttering marionettes and partly because it assumed *all* Sheridan's characters to be interesting and important. Never before have I seen a *School for Scandal* in which the allegedly minor characters achieved such a full-blooded reality: Denis Quilley's Crabtree became a striped-stockinged exquisite for ever archly capping his nephew, Sir Benjamin Backbite's, latest piece of gossip with con-spiratorial glee and Benjamin Whitrow's Snake, servant to Lady Sneerwell, become an oleaginous time-server who might have stepped straight out of *Humphry Clinker*. This production went a long way to justify the old theatrical saw that there are no small parts—only small actors.

I also see grounds for optimism in the National's creation of Mobile Productions designed to tour theatres and halls up and down the country. The advantage of this kind of work—as with the Royal Shakespeare Company's Theatre-goround—is that it gives actors who might otherwise spend much of the season spear-carrying a chance to flex their muscles and that it encourages ensemble spirit by often assigning leading players to secondary roles. For instance I saw the National offering a highly presentable version of *Tis Pity She's a Whore* to an audience in Bury St Edmunds and got a much greater feeling of a company at work than I sometimes get in the Waterloo Road: not least because an actress of Diana Rigg's standing was playing the sexually lethal Hippolita rather than the primary role of the in-cestuous Annabella. Moreover the very simplicity of the presentation—the set here being nothing more than an arrangement of folding hospital-ward screens—forced atten-tion on the play and the company rather than on the elegant trappings.

I feel also the National has recovered its nerve because of a succession of very fine productions: apart from *The School for Scandal* there has been *Long Day's Journey Into Night*, Tom Stoppard's *Jumpers*, and Hecht and MacArthur's *The Front Page*. But the crucial fact is that the company has come increasingly to rely on its own resources. One cannot go on indefinitely importing new actors, new directors, new designers (thirty-four separate directors and thirty-five designers were responsible for the fifty-seven productions mounted from 1963 to 1971) and hope to achieve any artistic consistency. Now, at long last, the National is beginning to rely more heavily on the internal promotion of actors and on the strength of a permanent directorate. Admittedly neither the National nor the RSC has fulfilled one of the basic functions of a repertory theatre which is to build up a collection of permanently available productions (if only one could still see the National's *Love for Love* or the RSC's *Enemies*, for instance!). But at least both companies are now competing on equal terms and proving that the English actor's traditional fear that the company system will somehow undermine his virile independence is shallow, groundless and ludicrously out of date.

4

THE GREAT ONES

'What great ones do the lesser
ones will prattle of.'
(Shakespeare)

I HAVE dwelt so far on the way we train our actors; on the
set-up that greets them when they arrive in the profession;
and on the virtues and vices of our twin, large-scale ensembles. But, of course, what many people seek from the
theatrical experience cannot be found in the disciplined
teamwork of a close-knit company. They hunger for the
certainty that they are in the presence of star quality or
the knowledge that they are about to witness a great solo
performance. And if they cannot find what they are looking for in conventional West End productions, they seek
it out in heavily priced charity concerts, in one-man
shows and in a Fonteyn or a Christoff night at Covent
Garden.

But my theme here is great acting—admittedly not
something that can easily be measured or even defined.
You cannot relate it to queues at the box-office, columns
of newspaper print or volleys of applause: it is something
that you recognise the moment you see it and that can
make its presence felt by a slight chill at the nape of the
neck, an unforeseen tingling of the spine, a sudden quickening of the senses. Great acting is demonstrably physical in
the means it employs and physical in its effect on the

Paul Scofield as Wilhelm Voigt
in *The Captain of Köpenick*.
Above, on release from gaol;
below, when he first put his
uniform on . . .

Laurence Olivier as Shylock in
The Merchant of Venice, Act 3
Scene 1, in which Shylock hears
both of Antonio's disasters at sea
and Jessica's extravagance on
land. 'The veneer of bourgeois
amiability has now been torn
aside to expose the naked racial
hostility underneath.'

Donald Sinden as Sir William Harcourt Courtly
in *London Assurance*.

spectator. And while I know of no pleasure in life comparable to that of trying to describe it, I also know of no task more difficult. For when a performance is in progress one's temptation is to surrender to its immediate excitement rather than note the techniques employed. Consequently the following descriptions of great performances are usually the result of more than one viewing: the first occasion was a chance to absorb, the second or third to make notes.

The two best critics of acting over the last few decades have been James Agate and Kenneth Tynan. And one can fruitfully study both for some indication of wherein greatness lies. Not that either is infallible. Agate, for instance, was astonishingly wrong about Sir Ralph Richardson, who, in 1945, he amazingly described as lacking vivacity or melancholy; and who, he suggested, could never play Solness in *The Master Builder* on the grounds that 'Solness is as mad as a hatter whereas Ralph is as sane as all the hatters in London'. Considering that Richardson is an actor who has what Stephen Potter once called 'a remarkable capacity for existing in two dimensions at once' and who manages to invest the most ordinary-seeming character with a wealth of eccentric mannerisms (the nodding head, the constantly twitching stick, the spring-heeled walk on apparently electrified soles), this seems to me totally wrong-headed. Agate knew well enough, however, that greatness was not something that could be achieved purely by industry, application or sweat; that it was something incalculable that took you by surprise and left you no liberty to reason. 'The alleged modern approach to great acting?' he once wrote. 'Whoever has seen a great actor knows that he is not an animal to be stalked in its lair but a tiger leaping out on the spectator from the bush of mediocrity and the brake of competence. That if there is any approaching to be done, it is the tiger who will do it.'

At his best, Tynan showed a comparable response to the purely physical impact of great acting plus a rather more persuasive analytical power. In writing about Olivier's Othello, he even listed what he considered the seven essential attributes of greatness. These were 'complete physical relaxation, powerful physical magnetism, commanding eyes that are visible at the back of the gallery, a commanding voice that is audible *without effort* at the back of the gallery, superb timing which includes the capacity to make verse swing, *chutzpah*—the untranslatable Jewish word that means cool nerve and outrageous effrontery combined and the ability to communicate a sense of danger'. I would add only one more gift: acute interpretative intelligence. While I do not believe anyone can work his way towards greatness purely by the application of rational thought, I do believe a component of great acting is an intuitive reappraisal of a role. Olivier's Othello was great not merely because of its extraordinary emotional dynamic but because Olivier went further than any other modern actor in showing Othello as self-regarding, arrogant and vengeful; Kean's Iago was vigorously championed by Leigh Hunt not merely for its hair-raising audacity but 'because, instead of the Saracenic grimness usually adopted, he had personated it with the familiar air of a man of the world'. And, of the performances I propose to discuss here, McKellen's Richard II was remarkable for its radical rethinking of a role that had been swamped in effeminate glitter, and Williamson's Hamlet for its decisive and sometimes discordant break with the Gielgud tradition.

One other point. I have included in this chapter a postscript on a noted vaudeville performer: Ken Dodd. This is not because I regard him as a great actor or a potential

King Lear but because he brings to the music-hall or revue stage the same kind of hypnotic power that an Olivier or McKellen brings to the legitimate stage—what Tynan once called 'fingertip control over the emotions of a large number of people gathered in one place to witness a single unique event'.

Leonard Rossiter in 'Arturo Ui' at Nottingham Playhouse and the Saville Theatre

Until the eruption of this superb Chaplinesque performance, Rossiter had always been something of an actor's actor: men who had worked with him in the provinces gave frankly admiring accounts of his ability but even to the theatregoing public his name meant relatively little. I had first glimpsed his enormous comic potential when I saw him play Fred Midway in David Turner's robust Jonsonian satire, Semi-Detached: whereas Olivier in London played Turner's Midlands Machiavel with an alert but misplaced naturalism, Rossiter made him a scheming, lunatic grotesque. The key line in his interpretation became Midway's 'We'll have nothing spontaneous here' and indeed in Rossiter's performance there was nothing loose, undefined or uncalculated. In moments of pressure his enormous, stiff-jointed legs shot out like pistons, the arms revolved like a berserk windmill and the eyes took on a hard, basilisk stare. Olivier offered us a feat of impersonation. Rossiter gave us stylised transformation.

In Arturo Ui the same process was at work. Brecht's play equates the Nazi party with a mob of Chicago gangsters and Hitler with a daemonic Al Capone: it is a not altogether convincing parallel since it omits any reference to Nazi anti-Semitism and takes the rather simplistic party line that Fascism was really an attempt by the capitalists to stop the seizure of power by the working-class. It does, however, boast a mordant, rasping gaiety that tends to win over even the most ardent of Brecht's detractors and it gives a magnificent opportunity to a star performer. And that Rossiter undoubtedly is.

The essence of the performance was contained in the first entrance: Rossiter's Ui sprang dramatically through a paper screen like a clown at the start of a circus, spoiling the effect only through the fact that he left a mass of brown paper clinging obstinately to his mouth. From that instant we knew we were in the presence of a man who could never live up to his own mental image of himself, a man for whom there was always a fatal gap between the imaginative intention and the end product. Physically, he was grotesque: the vast-brimmed, top-heavy felt hat made him look like a walking advertisement for Spanish sherry; the wide, board-stiff shoulders suggested a coat from which the hanger had, uncharitably, not been removed; the ungainly, outsize feet splayed out like a pigeon's and had to be picked up whenever he moved as if lead weights were attached to the soles. His walk was a trudge through a ploughed field after heavy rain. But there was also danger and venom behind the grotesquerie. Asked to leave a restaurant by a pin-striped capitalist, he emitted a steam-iron hiss, his head spiralled up like that of a cobra about to strike and then, exercising an iron control, he contented himself with raising his hat in exaggerated mock-politeness. His corkscrew body constantly seemed to be in the grip of some barely restrainable animal force but, at the same time, the absurdity balanced the menace: resting his finger delicately on a chair-back, he let forth a pig-like squeal of pain when someone actually sat down on the chair.

To make evil funny is a singular achievement; and this is precisely what Rossiter did. And nowhere was the technique of balancing the laughter and the absurdity better demonstrated than in the classic scene where Ui is given lessons in deportment and declamation by a veteran Shakespearean actor. The actor firstly showed him how to enter a room, flinging his right arm over his left shoulder as if wrapping a cloak about himself: Ui imitated this with passable effectiveness. He was told to walk on the points of his shoes: he dutifully did so, shooting out his legs like a demented chorine until we saw the evolution of the goose-step. Instructed to stand with his hands neutrally folded in front of him, he seized his crotch with rabid intensity and shot white-toothed, manic smiles at his colleagues as if seeking approbation. Taught to speak with theatrical clarity, his tongue stumbled over the word 'hath' and then flicked out like a lizard's as he tried to master the insuperably difficult verb. Movement and speech thus mastered, next came the art of sitting with the legs placed wide apart and the hands planted firmly on the thighs. From this position he essayed a multi-purpose, Roman-history-play gesture of authority; gradually he realised it was more impressive if the arm was stiff and unbent; and with a gleaming and delirious self-approval he achieved the first-ever Nazi salute. Thus the most remarkable transformation-scene in the whole of modern drama took place.

As in all great performances, one was struck by the actor's ability to take—and get away with—the most hair-raising risks. Crossed by Dullfeet (the equivalent of the Austrian Chancellor, Dollfuss) Ui's hands rose unbidden from his sides and made as if to strangle the stricken grocer. But, as in the restaurant scene, some cautious instinct checked the impulsive animal gesture and, slowly and just as menacingly, the hands fell and resumed their original position. As Ui gazed at the movement in frozen fascination, one was reminded of Craig's description of Irving's arrested gestures of taking off his snowy boots in *The Bells* ('We suddenly saw these fingers stop their work; the crown of the head suddenly seemed to glitter and become frozen—and then, at the pace of the slowest and most terrified snail, the two hands, still motionless and dead, were seen to be coming up the side of the leg'). Even greater risks were taken in the scene that parallels Richard III's wooing of Lady Anne over the burial-chest: Rossiter, publicly seducing Dullfeet's widow, actually rested his foot on her husband's coffin and at one point knocked on its glittering surface, put his ear attentively to the wood and cried, 'Dullfeet is gone'.

The final image, however, was the most memorable of all. A vast mobile tower was wheeled on to the stage and pushed down towards the footlights. Suddenly the sweating, sleek-haired figure of Ui coiled up at the top of the tower like a jack-in-the-box with a broken spring. Instead of the expected rational address one was confronted by the drivelling ravings of a screaming maniac. One laughed first and then was chilled into silence. Finally Rossiter himself appeared at stage level in his own person and, mopping his brow, presented us with the salutary moral tag that the bitch that gave rise to Ui was in heat once again.

A great performance. Partly because of its sheer mimetic vitality; partly because it left behind an ineradicable physical image as of an animated Grosz cartoon; partly because of its truth to the Brechtian ideal in that it revealed the abject cowardice and fear behind the character's public mask of brutality. 'The actor,' wrote Brecht, 'must make himself observed standing *between* the spectator and the text.' And in the most imaginative and potent way possible that is precisely what Rossiter did.

Nicol Williamson in 'Hamlet' at the Roundhouse

No doubt about it: Nicol Williamson's Hamlet undoubtedly leaves a lot out. The observer's eye is mercilessly there but scarcely the scholar's tongue or soldier's sword; 'Sweet prince' seems the strangest of appellations for this testy, penetrating member of the blood royal; and he was like, had he been put on, to have proved most costive. Not for the first time it occurs to me that I would far rather live in an Elsinore governed by Claudius than one ruled by someone as mercurial as Hamlet.

And yet, for all its excess coarseness and over-reliance on a note of unmasked contempt, this is the most exciting Hamlet since Redgrave's 1958 Stratford performance. Its secret is not that it abandons the reflectively melancholic Gielgud tradition or that it offers the kind of angry young Hamlet with whom the Roundhouse audience can identify: it is, quite simply, that it combines a relish for grandiose romantic effect with a scrupulous attention to detail and to the sheer basic sense of the lines. The text has clearly been re-thought and re-felt: at the same time the door has been left open for the use of arresting effect.

In aspect, Williamson is not your conventionally good-looking Hamlet: the leonine head with its waves of light-blond hair gives him a slightly top-heavy look and the voice combines the slimy whine of Brummagem with the slightly pinched vowel-sounds of a puritanical Scottish lay-preacher. He looks more like Gertrude's elder brother than her son and has clearly been doing post-graduate work at Wittemberg, even heading possibly for the role of militant junior don siding with student complaints. From the start he is weighed down, more onerously than any Hamlet I have seen, with a prophetic sense of doom, with a far-sighted realisation that he is involved in some kind of ritualistic dance of death: thinking of his mother's marriage he warns us, emphatically and fatalistically, that 'it is not nor it *cannot* come to good'. The contradiction in Hamlet is, however (and it is this more than anything that explains the character's obsessive fascination down the centuries), that his instinct for death and destruction is combined with a paradoxical enthusiasm for life: the uses of the world may be weary, stale, flat and unprofitable but yet the players must be well-bestowed; women may be painted deceivers but 40,000 brothers could not, with all their quantity of love, make up his sum. This sublime contradiction Williamson expresses perfectly. At the news of the Ghost's nocturnal presence on the battlements he rubs his hands together in delirious anticipation and paces the stage like a demonically possessed sentry letting his words tumble over each other. And he delights in mimicry and play: he gets caught up in the emotional excitement of the 'rugged Pyrrhus' speech, abandoning it only with reluctance to the First Player, and in private converse with Horatio he fastidiously and exactly apes other people's accents and mannerisms.

The romanticism? This comes out in key moments like the leap into Ophelia's grave on 'This is I, Hamlet the Dane', cloak being flung back over left shoulder as if it were the Red Shadow finally revealing himself. The realism? *Passim*. Never before have I been made to realise that Hamlet has always been an impassioned railer, that when he advises Ophelia to betake herself to a Nunnery this is part of a familiar stream of invective at which Ophelia can indulgently smile. Never before have I seen a Hamlet who communicated such a strong sense of physical disgust: 'nay but to *live* in the rank sweat of an enseamed bed', he retchingly observes, the point rubbed home by the fact that Claudius and Gertrude seem to conduct much of their diplomatic business from a fourposter. Never before have

I felt a Hamlet establish quite such a fearsome and direct contact with his audience: the soliloquies have a strong element of challenge about them ('Who does me this, HA?') and Yorick's skull is held up for our inspection so that the moral to be drawn from it ('Now get you to my lady's table and tell her, let her paint an inch thick, to *this* favour she must come') is inescapable.

This is not a complete Hamlet. On the debit side, it reminds me of Agate's description of Wolfit: 'There is very little suggestion of weakness and Hamlet's reluctance to put paid to his stepfather's account is almost as inexplicable as it would be in the case of a heavyweight boxer or Woolwich Arsenal centre forward'. It lacks irony, delicacy, gentleness. Its virtues, however, plead trumpet-tongued on its behalf. It matches the play's questing feverishness with a bottled hysteria of its own. It informs the lines with a bristling, bruising intelligence and is constantly showing Hamlet to be testing those around him—'How if I answer No?' he suddenly asks Osric when confronted with Laertes's challenge, as if genuinely anxious to get a reply. And it provides that rarest of all sensations: the feeling that the actor rejoices wholeheartedly in his presence on the stage. After David Warner's Hamlet (too lymphatic by half) and Richard Chamberlain's (a handsome head-boy with deep personal problems) it is refreshing to find a man-sized, ravenously hungry attack on the part. Some actors take the stage by default: Mr Williamson invariably takes it by storm.

Ian McKellen as Richard II and Edward II at the Mermaid and the Piccadilly

Is McKellen a great actor? On the strength of his Richard II and Edward II, I would say potentially Yes. He brings

on to the stage with him an extraordinary physical magnetism, an ability to find the external gestures to match his
emotional impulses, an Olivier-like gift for seizing on a key
line and making that an interpretative cornerstone, and a
strong intellectual flair. His greatest weakness at present is
that he sometimes imposes the emotions on to the words
instead of letting them emerge through the lines so that he
occasionally seems to be acting alongside the text. This
may be the result of a lack of formal training and is, in any
case, the kind of thing that can be easily remedied. The
things that cannot be taught McKellen has in abundance.

The clue to his Richard comes from his first appearance:
he glides into the court stepping lightly on the balls of his
feet, holding his warder delicately between thumb and
forefinger as if it were a sacred wand and his orb in the left
hand with the wrist as rigid as can be. He might have
stepped from a Bayeux tapestry; and from the smoothness
and formality of his movement he could be gliding on
casters. I have seen Richards who have begun with their
left leg idly hooked over the throne as if they were in their
own backyard: McKellen, however, makes it instantly
clear that Richard is steeped in ceremony and that through
the years he has come to accept it as proof of his physical
inviolability. The court itself has become so used to this
that it applauds politely when, in the lists, the king utters
sentence. But from the heartless reaction to Gaunt's death
we see that the form and ceremony are devoid of real
feeling; and the faint sighs and lowering of the eyebrows
that accompany York's hymn to the virtues of the Black
Prince suggest an insensitivity to anyone outside himself.

The interpretation is developed consistently and with
linear clarity. There is comparatively little here of Mon-
tague's artist-king, tipsy with grief. Rather, this Richard is
a man engaged in the process of discovering his own vulner-

ability and genuinely appalled at the collapse of his unquestioning belief in the divine right of kings. When he
comes to the Welsh coast and news of fresh disasters arrive
with every messenger, he is completely and utterly pole-
axed:

> Throw away respect,
> Tradition, form and ceremonious duty;
> For you have but mistook me all this while.
> I live with bread like you, feel want, taste grief,
> *Need friends.*

These last two words become a cry of anguish, the vowels
stretched out to breaking point like pieces of elastic and
all the world's pain and desolation suddenly seeming to be
momentarily compressed into a few seconds.

McKellen has not yet got a Gielgudian feeling for the
architecture of a speech: what he does have is the impressionistic ability to make a line or phrase convey a great weight
of meaning. Take the scene at Flint Castle:

> For well we know, no hand of blood or bone
> Can gripe the sacred handle of our sceptre,
> Unless he do profane, steal or usurp.

In the last line his voice soars to a high-pitched scream on
usurp: a word with sacrilegious connotations for a Plan-
tagenet. For a moment he cannot go on; tears start to
drown his words; and he recovers himself only with the
boast that 'God omnipotent is mustering in his clouds on
our behalf, armies of pestilence'. Compare Gielgud's treatment of the same passage. He ignores the terror behind
particular words like 'usurp'. He begins with a breathless,
stricken 'We are amazed' and gradually increases volume
and tempo until he comes to the 'armies of pestilence
which shall *strike* your children yet unborn'. Having thus

established himself at base camp, as it were, he goes on to assault the summit of the speech with its threat of civil war and its terrifying image of lush pastures bedewed with faithful English blood.

What makes McKellen's Richard so moving is that the residual belief in ritual constantly clashes with the sheer weight of feeling. At Flint feeling gets the better of respect for form. In the deposition scene at Westminster form finally conquers feeling. When Richard makes as if to surrender his divine authority ('Here cousin seize the crown') he actually tightens his grip on the symbol of his power at the very second Bolingbroke catches hold of it; but after luxuriating in all the verbal conceits attached to the act of surrender he finally turns the act of deposition into a solemn ritual matching the formalistic nature of the text. Even in the prison scene at Pomfret we see Richard on the bare, open stage rigidly defining the limits of his cell while at the same time literally beating his brains to hammer out the appropriate images.

I saw McKellen's Richard three times: at Cambridge in the autumn of 1968, at the Mermaid in the autumn of 1969 and at the Piccadilly in the spring of 1970. Each time McKellen seemed to be refining, improving, wiping away the superfluous decoration. Listen to Gielgud's recordings over the years and you will notice how, with each new version, he cuts away more of the dead wood. He himself has said that the art of acting—like the art of living—is a matter of selectivity. As long as McKellen appreciates this, he will grow into a still greater actor.

Meanwhile his Edward II had slightly less linear clarity— in keeping with the fragmented, episodic nature of Marlowe's play—but no less moment-to-moment physical excitement. It began with a vivid, impressionistic portrait of Edward the infantile lover: shrill, restless and quivering with frustration at the slightest check to his instinctive impulses. At one point McKellen chewed hard on a bronze medallion round his neck as if to try and suppress the bubbling feeling within. Thus he broke one of the cardinal rules of acting which is that one must never start on too high a pitch for fear of being unable to maintain the level; and he broke it successfully. He dispensed titles and offices like a Selfridges' Santa Claus dishing out Christmas presents; was truly frantic; and conveyed the character's physical weakness by staggering under the weight of the ornate broadsword he used to invest Gaveston with the title of Lord High Chamberlain.

Checked and restrained by his nobles in his homosexual passions, we saw Edward transformed into an exultant warlord glorying in his new-found physical strength and at one point wristily brandishing above his head the very broadsword that he had earlier found impossible to lift. Sometimes the approach was too eclectic: thus after Gaveston's death McKellen essayed a silent cry too reminiscent of Weigel's in *Mother Courage* for comfort. Sometimes a few too many fruity Olivier cadences strayed into the performance. But the overriding impression was of a fantastic nervous energy being fuelled into military activity. Intelligent, detailed contrasts were also made with the Richard: thus instead of clinging tightly on to the crown, Edward literally tossed it away in despair on 'Here take my crown'. The death scene was also superbly handled, thanks partly to Robert Eddison's brilliant Lightborn and the skilful realism of Toby Robertson's production. In fact an explicitly sexual relationship was suggested between the emaciated king and his voluptuous assassin, with the latter washing the king's body before death with a sensual thoroughness and with Edward to the last hungering for physical contact.

McKellen is an actor who holds all the court cards: intelligence, physical flexibility, a strong commanding physique, mobile, expressive features. Given the determination to cut away some of his vocal excesses and the feeling that every rift must be loaded with ore, he should go on to scale the heights of his profession. He is already pre-eminent amongst the actors of his generation.

Laurence Olivier in 'The Merchant of Venice' at the National Theatre

'One talks vaguely of genius,' wrote Matthew Arnold, 'but I had never till now comprehended how much of Rachel's superiority was purely in intellectual power, how eminently this power counts in the actor's art as in all art, how just is the instinct which led the Greeks to mark with a high and severe stamp the Muses.' Arnold was right. For, although several things conspire to make Olivier's Shylock the best of its generation, the greatest of these are its 'high intellectual power' and sheer interpretative originality.

The key point about Olivier's Shylock (a frock-coated prosperous Jew with a skull-cap under his top-hat reminiscent of George Arliss as Disraeli) is that he knows his revenge upon Antonio is inextricably tied up with Venice's credibility as an international trading area (a point highlighted by Julia Trevelyan Oman's realistic nineteenth-century setting with its hint of St Mark's Square). Antonio himself realises that if the course of law be denied it 'will much impeach the justice of the state Since that the trade and profit of the city consisteth of all nations'. And therefore in the Trial Scene Shylock's 'If you deny me . . . THERE

IS NO FORCE IN THE DECREES OF VENICE' is driven in like a series of hammer-blows. Allied to this implacable conviction that he has the city by the short hairs is Olivier's conception of Shylock as an outsider who is tolerated by Venetian society just so long as he continues to play the role that is expected of him. I was reminded of something James Baldwin wrote in *Notes of a Native Son*. 'It is part of the price the Negro pays for his position in society that he is almost always acting. A Negro learns to gauge precisely what reaction the alien person facing him desires and he produces it with disarming artlessness.' So it is with Olivier's Jew.

A second reason for the performance's power is Olivier's familiar ability to seize on a line or a moment and impale it forever on our memories. Thus Shylock's last words to the court—'I am content'—are delivered with rigid, poker-stiff back, eyeballs bulging and hands clapped firmly to the sides like a carefully-welded toy soldier: clearly the man is undergoing some kind of fit and so we are prepared for the earth-shaking, off-stage death-cry that follows his exit. And a third reason for the performance's magnetism is that it offers us the terrifying and exhilarating spectacle of a full-scale piece of heroic acting being given in an orderly, mercantile late-nineteenth-century setting. It is like seeing a tiger unleashed in a drawing-room. It would be a great performance in Renaissance costume; it becomes even greater because of the tension between period and style. But to show how the performance works in detail let me analyse it scene by scene.

ACT I. Scene 3

First impression is of a wealthy urban financier who has adopted the alien's mask of politeness and false *honhomie*. He is constantly laughing (after 'Antonio is a good man' he emits a dangerous chuckle) and making weak Gentile puns (like the one about the 'pi-rats') which drop into the conversation like boulders into a garden-pool. He is the smiler with the knife under the cloak. And early on he plants the verbal mannerisms: the dropping of the final 'g' on verbs ('I was debatin' of my present store'), the pinched strangulated vowel sounds that evoke the ghetto origins ('For sufferance is the badge of all *ower* tribe'). And, as always with Olivier, one is struck by the mimetic vigour. 'Your worship was the last man in our mouths' is accompanied by a rolling masticatory jaw movement. Likewise when he describes how Jacob, while Laban's ewes were breeding, 'peeled me certain wands', he inserts his stick with a corkscrew movement through his outstretched left hand brilliantly summoning up both the peeling-process and animalistic copulation. The element of icy racial fury under the bland exterior only emerges in the speech to Antonio about the insults he has repeatedly borne —and he highlights this fury simply through a sharp emphasis on the word 'You'. '*You* come to me and *you* say "Shylock, we would have moneys"—*you* say so; *you* that did void *your* rheum upon my beard.' Yet in proposing the bond he resorts to the mask of joviality that he has adopted for purely commercial transactions. In talking of a 'merry sport' he jauntily puts his stick over his shoulder like a young Chevalier. And he does a marvellous false exit when it looks as if the bond will not be unanimously accepted, spinning round on his heel the very split second Antonio cries out, 'Yes, Shylock'. Thus the scene comes full circle and returns to the note of benevolent amiability on which it began. In the course of ten minutes Olivier has given us the complete architecture of the scene; filled in the outline with some staggering detail; and laid the whole basis of the characterisation for the rest of the play.

ACT 2. Scene 5

The scene where he bids farewell to Jessica. Decked out in white tie, tails and with a watch-chain across a spreading corporation, he resembles more than ever a role-playing alien. Immediately he introduces a note of menace by asking of Gobbo 'Who bids thee call?' and then dropping his voice to a whisper on 'I did not bid thee call'. And he introduces a typically eccentric touch by placing the keys for Jessica on the thumb of his right hand where most actors would simply hand them to her. He also introduces a whole new concept of Gobbo on 'the patch is kind enough but a *huge* feeder', suddenly producing an image of a boy with a gargantuan Dickensian appetite (scarcely borne out, one must admit, by Jim Dale's attenuated, bird-like frame). It is a short scene but Olivier reinforces the earlier impression of a stern patriarch prepared to dissemble in front of the Christians just so long as it suits his purpose: in the previous scene, do not forget, Shylock has told us that he will not eat with the Christians, yet here he is going off to supper with them.

ACT 3. Scene 1

This is the key scene where you really know what a Shylock is made of. As I mentioned before, O'Toole did it brilliantly in Michael Langham's 1960 Stratford production, rending his gown of watered silk and allowing the desire for revenge to increase in direct proportion to his disgust with his daughter's behaviour. Olivier's treatment has less of a straightforward linear curve; but he leaves particular moments branded on the memory. He begins the scene on the balcony of his house eavesdropping on Salanio's news of Antonio's misfortunes and feverishly searching for his daughter. He comes down to street level visibly distracted and confused. He rests for support on a side rail with his

D

back to us and is obviously more obsessed by news of his daughter's flight than anything else. Antonio's name is mentioned and he then turns slowly round on 'Let him look to his bond' so that we see the dawning realisation of the consequences of the merchant's loss. He prowls restlessly round the stage like a caged wolf itemising Antonio's insults and stiffens suddenly on 'I am a Jew' as if summoning up all his racial pride. In this context, 'Hath not a Jew eyes?' becomes not a sentimental plea for pity but a clarion-call to revenge—the word Olivier insistently emphasises. And for that key word he devises an extraordinary gesture that consists of slapping the right hand into the palm of the left and shooting the thumb of the left hand outwards: it suggests a butcher slapping a piece of meat on to a weighing machine and has exactly the right blend of coarseness and brutality.

With Tubal's arrival he retires to his house and emerges with Jessica's dress draped over his shoulder, stroking it gently as if to console himself for the loss of two thousand ducats. On 'I would my daughter were dead at my feet' he hurls it to the ground as if the folds of cloth did indeed contain Jessica and tramples on it as if to exorcise her spirit for ever. His frame bursting with a flood of contradictory emotions, he breaks into some ancient Sephardic dance on the news of Antonio's ill-fortune; and as suddenly snaps out of that by picking up Jessica's dress and twirling it rapidly round his arm like a bandage on the news of the ring that was exchanged for a monkey. Telling Tubal that he would not have given it for a wilderness of monkeys, he elongates all the vowel sounds on the word 'wilderness' as if to suggest an eternity of pain and anguish. At this point one suspects he has studied carefully what Irving did with the role. 'He contrived to suggest,' according to his biographer, 'in his delivery of the word "wilderness" of monkeys a vast emptiness signifying Jessica's life of frivolous and trifling amusement and his contempt for it—an example of his ability to make an effective point out of an apparently insignificant word.' Olivier's final touch is masterly. For 'Go Tubal and meet me at our synagogue' he takes up his Jewish prayer shawl, holds it up to his face and lightly kisses its hem; and then drapes it round his head before setting off to his devotions. The veneer of bourgeois amiability has now been torn aside to expose the naked racial hostility underneath.

ACT 3. Scene 3

Sixteen lines only for Shylock in this short scene with Antonio and the Gaoler. Yet Olivier still manages to reveal a new facet of the character: an implacable, iron resolve. He signifies this by a harsh, reiterated emphasis on the word 'bond'. And he fortifies it on 'I'll have no speakin'', ramming the point home by forming the shape of a mouth with a rounded thumb and forefinger. He exits with sublime confidence using one of his favourite tricks: that of leaving part of himself trailing behind as he departs. In *Rebecca* there is an extraordinary shot of him going out of a door momentarily leaving his hand caressing a support; in *Coriolanus* he let a hand linger on a pillar after his body had already gone past; and here he places his stick on his shoulder as if it were a rifle and exits slowly upstage so that for a second or two all we can see is the tip of the stick after he has gone out.

ACT 4. Scene 1

A stony adversary: Olivier here exemplifies the Duke's words. And the reason, as I suggested earlier, is that Shylock knows that it is the integrity and honour of Venice that is

on trial. Thus he enters jauntily, swinging a black brief-
case, as if off for a day at the races. Confident of the out-
come, he is anxious to get on with the business, drumming
his fingers on the table and scarcely bothering to turn
round to answer Bassanio's queries. Like Irving, Olivier
also unerringly hits the key word in any speech. The
slaves purchased by the Christians are abjectly used because
'you *bought* them'. And in the same speech the pound of
flesh he demands of Shylock is also 'dearly *bought*'. He
chuckles knowingly on Antonio's 'I am a tainted wether
of the flock' which instantly tells us that the Merchant's
homosexuality was a common secret. And his reaction to
the 'quality of mercy' speech is a derisive 'Huh'. This is a
man who can at last afford to show his true religious and
racial animosity.

Olivier brings his exultation to the boil on hearing
Portia's initial declaration in his favour, even doing a
spring-heeled leap. But this is the turning-point in the scene:
from here on Shylock's fortunes trace a downward curve
which Olivier plots with startling intensity. He has Antonio
halfway out of the door to execute sentence before Portia
halts him with 'Tarry a little'. Learning that his lands will
be confiscated if he sheds Christian blood, he enquires
anxiously 'Is that the law?' peering at a dusty legal tome.
He realises that he cannot even retrieve his initial capital,
hurries towards the door and is stopped just as he has
reached the side-rail. Portia puts the boot in by telling him
of the legal penalties against an *alien*. The last word is like
a dagger in his heart. He obviously knows exactly what is
to come: jaw sagging, he turns round to utter a cry that
just will not come like that of Weigel in *Mother Courage*.
His quivering hand reaches out for the rail to steady himself; he can stand everything except Antonio's vicious
demand that he become a Christian, at which he flops over

the rail, his head hurtling towards the floor until he is rescued by two Jewish friends. They prop him up while he says 'I am content', and his rigid frame is carried from the court. A few seconds elapse before a cry is heard—sharp and intense at first and then barbarically extended—that reminds one of a wolf impaled on a spike and dying a slow death, or of some savage mastiff gradually having the life squeezed out of it as it is forcibly put down. Shylock has returned to his forefathers.

Paul Scofield in 'The Captain of Köpenick' at the National Theatre

After Olivier no living actor is more endowed with mimetic vigour than Paul Scofield. He relishes disguise; can ring the most unearthly changes on his voice and physical presence; and yet always projects through every performance something that is quintessential Scofield. And one saw all this in Carl Zuckmayer's extraordinary *Captain of Köpenick*: a picaresque fable about a worn-out old jailbird who astonished the Germany of 1906 by donning an army captain's uniform, taking over a company of soldiers and marching into the town-hall at Köpenick to get a long-withheld work-permit. The tragic irony, of course, was that he had come to the wrong place: work-permits were dealt with elsewhere.

'How came it,' asked Carl Zuckmayer in his introduction to the play, 'that this ex-convict Wilhelm Voigt, who could get neither permit nor passport, instead of drowning himself or sinking into an inebriates' home, decided to adorn himself with a shabby old uniform and suddenly become a new and different being? How came it that this poor victim of officialdom, as soon as he was in uniform, was able to

treat officials as their undisputed lord and master? How
came it that he, Wilhelm Voigt, happened to notice something which sixty million good Germans had seen without
noticing?' These are questions to which Scofield—who had
earlier played that other great impostor, the Government
Inspector—provided all the answers.

To begin with, he provided a meticulously accurate
naturalistic portrait of a man who had spent all his life as a
bureaucratic victim. All the lines in his body and deportment inclined downwards as if he were struggling under
the weight of some invisible load. The walrus-moustache
was like a sagging parody of Kaiser Bill's; the shoulders
sloped in a jacket that was several sizes too large; the
withered fingers were constantly thrust into the pockets of
a crumpled, stained fawn waistcoat; even the slack-jointed
knees looked as if they could barely support the fragile load
they were being asked to carry.

But having carefully laid the naturalistic foundations,
Scofield then proceeded to build on them with all his
characteristic love of extravagant, revelatory detail. I was
reminded, in another art-form, of the Hogarth of 'Marriage
à la Mode' or 'The Four Stages of Cruelty' where a love
of observable reality is combined with a passion for
grotesque detail. Soliciting a work-permit from the police
chief at Potsdam, his leaden shuffle was transformed into a
gliding waltz as hope momentarily surged up in him and
the palsied arm executed circular flourishes as he tried to
establish his own importance. The curious sartorial fas-
tidiousness often found amongst the down-and-out was
also suggested by a momentary shooting of the cuffs as he
took tea with his brother-in-law after emerging from prison.
The first stirrings of the military instinct were evoked by a
kicking-up of the left heel and a barely perceptible stiffening
of the back at the mention of the Army.

Zuckmayer himself says in the published preface that the play moves along two tracks: the story of the hapless man slowly waking up to the use of his wits, and the story of the uniform's slow degradation. And the brilliance of Scofield's performance lay in the way it embodied the two. He presented us with a man who was totally transformed once he donned the captain's gear: the crab-like gait was turned into the delicate prancing of a Bertram Mills liberty-horse, the hitherto sloping shoulders became board-stiff and the lustreless eyes shone with dreams of Prussian grandeur. At the same time he retained enough of the ex-convict's lifelong mannerisms to reinforce Zuckmayer's general social point: thus, nervously raising the matter of a passport once in the town-hall at Köpenick, he produced the most bizarre series of vowel sounds which seemed to go 'Ooo . . . eeee . . . aw . . . eh . . .' and when he awoke to the terrible fact there was no passport office at Köpenick his body seemed miraculously to shrivel inside the uniform.

In any discussion of great acting enormous stress is always placed on the purely physical aspects; but, as Scofield's performance reminded us, unless these are to become external and arbitrary they must always be placed at the service of acute interpretative intelligence and a controlling imagination. This was a great performance not simply because it was crammed with exciting detail but because it also illuminated the play. Stanislavski once described intuition and emotion as helmsmen of the ship of acting; but I would argue that sheer intelligence is usually doing the navigation.

Ken Dodd

It was Arnold Bennett who said that a filthy mind is a source of constant pleasure. Ken Dodd, I feel sure, would agree. His act is a close-knit and carefully planned succession of *double-entendres* with endlessly phallic connotations. 'For all those people who like good clean fun,' he announces early in his act, 'we have the exit.' Believe me, he's not joking.

Doddy first captured the town in the summer of '65 when he did a memorable season at the Palladium. John Osborne reputedly went back again and again to see him; Jonathan Miller wrote a deeply serious analysis of him in the *New Statesman*; the public flocked. He came back a year later but since then has spent most of his time doing either summer seasons, pantomimes or television. I caught him at Bournemouth in the summer of '69 and was glad to see that he had lost none of his capacity to reduce an audience to hysteria. A Doddy evening is like a giant fertility-rite, an act of riotous penis-worship conducted with the happy co-operation of up to 2,000 people. He liberates our dark recognition of sexual power, ridding us of Pauline guilt about our physical organs. The atmosphere at a Dodd show is, I should guess, similar to that at the kind of bawdy comic relief offered by the Greeks at the end of a tragic festival.

His appearance is, of course, half the battle. With a combination of buck-teeth, saucer-eyes and hair that often proceeds dramatically upwards, he looks like a startled Chinese rabbit. His apparel too is outlandish. For Bournemouth he first appeared in a mustard-yellow suit with bowler to match and sporting an outsize sunflower with obvious connotations. 'All the ladies look tickled tonight,' he cried. 'Well done, lads.' In his first act he cruises along gently. An idiot fashion-show takes place in front of the tabs with one male model daintily lifting his kilt to reveal a fan-heater underneath—'He starts off as Angus and ends up as Agnes'. For some reason the monologue turns to

Mr Dodd's dimple—'a moon-crater in a sea of tranquillity'. Later he tells us, irrelevantly, of a man who sits on a walking-stick and yodels. Pause. 'You'd yodel too if . . .' (the rest is drowned in laughter). We also hear of a man who does splits over a blow-lamp and sings 'Tears'. There is even reference to a lion-tamer: Claud Bottom.

For his second appearance he sports a maroon maxi ('It's taken twenty-eight moggies to make this—all toms') and a phallic, high-domed hat. At this stage he produces his notorious tickling-stick, a long pole with what looks like a feather duster sprouting from the end of it. Informing us that he's had his tickling-stick re-fluffed, he proceeds to touch up the ladies in the third row. 'I've tickled people in remote parts. I've tickled people in some very out-of-the-way places.' An even bigger stick stretching roughly to Row L is then produced. 'The size of it,' proclaims Mr Dodd, seeking our earnest admiration. From then on the fun gets gradually more lunatic. 'I've got a ladder in me socks,' says Doddy, producing precisely that from inside his left trouser-leg. He essays a version of 'Granada' wearing a gaucho hat with ping-pong balls suspended from the side to suggest Andalusian gaiety. Surrealism blends with vulgarity when he gets on to the subject of his grandad. 'He's in the Darby and Joan club. I don't know what he does but he's got three notches on his walking-stick. . . . Me grandad stood all winter with his back to the fire. . . . We had to have him swept. . . . I wonder if he can hear us now . . . (a reverent pause and a solemn hush from the audience as Mr Dodd gazes skywards). . . . He's on the roof picking lead.' The jokes become more anatomical and even more Daliesque. 'Men's legs have a very lonely life. Standing in the dark in your trousers all day. . . . Be nice to have another mouth under your arm, you could eat a bacon sandwich on your way to work.' But by this stage Doddy has got to the point where we will laugh at almost anything. He never allows us to relax for a second. Whereas most comedians signal that a joke is coming, tell it and then wait or even beg for applause, Ken Dodd piles gag on gag like a man possessed. Hysteria is never far away at the end as he gets us to stand up for the National Anthem which turns out to be rude and un-Anthem-like; as he beats a Sally-Ally-style drum announcing that he has something in a more jugular vein; and as he melodically pays tribute to 'Happiness, happiness, the greatest gift that I possess'.

Dodd is a manic comedian. He stands up in front of an audience not in order to confide his injuries and stories of maltreatment like Frankie Howerd; nor like Tommy Cooper to demonstrate his own glorious, fuddled incompetence; but simply because he could not conceivably be otherwise employed. He does not tell a joke: he detonates it. He does not constantly tell one that he is a paid-up comic by reference to how many minutes he has got left or the comparative behaviour of audiences in Slough or Glasgow: he just fires off a heady blend of one-liners, Archie-Rice quips and wry, surrealist observations. He is a comedian who works, in fact, in terms of images. He presents you with a snapshot of his Grandad, who apparently works in a savoury factory, wading neck-high through a jar of piccalilli groping for the cauliflower. He then cuts to another image of men in hiking-shorts whose white legs look like 'two sticks of celery sticking out of a paper bag'. In that sense, he is perhaps the most cinematic comedian we possess. More important, he is also one of the funniest, one of the few who can transform a bunch of strangers into a half-crazed and uproarious assembly. And that is a mark of greatness.

5

IDOLS OF THE SCREEN

'Acting is largely a matter of
farting about in disguises'.
(*Peter O'Toole*)

I HAVE concentrated so far mainly on acting for the stage;
but of course for most people acting is something they see
on a screen, large or small, and so in the next two chapters
I want to concentrate on the state of film and television
performance.

With the cinema, however, one immediately runs into a
problem: how much one can talk of 'acting' in a medium
that is so heavily dominated by the director. 'Actors,'
wrote Josef von Sternberg in *Fun in a Chinese Laundry*, 'are
dolls who look as if they could move and speak by themselves. When a film actor, who undergoes considerably more
manipulation than any duck or dummy, begins to appear
to function, he is judged even by the shrewdest critic on
the basis of being a self-determining unit of intelligence.
This is not so . . . the more I ponder on the problems of
the artist, the less they resemble the problems of the actor.'
This is obviously a somewhat extreme, arrogant and brutal
viewpoint, but it does contain more than a grain of truth:
that directorial manipulation combined with the skills of a
good editor can 'create' the kind of performance the film's
auteur wants and that the actor's control over what finally
appears on the screen is absolutely minimal. Even a director

like Billy Wilder, who gives a lot of attention to his actors, has an absolutely clear mental picture of the kind of performance he wants from them: on the set of *The Private Life of Sherlock Holmes* I watched him giving minute inflectional readings to his actors and him and his script-collaborator, I. A. L. Diamond, quietly mouthing the dialogue to themselves during each single take. Like it or not, we are living in an age of director's cinema; and the more power accorded to the director, the less will be granted to the actor. 'An two men ride a horse, one must ride behind.'

Before one can discuss screen acting, one must also acknowledge the performer's dependence on the writer. Frederic Raphael, in his preface to the published script of *Two For The Road*, draws attention to a writer on a woman's magazine coming to interview Audrey Hepburn and asking her if she was deliberately trying to change her image by playing a woman whose marriage was heading for the rocks. The assumption, as he says, was that Miss Hepburn when the mood took her commissioned a writer to provide a part specially tailored for her. A few exceptionally fortunate performers may work in this way. But the truth is that a writer is not these days concerned with providing star fodder but with creating an intelligent script that will simply be cast as well as possible. Yet almost every film-star interview one sees on television or reads in the press still rests on this precarious belief that actors are totally autonomous creatures royally dictating the state of their career: indeed I recently watched an interview with Telly Savalas who could scarcely disguise his impatience with his naïve girl interrogator's assumption that he set out to play the screen heavy at an early age and had since pursued this idea with relentless determination. Actors, particularly these days, are grateful for whatever work they can get.

But, granting that screen actors are even more dependent than their theatrical colleagues on directors and writers, one still comes up against a number of myths that surround the mysterious art of acting to a camera. And of these the most pernicious and destructive is the one that assumes that less automatically means more; that in the cinema all one needs is the minutest tremor of an eyebrow to communicate passion or the merest twitch of a cheek muscle to indicate some volcanic internal eruption. The origins of this attitude are, of course, not hard to discover. In the early days of the talkies when silent-screen extravagance had necessarily to be muted, the idea inevitably grew up that the less facial and physical activity an actor displayed the more sincere his performance was likely to be. And undeniably a really great screen actress, like Garbo, could communicate intense emotion with the utmost economy of means. Clarence Brown, who directed many of her silent films for MGM, has said: 'Garbo had something behind the eyes that you couldn't see until you photographed it in close-up. You could see thought. If she had to look at one person with jealousy and another with love, she didn't have to change her expression. You could see it in her eyes as she looked from one person to another. And nobody else has been able to do that on the screen. Garbo did it without the command of the English language.'

For Garbo less may have meant more. For many of her successors, however, less has emphatically meant less. And the curse of much screen acting today is the belief (*a*) that one simply has to act with the head and never with the whole body, (*b*) that any element of impersonation looks phoney when subjected to the camera's X-ray analysis, (*c*) that thought and intention will be communicated provided the actor screws up his eyes and simply concentrates hard enough. It takes an exceptional personality, however, to get away with the business of simply presenting himself on the screen. A Spencer Tracy can do it. Indeed when once ill-advisedly asked 'Why do you always play Spencer Tracy?' he replied: 'Who do you want me to play— Humphrey Bogart?' But even he subtly modulated his personality from film to film: thus his Runyonesque sports promoter in *Pat and Mike* had a dapper flashiness far removed from the sinewy integrity of his computer expert in *The Desk Set* a few years later. Too many of today's actors, however, use only a limited fraction of their personality or assume that a be-yourself style of acting is sufficient to carry them through, say, a costume epic, a caper movie and a sophisticated comedy.

The myth that screen acting consists largely of knowing what *not* to do and of a cool serene inactivity is exploded simply by mentioning some of the most potent screen presences of the last forty years: Chaplin, Cagney, Laughton, Fields, Brando, Scott (George C. not Randolph), Swanson, Davis, Crawford. All are distinguished by an intransigent selfhood and by a fundamental belief that a screen per-formance can afford to be larger than life. Take Cagney, for instance. While his grossly overrated contemporary, Bogart, offered a standardised, tough-guy performance built up out of certain mannerisms (the vulpine stare, the sibilant rasp, the shoulders protectively hunched), Cagney offered a rich variety of character-traits and made his blood-soaked hoodlums seem more interesting by endowing them with a dancer's fleetness of foot: at his best he was Fred Astaire with a machine-gun. Tynan once listed his super-abundant qualities: 'The spring-heeled walk, poised forward on the toes; the fists clenched, the arms loosely swinging; the keen roving eyes; the upper lip curling back in defiance and derision; the rich, high-pitched hectoring voice; the stubby, stabbing index-finger, the smug purr with which he accepts female attention—Cagney's women always had to duck under his guard before he would permit them to make love to him.' A. Alvarez said to me on radio on one occasion that the difference between Bogart and Cagney was like the difference between J. F. Kennedy and Lyndon Johnson. Johnson may have done more but it was Kennedy who had all the charisma. Similarly, he argued, Cagney may have acted better but it was Bogie who had all the magnetism. To this I would only say that the Bogie-cult is a somewhat exaggerated one and that when it was put to the test with a revival of his main films in repertory at the London Pavilion in 1971, the cinema-going public was shown to be noticeably indifferent.

The second myth about screen acting—and it is one that stems from the first—is that there is a mystery surrounding the process that yields up its secrets only to lifelong devotees and that it is withheld from people coming to the cinema from the stage. Again the historical origins of the myth are clear. As Alexander Walker points out in his admirable book, *Stardom*, producers like Adolph Zukor believed in the second decade of the century that the whole-sale importation of stage actors was of itself sufficient to guarantee quality. In 1912 Zukor set up his Famous Players Company in Hollywood headed by theatrical stars like James O'Neill and Lily Langtry: 'Famous Players in Famous Plays' was the group's vaunting slogan. The prime intention was to show stage actors in their best-known roles and, only secondarily, to make films starring 'well-known picture players'. However the moment they were pitted against stars of the calibre of Mary Pickford—who had worked for four years under Griffith's direction —the Famous Players lost some of their prestige. And, of course, throughout screen history there have been instances of excellent theatre actors not managing to bridge the gulf between stage and studio. Beerbohm Tree was paid $100,000 for six months' work in Hollywood but proved so unacceptable that a picture player had to be used in his place in many sequences. In the 1930s plenty of Broadway stars looked towards Hollywood for an enlargement of their fame and fortune and all too literally went west (a process buoyantly satirised by Kaufman and Hart's eminently revivable comedy, *Once In A Lifetime*). And again there are always dynamic stage personalities like Ethel Merman whose bravura and attack require the protective barrier of the footlights to be totally disarming.

But although the myth that screen acting is a mysterious craft ultimately impenetrable to stage actors has some historical substance, it is today visibly disproved by the large number of theatre-trained players dominating the screen. The dreary acting in the modern cinema invariably comes from people who are 'pure' movie actors: the best from men like George C. Scott, Walter Matthau, Alan Arkin, Dustin Hoffman and Gene Hackman or girls like Glenda Jackson, Janet Suzman, Vanessa Redgrave, who have a strong grounding in theatre. Lacking the complex, deep-rooted Hollywood studio system, Britain has of course nearly always looked to the stage for its movie-actors; and it is fascinating to see how expertly and daintily the gap separating stage from screen acting has been crossed. Some actors do it by successfully transferring from one medium to another many of the mannerisms and idiosyncrasies for which they are famous. Sir Ralph Richardson, for instance, transfers to the cinema that same look of baffled, mooncalf simplicity, that same extravagant handling of props, above all that same multi-dimensional quality that delights us in the theatre. Whether playing a lead role—as in *The Fallen Idol* or *Long Day's Journey Into Night*—or simply lending a touch of buoyancy to a heavyweight epic, he invariably leaves behind a memorable physical imprint. In a piece of Hollywood hokum like Fox's *300 Spartans*—where he plays a grey-bearded political leader— he will suddenly inject a bit of individuality into the proceedings by inserting an extraordinary 'Brrrrrm . . . Brrrrrm . . .' into the middle of a speech illustrating the importance of infantry tactics. And no one who saw *The Wrong Box* can ever forget the scene where John Mills, having made numerous unsuccessful attempts to kill him, finally launches at his totally unsuspecting and departing head a vase of flowers which Richardson adroitly catches with a cry of 'Too late . . . too late to apologise'. Meanwhile, to a role like Buckingham in *Richard III* he brought all his familiar gifts for investing the ordinary man with a wealth of unsuspected interior life: this was, as Paul Dehn said, a Mr Baldwin who had read Machiavelli.

An entirely different approach comes from Sir Alec Guinness, an actor who has spent so much of his time in the cinema that he may almost be regarded as a home product. But all his early training was in classical theatre and it was only after more than a decade spent in the West End and at the Old Vic that he turned to the movies. Yet his innate understanding of the medium is visible even in a mediocre movie like *Cromwell* where he played Charles I. Richard Harris in the name-part displayed a blustering, hit-or-miss earnestness and sincerity but some idea of his technical adequacy could be gleaned from listening to his vocal variations from scene to scene. Sometimes he was a full-throated roarer, at other times he gave the impression that Cromwell was engaged in a desperate fight not with the monarchy but with creeping laryngitis. Guinness, however, flawlessly established from the start the king's character and mannerisms—his faint stutter, his habit of letting his eyes roam while his features maintained an outward composure—and deployed them at the essential points in the narrative. Thus the stutter lent emphasis to the scene in which he arbitrarily prorogued Parliament ('This Parliament is by my a-a-authority dissolved'—he chose the one word in the sentence that highlighted the very weakness of that authority). And in the scene of the king's trial the use of the restless eyes, apparently searching the hall for sign of a friendly face, instantly belied the impression of serenity and cool that his body gave. Harris, one felt, attempted to take the picture by storm: Guinness took it by stealth. And looking at the movie careers of men like Olivier, Redgrave and Gielgud, one is tempted to produce a general rule: that a great stage actor can often adjust to the screen with relative ease but that a great screen actor all too rarely manages the journey in the other direction.

Despite some of the exceptional performances I shall deal with shortly, film acting today is still in decline. The most obvious reason why is that the whole star system is on the wane. When it was flourishing, people attacked it; now that it is passing everyone seems conscious of its virtues. But it was one of the products of the system, Joan Crawford, who put her finger most concisely on what it had to offer in the course of a *Times* interview: 'I don't think anything can quite replace the sort of repertory system we had then, in which each studio had its own group of stars, directors and so on, and you would go from role to role playing with first one star, then another, then perhaps with both together, but in the sort of stable, secure atmosphere which let you grow, and learn, and use what you had learnt to build something more. I know what people say about the studios and their limitations now but I tell you at MGM in the Thirties we were spoilt rotten.' It was, as she says, a repertory system; and, like all repertory systems, it produced a far better quality of performance than the *ad hoc* approach to casting which often yokes together wildly improbable and unsuitable actors. And even when chance does throw up a potentially good star combination—like Jim Hutton and Paula Prentiss in some early 1960s Hollywood comedies—you know these days it will never be successfully exploited.

With the decline of the player has, of course, come the rise of the director and his elevation to the status of auteur —the man whose unmistakable imprint is on every foot of the finished film. I have heard it argued, with some justice, that the auteur system is the product of literary-oriented movie critics who cannot believe that any work of art is not ultimately the product of a single creative imagination. And there is no denying the auteur theory overlooks a number of elementary facts about movie-making: that more writers than one might imagine specify in their scripts precisely what kind of cuts, dissolves, even camera angles they want; that, in practice, the lighting cameraman often dictates the mood and atmosphere of a scene as much as a director and may also help determine the camera positions; that all film-making is necessarily a creative enterprise. As Ernest Lehman, whose credits as a writer include *North by Northwest* and, as a producer, *Hello Dolly*, once said to me in an interview: 'Every time a director claims sole credit for a movie, he buries 100 people in the process'. In an age of fanatical director-worship (where even a second-rate talent like Samuel Fuller is incredibly compared by an intelligent critic like Tom Milne to D. W. Griffith) great screen acting is inevitably at a premium.

The way movies are now financed also militates against great acting. Each picture is now the result of a deal usually made by an independent producer with a major studio as distributor. Stars are seen less frequently, get less chance to build up an interesting repertory of performances and, above all, know full well they are part of a declining industry. In addition to formidable talent, great screen acting also requires a magical combination of circumstances: an instant sympathy between actor and director harder to create in these days of piecemeal movie-making, confidence in one's material and, especially, a climate of opinion in which the art of acting is respected. Since even the best film critics these days usually dismiss the performances in a sentence, this last is hard to achieve. The one overwhelming consolation is that in recent years we have seen the rise of a small, select band of players who combine star-quality with technical prowess; and at the top of that list I would place George C. Scott, Walter Matthau and Alan Arkin. And I propose to examine some of their recent work to see what it tells us about the art of screen acting. I also intend to take a close look at one of the most durable and glittering products of the old-fashioned star system, Katharine Hepburn.

Scott, after remarkable performances as the unctuous gambler in *The Hustler*; the cool sleuth in *The List of Adrian Messenger* and the murderous hawk in *Doctor Strangelove*, laid claim to greatness with his portrayal of Patton in *Patton: Lust for Glory*. And the fascinating thing about that performance was that it followed none of the conventional ground-rules for film acting. Firstly, it had a strong mimetic element. Scott had clearly studied Patton's appearance, mannerisms and personal style and attempted to reproduce them without submerging his own identity. It is typical of his approach that when in the course of research he noticed Patton's upper teeth were showing but not his lower ones he asked the studio to seek out Patton's dentist and find out why. And in the movie it is noticeable that Scott smiles a crooked smile that tilts the left part of his mouth upwards, thus concealing the flawed lower teeth. Secondly, the performance had an outsize audacity rare in movies and a use of arresting detail also relevant to character. And thirdly it had a magnetic combination of apparently irreconcilable qualities. By this I mean that Scott endowed this bullish, aggressively masculine militarist with any number of gentle, feminine qualities. He thus reinforced the view that all great acting has about it an essentially bisexual quality; to prove my point let me examine the performance in some detail.

The first appearance was stunning. Against a mammoth Stars and Stripes occupying the whole Cinerama screen a miniscule figure was suddenly manifest: Patton. (One of the recurring images of the film was that of Patton as a pygmy when seen against the broad horizon of history and as a Titan when seen against his contemporaries.) The camera cut to a close-up on the medals, the ivory-handled revolver, the blue military sash. Vocally Scott combined an exhortatory Churchillian quality with the crude bull-swagger of a man speaking to man. 'We're going to go through the enemy,' he announced, 'like crap through a goose', making sharp, stabbing movements with the left hand as if the enemy were a visible punchbag. As Alexander Walker noted, sadism, narcissism, exhibitionism (the three qualities of military leadership, according to Freud) were all implicitly present in a speech of withering sarcasm and deadly logic.

The first hint of Patton's sly feminine streak came when he announced to General Bradley that he had designed a uniform for the tank crewmen and he registered regret that it had not been adopted: Scott's tone was that of a singularly aggressive couturier. He built on this element in the character in the scene where Patton visited the battlefield where the Carthaginians defended themselves against the Romans. Surveying the empty landscape he hitched up his trouser-crotch as if there were literally a pleasurable feeling stirring in his loins. And as he recited to Bradley a poem he had written about death and military glory, his left hand was compulsively tightening the glove on his right hand as if he wanted to assert his masculinity in defiance of his gift for poetry: a brilliant shorthand device for conveying the internal conflicts of a warrior with a feeling for the soft arts of peace. Scott also gave us the man's self-dramatising vanity. Being ceremonially dressed by his batman in preparation for his first encounter with Rommel, he raised the index fingers of each hand delicately skywards as the pistol was strapped round his waist. Most actors would have just raised the flat of the hand; but that typically Olivierish gesture gave clinching proof of Patton's concern for effect.

The leitmotiv of delicacy and gracious femininity was especially apparent in the crux of the film: the famous scene where Patton slapped a soldier suffering from combat fatigue. On his tour of the hospital-tent, the first man Scott encountered was suffering from a chest complaint and he received a kindly, reassuring pat. The second man was clearly dying, to judge from the way the respirator round his face heaved slowly up and down. Scott pinned a medal on his pillow, whispered confidentially in his ear and then wiped his own nose with the back of his hand as if to staunch the flow of tears. He thus showed us a man who was prey to sentiment and emotion; and he paved the way immaculately for the violent alternation of mood when Patton encountered a third man he regarded as a malingerer and struck him violently across the face. You felt he was not being cruel: he was simply trying to compensate for the feminine display of emotion to which he had publicly surrendered. The whole key to Scott's performance lay in this constant tension between the man's physical appearance and his inner nature. He was built like a barn-door; had the noble head of one of the Roman Emperors outside the Sheldonian at Oxford; had a stance as aggressive and menacing as that of a bull mastiff scenting danger. At the same time he loved poetry, cared deeply about his men, hungered for glory. Coming across a soldier wounded in combat he kissed his head gently like a friar administering extreme unction; yet in the great drive towards Berlin he swaggered in front of his troops telling them he was personally going to shoot 'that paper-hanging sonovabitch'. On top of this conflict between gentleness and aggression, Scott also gave us the feeling that this man existed on a different plane from his colleagues. Patton believed in reincarnation; and when, at a dinner party, he assured General Alexander that he had previously lived in the eighteenth century, Scott's face joined in the general laughter but his eyes retained their steely seriousness. Even when his friend, General Bradley, finally reassured him that the soldier he slapped did more than anyone to win the war in Europe, he again smiled a smile that had no direct contact with the rest of his body: the eyes registered a painful blank at the thought of the humiliations he had endured.

In sum what Scott gave us was a man who was a strange combination of Shaw's Sergius and Bluntschli in *Arms and the Man*: a man who embodied the romantic concept of a soldier and yet who underneath was a plain, straightforward realist. And like Shaw's two characters—representing opposite sides of the military temperament—he was also a performer whose mask occasionally slipped. It seemed to me a classic piece of screen acting in that it made no moral judgements on the character but allowed us to form our own conclusions; in so far as it restored the

element of impersonation to screen acting with giant confidence; and in so far as it reminded us that one of the
pleasures in watching acting lies in seeing a man—or
woman—embodying the kind of sexual conflict that psy-
chiatrists say resides in all of us.

I get a similar pleasure from watching Katharine Hepburn
at work. She is blessed with a poise and charm that are
entirely feminine; yet one also senses in all her work a drive,
authority and energy that are implicitly masculine. Peter
O'Toole recognised this when he told one interviewer that
'Kate's a combination of Tugboat Annie and Medusa. You
need your wits about you when you're with her. She fights
fair but she fights'. And she herself has told how when she
first arrived in Hollywood in 1930 in a Quaker-grey riding
habit and pancake hat, with a steel filling in one eye and
the other red in sympathy, Myron Selznick took one look
at her and said, 'Is this what we paid so much money for?'
Part of the perfection of her working relationship with
Spencer Tracy lay in the fact that they seemed, physically
and temperamentally, to complement one another. His
craggy features and granite-like Mount Rushmore-profile
concealed a good deal of gentleness: and under her slender,
fashion-plate frame one senses a wiry toughness and re-
silience. As Penelope Gilliatt once wrote, à propos Phila-
delphia Story, 'her faultless technical sense makes one feel
that she could play a scene with a speak-your-weight
machine and still turn it into an encounter charged with
irony and challenge'.

In recent years her best performance has come in The
Lion in Winter and it is the one, I think, that reveals most
about the nature of her talent. I should begin by saying
that I am extremely dubious about James Goldman's play

and movie-script: a desperately self-conscious account of the complex domestic bickering that took place at Henry II's winter court in 1183. Confronted with a convoluted historical episode—such as Henry's choice of a successor— a writer has two courses open to him. One is to unearth the episode's genuine relevance to the present day and the other is to paste modern mannerisms and speech patterns on to the characters in an attempt to suggest there is a link between them and us. Mr Goldman adopts the latter course. Although Eleanor vigorously protests that 'it's 1183 and we're barbarians', the dialogue suggests that it's 1972 and they're all living on Long Island.

The virtue of Miss Hepburn's performance was that it recognised and took advantage of that fact. While O'Toole as Henry tried to lend the character a Shakespearean density and grandeur, Miss Hepburn astutely realised that what Goldman had tried to write was a modern comedy, a *Who's Afraid of Eleanor of Aquitaine?* Although she successfully conveyed the intensity of Eleanor's love-hate relationship with Henry, she played throughout in a vein of wit-cracking irony. Surveying her puny, bedraggled, tow-haired younger son on alighting from her royal barge, she murmured from between clenched teeth, 'John, you're so clean and neat'. When she and Henry, following a little preliminary sexual sparring, advanced into the banqueting hall for dinner, she fixed a smile on to her features like a boxer putting in his gumshield. She then looked amiably at the barons while uttering sidelong asperities in a manner that exactly recalled Bob Hope, in a *Road* film, whispering to Crosby that it was time to vacate some trouble-spot while still managing to keep a weather-eye on the natives. And she actually let her wrists go perversely limp when obliged to utter a line like 'In a world where carpenters get resurrected, anything is possible': she seemed intuitively to appreciate that what Mr Goldman had written was a kind of codpieced Broadway camp. If her timing was that of Hope and Benny, her intonations were, surprisingly, those of Mae West. There was the same habit of biting off the consonants in the key word in a sentence ('How old is *Daddy* then?' she enquired when weighing up Henry's chances of getting another heir); there was the same languorous supine drawl ('We shattered the commandments on the spot' was a line that escaped from her lips with the authentic Westian drawl); and even the rise and fall of her intonations had the same pattern ('You have too many sons' was taken on an upward curve. 'You don't need more' was like coming down the nether side of a ski-run).

I do not want to push the parallel too far. I only want to suggest that Miss Hepburn has the experienced actress's ability to relate means to ends, the nous to heighten comedy where it undoubtedly exists. But she also here had the sexual ambivalence that is a hallmark of fine acting and that presumably was a quality of the real-life Eleanor since she had, on the one hand, raised armies against Henry and, on the other, gone on crusades half-naked to Damascus. The costume helped. A comb on the crown of her head thrust her hair forwards in an aggressive, dangerous-looking peak; yet her white medieval veil framed her face and seductively followed the contours of its hollow cheeks. When she clutched at Henry it was with a prehensile talon that, on closer inspection, turned out to be her hand; and yet when tauntingly suggesting that she had slept with his father, she stretched out on her bed like Monroe in a pin-up calendar. It was again a performance that embraced opposites: masculine and feminine, emotion and irony, aggression and submissiveness. George S. Kaufman, hearing that Miss Hepburn put up blankets in the wings during the Broadway run of *The Lake*, wrote that 'she's afraid she might be catching'. *The Lion in Winter* was one of many films that showed she had the disease through and through.

'He could play anything from Rhett Butler to Scarlett O'Hara,' Billy Wilder once said of Walter Matthau; and in the last few years he has come close to proving this true. For, like Scott, he is an actor who proves that movie-playing is not simply a question of behaving naturally in front of a camera but can involve impersonation, disguise and the creation of a character. Yet he also shows that even the most Protean actor retains an essential, irreducible quality of self whatever the role he is playing. I am reminded, strangely enough, of the character of the arch-criminal Vautrin as he appears in Balzac's novels. In *Splendeurs et Misères des Courtisanes* he may crop up as the respectable Spanish priest, Herrera. In *Père Goriot* he may be a lodger in a cheap boarding-house in the Rue Neuve-Sainte-Geneviève. Yet, however artful the impersonations, your pleasure lies in knowing all the time that it's still Vautrin, with that phenomenal red hair on his chest, those piercing eyes and with what one critic called 'that strong smell of brimstone' about him. What Matthau has is the true smell of the comedy actor.

Three things, I would say, are essential for a supreme comedy actor: a wayward appearance; an ability to time a phrase with the aplomb of a Billie-Jean King scooping a shot off the base line; and a suggestion that, behind the lines, there lies a personality with an omniscient, possibly jaundiced view of human endeavour.

Matthau has them all, but the appearance most especially. He has a wall-to-wall grin, a nose like an unpeeled banana and ears that an elephant would not be ashamed of.

And all these came into play in his performance as Oscar Madison in *The Odd Couple*, Neil Simon's blissfully funny account of two divorced husbands shacked up together. Before that Matthau had spent many years in Hollywood proving himself to be an invaluable character-actor: as the psychopathic killer in *Charade*; the hawkish Presidential adviser (equivalent of *Strangelove's* Buck Turgidson) in *Fail-safe*; the stone-faced sheriff in *Lonely are the Brave*. But it was the role of Neil Simon's greasy, sports-writing slob that lifted him out of the Best Supporting Actor rut. As he himself once said: 'Every actor looks all his life for a part that will combine his talents with his personality. *The Odd Couple* was mine'.

He was first glimpsed in blue baseball cap, stained T-shirt and begrimed bell-tent slacks dusting the ash off a piece of bread he had dropped on the floor. And, picking up a hand of cards for a poker game he was immersed in, his natural reaction was to stuff the tomato-and-mayonnaise sandwiches he was carrying under his capacious armpit. Within thirty seconds of seeing him, you knew just what sort of man he was. But Matthau's singular achievement was to integrate all the comic business into the character of Oscar. Thus, during the stag card-game, the phone rang. Matthau purred sweetly into the receiver, laughed coyly as if ravished by endearments and allowed his watermelon mouth to form the widest of grins as he murmured: 'Yes, darling. . . . No, darling. . . . I told you not to call me during the game.' He then turned from the phone, abruptly switched off the charm and rapped out to a bald-pated guest: 'Murray . . . it's your wife'. An old gag; but Matthau made it look as if Oscar had just invented it.

He also suggested very subtly that Oscar, just like the rest of us, changed his personality to suit his environment: a swaggering hearty with the boys, a venomous mate

when left alone with Felix, and a devilish Don Juan when
confronted by a female. When a pair of British birds from
the flat upstairs came down for the evening, for instance,
he assumed a cuddly amiability and essayed a few fresh
remarks. The girls complained of the heat in their flat.
Then why, he asked, didn't they sleep with an air-con-
ditioner? 'We haven't got one,' they gurgled. 'No,' he
replied, 'but we have.' Overcome with the outrageousness
of the joke, he punched the furniture in ecstasy and struck
the table with an iron fist. Not only funny in itself; but
providing just the right atmosphere for Jack Lemmon, as his
spinsterish partner, to step in with a classic conversation-
stopper about the possibility of rain on Friday.

Above all, Matthau's timing is as sweet and impeccable
as Hope's. Complaining that he found a note on his pillow
saying 'We're out of cornflakes, F. U.', he holds the pause
just long enough for us to get the point and for a ripple of
laughter to run round the audience. He then weighs in,
wearily, with 'Took me three hours to work out that
F. U. meant Felix Unger,' thus reaping the whirlwind. He
also throws away with the dexterity of a veteran poker-
player. 'How could you be in anybody's way?' one of the
nice girls from upstairs asks of a wounded-looking Lemmon.
'Want to see a type-written list?' retorts Matthau, barely
shrugging an eyebrow.

Since *The Odd Couple* Matthau's career has blossomed. In
Hello Dolly he was admirable, gazing on the proceedings
around him with a starchy disdain and joining in the song-
and-dance numbers with all the enthusiasm and visible
sense of commitment of a rural dean taking part in a peek-a-
boo routine. In *The New Leaf* he was a loping, narcissistic
playboy affianced to a rich and messy botanist ('She has
to be vacuumed,' he complained, 'after every meal'). In
Kotch he redeemed a somewhat sentimental fable about a

self-reliant, sturdily independent old man by investing him with a waspish asperity rarely visible in the script. And in *Plaza Suite* he did a triumphant three-card trick as a bourgeois philanderer, a Hollywood Lothario and an apoplectic father on his daughter's wedding-day. Combining the best elements of W. C. Fields, Mister Magoo and Thersites, he has an ebullient sourness welcome in these maudlin times and constantly suggests that his mordancy is more than skin-deep. Actors talk much about communication, contact, fellow-feeling: occasionally it is refreshing to find someone who looks as if he hates the human race and who can remind us that much of the best screen comedy taps a vein of misanthropy hidden deep in all of us.

Throughout this chapter I have stressed the importance of the mimetic element in screen acting and my boredom with the purist view that Gary Cooper, say, is a truer screen actor than Alec Guinness, or that you can learn more about acting to camera from Alan Ladd than Laurence Olivier. And today I suppose the smart thing to say would be that an actor like Robert Redford—who changes his costume more often than his performance—is more truly cinematic than someone like Alan Arkin, with his chameleon gift for altering his manner and appearance from role to role. Yet give me Arkin every time: the Arkin who transformed himself from the gimlet-eyed murderer in *Wait Until Dark* into the dapper, spring-heeled deaf mute in *The Heart is a Lonely Hunter* and into the volubly explosive Puerto Rican father in the raucous and sentimental *Popi*.

Like a lot of actors with an infinite flexibility, he has the kind of off-screen presence that would never cause a traffic-jam: as Shaw said of Irving, he has no face. Or, at least, what face he has lacks revealing contours. The hair, like that of Felix Unger in *The Odd Couple*, could best be described as clenched. And when we met for a Manhattan lunch appointment he arrived in sneakers, white slacks and blue fisherman's jersey. But what distinguishes his work is its mimetic relish, fastidious attention to detail and humanist understanding. Like Matthau (who developed his own miniature biographies for each of the characters in *Plaza Suite*) he believes in a scientific and methodical approach to the art of acting. 'I'm not basically an inspirational actor,' he told me. 'I don't think you can be inspired twenty shots a day over a ten-week shooting schedule.' Unlike Matthau, however, you feel he has a compassionate sympathy for many of the characters he plays: it seems to me no accident that his cinematic god is Renoir.

It was *The Heart is a Lonely Hunter* that showed this regard at its best. Adapted from a Carson McCuller's story about a deaf mute on whose shoulders everyone loaded their troubles but who himself had nowhere to turn, the film could easily have nose-dived into sentimentality. What prevented it doing so was Arkin's own refusal to milk the situation for a cheap penny-in-the-slot pathos. He turned the character into a neat, spry, dapper figure in lightweight suit and straw hat and endowed him with the sort of constant alertness you often find in people who are partially handicapped; and he developed a beautiful relationship with a fat, mute anarchic chum (Chuck McCann). They chuckled together over harmless japes like a pair of truant schoolboys and yet at the same time Arkin displayed the fierce protectiveness of a maiden aunt towards his delinquent friend. Arkin got our sympathy through the simple expedient of never appealing directly to it; yet, as Penelope Mortimer excellently remarked, the performance's understanding and control seemed to spring not just out of the actor's technique but out of his own understanding and compassion.

As Yossarian, the reluctant bombardier of Joseph Heller's *Catch-22*, he was no less remarkable, constantly revealing the abyss of panic and dread that lay underneath the precarious surface sanity. What made the performance even more interesting was that Arkin for the first time relied not at all on impersonation: instead of screening himself behind a disguise, or hiding beneath a concept, he simply used himself and played each scene for its own values. 'Not having a characterisation,' Arkin told me, 'I had nothing to fall back on except myself.' He proved, in fact, that that gave him ample room for manoeuvre.

Where then does screen acting stand today? In a state, I would suggest, of some confusion. Reassuringly, the actor (in the case of the people mentioned above) has taken over from the star. At the same time one rarely gets that sense of continuity achieved in the repertory casting of the old studio system and there are still plenty of movie-actors around who seem to drift through their films in a somnambulistic comatose condition. Indeed one of the advantages theatre enjoys over cinema is that by virtue of the working conditions the live medium shows you the actor the night before, whereas the camera preserves him for posterity the morning after.

But what really militates against the actor today is the gradual, and perhaps historically inevitable, disappearance of narrative cinema before the tide of mood-movies, directorial fantasies and 'specialist' films aimed at an easily definable market such as rock-lovers or solitary men in stained raincoats. The cinema has, of course, since its inception provided the possibility of escape into a trancelike condition: a film is, in Cocteau's words, 'a dream that can be dreamed by many people at the same time'. And anyone hooked on movies from childhood will scarcely need telling what a large part they play in one's own wish-fulfilment and private fantasy life. The difference is that in the past the dream was filled with outsize beings with whom one secretly identified; today films are much more like abstract paintings in which one admires the pattern, the rhythm, the colour, the general sense of design. In the past the cinema offered us characters; today it is inclined to offer us images. And indeed what one tends to remember in modern cinema is not any affirmation of humanist faith but some beautiful piece of shooting: the repeated shots of a house blown to smithereens in Antonioni's *Zabriskie Point*, the haunting rural lyricism of Bo Widerberg's *Elvira Madigan*, the energetic, Petrushka-like opening of Ken Russell's *The Music Lovers*, the tracking-shot round the oval counters of some shinily futuristic store in *The Clockwork Orange*. Even a film-maker like Joe Losey, who shows a heartening old-fashioned attachment to the problems inherent in the human condition, still defines people as much through the objects surrounding them as through their own personalities: in a Losey film you are what you own.

The logic of the new approach to movie-making is that the actor simply becomes a small part of the total aesthetic design, the human being less important than his surroundings. One could, in fact, write a fascinating thesis about the treatment of one specific machine in modern cinema: the car. Penelope Gilliatt noted in the *New Yorker* how in *Les Choses de la Vie* the death of the hero in a motor-smash was regarded as infinitely less important than the break-up of his auto: the car's demise was photographed lyrically, lovingly, slowly, gracefully and from many different points

E

of view whereas poor old Michael Piccoli (an excellent actor as a rule) was seen as perfectly expendable. What does one remember from *Bullitt*? Steve Macqueen's performance as a harassed San Francisco cop? No. The exhilaration of the car-chase over those undulating roads. Does one recall anything Michael Caine did or said in *The Italian Job*? No; but one instantly recalls the spectacle of Mini-Minors hurtling through colonnades and down precipitous flights of steps. Were there people in *The Love Bug*? Maybe; but all I can remember now are the splendid contortions of the automatic hero. And when it's not cars it's helicopters. Long after I have forgotten who played what in Peter Yates's *Hot Rock* (British title—*How To Steal a Diamond in Four Uneasy Lessons*) I shall remember the spectacle of a chopper threading its way through the silvery tops of New York's daunting skyscrapers. Even Gene Hackman's splendid performance in *The French Connection* has been talked about much less than the spectacle of a car racing to keep up with an overhead train at whatever cost to life or limb. Actors these days are not only parts of a director's abstract design: they are even being up-screened by the hardware.

Is there a future for the actor in the cinema? A severely limited one, I suspect. The fact is that films are now identified almost exclusively by the names of their directors and that the acting is often regarded as the least important ingredient in the composition of a movie. When Polanski makes *Macbeth* it is he who is the unseen star of the venture and it is an apt comment on the film's priorities that the central roles were played by two performers whose names can have meant little to the cinema-going public. When Hitchcock makes *Frenzy*, it is his name that goes out over the billboards. When Fellini makes *Satyricon*, total unknowns are again cast for principal roles and the film is stamped through and through with its maker's name like a stick of Blackpool rock. A director like Pasolini even casts almost exclusively from amateurs. And as the director's power gets ever greater, so I suspect the public will stay away from cinemas in ever greater numbers, turning out in force only to witness a thrilling and exciting narrative or the occasional eruption of an illuminating outsize personality. I believe cinema should be the product of a fruitful collision between the talents of writer, director and actor. When any one of these gets the upper hand (as the director has today) then the product will surely suffer. Although there are plenty of fine actors still working in movies, I find it sad to see them in many cases making a lesser contribution to the finished product than the art director or the lighting cameraman. Acting may, as O'Toole said, be a question of farting about in disguises. But today on the screen a lot of it is simply reduced to farting about.

6

DOES TELEVISION DESTROY ACTORS?

THE title of this chapter asks a dramatic question; but it has some point. For, the moment one starts to consider acting on television, one is struck by the fact that in this medium the performer is confronted by numerous pitfalls that do not present themselves in theatre and cinema. Admittedly television has created some very fine actors of its own and boosted the career of many more. It has also been virtually ignored by most of the leading stage actors of this generation (Olivier, Redgrave, Gielgud, Guinness, Richardson, Scofield) for reasons that cannot simply be attributed to green-room snobbishness. More dangerously, it has created a new breed of actor content to spend most of his working-life in front of the cameras appearing in work that he knows at heart to be trivial and second-rate. As that fine actor George Coulouris once said, 'Television has wrecked acting because it's impossible to make a stirring success. If somebody had told me thirty years ago that by this point in my career I'd be spending a lot of my time in some cheerless, dusty rehearsal room preparing for a single performance in something not very important I would have said that it could never happen.'

To start with the obvious, the first problem about television is that, like the old Windmill Theatre, it never closes. An actor in a play or a film has at least the consolation that an audience has made a special effort to see the work in which he is appearing: in television he is simply part of a continuous electronic flow or what Jonathan Miller once picturesquely called the grey mass of ectoplasm that pours unendingly off the screen. For years BBC 1's main drama spot—*Play For Today*—was sandwiched between the Nine O'Clock News and *24 Hours*. On Independent Television any play is necessarily interrupted by plugs for commercial products. A remarkable stage performance, like McKellen's Richard II, when presented on television, comes after a documentary about life in Tokyo and immediately before a late news summary.

An actor is thus seen in the context of the raw material he is interpreting. After *Cathy Come Home*—the very moving and powerful Jeremy Sandford play about homelessness—was shown on BBC 1 there was a discussion on BBC 2 about the work in which the genuinely homeless were represented. Confronted with competition of that sort, how could the leading actors (Carol White and Ray Brooks) appear anything other than over-glamorous, excellent as their performances were? And precisely because a play may be seen between a documentary on East End slums and a newsreport from Vietnam, the easiest condition of acceptance (as Philip Mackie once noted) is that 'it similarly shows real people behaving in a real way against real backgrounds'. If this led to a series of authentically Balzacian plays, series and serials, then one would have no complaint. What it means in practice is that one gets a string of programmes offering a substitute-naturalism in which one feels real life is being seen from the cosy, insulated atmosphere of a television centre. (Maupassant said of Zola that he took a victoria to see the peasants and I sometimes feel that television writers and directors have taken a taxi to see the working classes.) And the effect this predilection for sentimentalised slice-of-life drama has on television acting is immediately apprehensible: that the scripts require a muted realism, an imitation of the visible and audible surfaces of life and allow very little opportunity for the presentation of passion and suffering on the grand, heroic scale.

Actors are at the mercy of the context in which they appear and the material they are presented with. They are also affected, less obviously, by the technological changes that have come over the medium. Looking at the growth of British television drama since the war, it is possible to see it in terms of three distinct phases. Phase One covers the late '40s (BBC TV only restarted in 1947) and early '50s when television drama was usually transmitted live, was theatrical in origin and limited in scope. It now seems hard to believe but plays transmitted on a Sunday were normally repeated on a Thursday partly on the grounds, a paternalistic executive once remarked, that it was considered healthy for viewers to have a night away from television occasionally. The emphasis during this period, however, was very much on the actor, and certain favourites (John Robinson, Clement McCallin and Peter Cushing— who played Winston Smith in *1984*) were carefully built up and established as nationally popular figures.

Phase Two began with the creation of ITV in 1955 and, in retrospect, looks from the drama point of view like a golden era. The dominant influence during this period was Sydney Newman, a bustling and dynamic Canadian, who brought with him a firm belief in the supremacy of the writer and director rather than the actor and a distrust of theatrical drama on television. And this policy was borne out by his work as Head of ABC drama from 1958 to 1962 and of BBC TV drama from 1962 to 1966. This was also the period in which videotape gave television a recording process of high quality and consequently made live drama almost a thing of the past. Phase Three dates from the

mid-'60s when the medium's preoccupation with naturalism was increasingly called into question, when a filmic
approach to television drama was taken by young directors and when 'agitational contemporaneity' (Newman's
phrase) became an important factor in much of the best
writing. The artificialities of studio production, with all
the heavy electronic equipment involved, were regarded
with increasing suspicion and the emphasis was placed on
real locations, documentary-style authenticity and filmic
pace. 'The results,' wrote Stuart Hood in *Television: A
Survey*, 'were soon evident in The Wednesday Play on
BBC 1. At their best they achieved something quite new—
something technically freer than the normal television play,
something with more visual impact, more pace. At their
worst they used film tediously, inserting long action scenes
—a man running after a bus, a boy wandering through the
streets—to eke out a script. The script indeed became less
important than the director's shaping of it. . . .' The result,
predictably enough, was the final ousting of the actor from
the dominant role in television drama—though it is only
fair to add that in the early '70s the actor has staged something of a comeback principally through the BBC's preoccupation with long-running Harrison Ainsworth-type
history series.

Perhaps the most crucial factor working against the
actor on television, however, is the whole showbiz ambiance
of the industry itself. This manifests itself in many different
ways. If, for instance, an actor in a long-running series or
serial establishes a character firmly in the public mind, then
his own private persona will become inextricably entangled
with that of the character. And the press (and not merely
the popular press) busily and relentlessly exploits the fact.
Thus, for the headline writers, Stratford Johns is now
'Barlow'; for many years after the series finished Rupert

Davies was always 'Maigret', and even a theatre notice in the *Guardian* of the Royal Shakespeare Company's *Dr Faustus* actually said that it had David Waller, 'hitherto an impressive supporting actor, in the role created by Soames Forsyte' (meaning, of course, Eric Porter). And the attempt to exploit the popular success of a particular programme often leads to a blurring of the line between fantasy and reality. Some years back the *Radio Times* published a massively detailed quiz entitled 'How Well Do You Know Angleton?' (Angleton was a mythical East Anglian town in which a series called *The Newcomers* was set) and the BBC has actually published copies of *The Ambridge Times*, a newspaper deriving from the radio programme, *The Archers*. With this kind of idiot practice going on, what chance does the poor actor stand?

The contrary danger is that success for an actor may lead to an exploitation of him by other departments of the television industry. In particular Light Entertainment seems to have a voracious appetite for using straight actors who have made a name for themselves in series. Thus we have seen the late, lamented Patrick Wymark stooging for Frankie Howerd; Glenda Jackson, Eric Porter, Edward Woodward, Francis Matthews, Ian Carmichael, Peter Cushing and many others fulfilling the same function for Morecambe and Wise; and singing actors such as Mr Woodward, Keith Michell and Patrick Cargill given their own hour-long variety shows on the strength of success in series like *Callan*, *The Six Wives of Henry VIII* and *Father, Dear Father*. I do not want to become too pompous about this and suggest that actors should never do anything other than hide behind the characters they are playing; and one could even argue that guest-appearances on comedy and variety shows help to establish in the public mind the fact that the actors are human beings with lives and personalities of their own. Yet there is an obvious danger in performers of the stature of Glenda Jackson clowning around on, say, *The Morecambe and Wise Show*; and that is that the really valuable work they have done on television drama merely comes to seem another part of the medium's unceasing electronic flow or, worse still, an extension of the light entertainment atmosphere which increasingly pervades the box from dawn to dusk. I am all for actors letting their hair down occasionally; but when, say, Laurence Olivier, Vivien Leigh and Danny Kaye did their famous *Triplets* number at showbiz benefits it was always for strictly limited theatre-going audiences. When actors get jovially insulted by Eric and Ernie, it is in front of several moderately attentive millions.

Advertising also plays its part in the process of altering our conception of an actor as a man who is an interpreter of the finest thoughts and emotions ever penned when it offers us the spectacle of the incomparable Michael Hordern cavorting round a Crosse and Blackwell's tin or the honeyed sound of Patrick Allen recommending to us a wide assortment of goods. But while a leading actor can survive involvement with commercials a relatively little-known actor or actress may find that their association with a particular product dogs them for some time to come. For instance an actress who played a somewhat harassed middle-class housewife called Katie in a sequence of cooking ads appeared, when these were at the height of their exposure, in a drama series about ecology called *Doomwatch*. More than one critic commented on the difficulty of responding seriously to someone they instantly associated with the world of Oxo cubes.

All these factors—the surrounding actuality, the mini-naturalistic scripts, the changing technology, the showbiz exploitation and the commercial temptations—conspire to make television a medium that, on balance, does more harm than good to the art and craft of acting. But lest anyone should think I was being too harsh, I decided to monitor a typical evening's television to see precisely what creative opportunities the medium offered the actors at its disposal. In the event I chose the evening of Friday, January 21, 1972, chiefly because it offered a fair selection of dramatic entertainment: no less than five drama series on ITV, a solo performance and an arts magazine on BBC 2 and a drama series plus an old Hollywood movie on BBC 1. This was how the evening went:

7.30: ATV's *The Persuaders* starring Tony Curtis and Roger Moore as a tough New Yorker and an English milord both involved in the secret agent game. Curtis comes to the series with a distinguished Hollywood pedigree (*The Sweet Smell of Success, Some Like It Hot, The Boston Strangler*) while Moore has built up a reputation chiefly through long-running television series such as *The Saint*; and the most immediately striking thing about the programme is the way Curtis uses all his Hollywood experience to bring a certain credibility to some paper-thin dialogue while Moore is left panting pluckily in the rear. This particular episode by Walter Black was the old one about the man who wakes up dozily one morning to find himself inadvertently married. He can't remember a proposal, a ceremony or even a honeymoon. But married he is to a beautiful Swedish girl who returns to England with him to act as hostess during a top-secret week-end meeting at his country pad: a meeting between an English intelligence chief and a high-ranking diplomat about to put some startling new proposals to the UN. No one ever tells us precisely what these proposals consist of; but we have to believe that they are of such significance that they merit an assassination attempt engineered by the bogus bride.

The plot, as you will see, is rubbish that might have come straight from a period boy's comic rather than the present day: in fact, more *Wizard* than *Oz*. And one notices how, despite the expensive casting of Curtis and Moore, there is elsewhere an impression that every expense has been spared. Thus two-thirds of the story is allegedly located in Stockholm; yet all we ever see of that city is a few stock shots of cars driving up to bleakly anonymous public buildings. Curtis, however, survives it all principally through following the old vaudeville maxim of never staying long enough in one spot to present anyone with a target. Visiting his chum's Stockholm apartment he does a dexterous, George Best-like weave to avoid a vacuuming chambermaid; at a judo club he attempts to carry on a Cary Grant-style conversation while being tossed over a girl's shoulder; and punching one of the heavies in the stomach he meets an iron wall of resistance, cries 'uh-uh' and dodges nimbly out of range. So invisible is the actual character, however, that he is reduced to weird eccentricities (like keeping a pair of black gloves on throughout) to lend it a little weight and substance. He does a good job; but it is regrettable that an actor of Curtis's standing should have to bolster up such an empty, unrewarding part. The rest of the episode was conspicuous chiefly for the crudity of the acting. The two actors playing the Swedish heavies adopted a mannered sing-song that sounded like Spike Milligan parodying an Ingmar Bergman movie; meanwhile the actor playing a Stockholm registrar made no attempt to alter his impeccable English upper-crust accent. Frankly, if I had been the Swedish cultural attaché in London, I would have been on the telephone to Sir Lew Grade straightaway to complain about this grotesque treatment of my native tongue.

8.30: London Weekend's *The Fenn Street Gang*, a spin-off

from the very successful series, *Please Sir*. This new programme shows a gang of teenagers just after they have left
school and are making their first contact with the harsh
outside world. It is not by any means a star-oriented series:
the focus shifts each week from one to another of the six
leading characters all played by relative unknowns. In this
particular episode we saw Dennis Dunstable, the softest-
hearted member of the gang and totally obsessed by horses,
attempting to save an old nag from the knacker's yard,
losing his job as a stable-hand in consequence but finally
selling the horse to his boss at a profit *and* getting his job
back. Peter Denyer admittedly gave quite a touching performance as the fuzzy-haired, seraphic-faced innocent; but
for me he could not disguise the melancholy fact that a boy
who was mentally defective was being presented by the
scriptwriters as eccentrically charming. Anyone who has a
compulsive urge to draw horses over every piece of paper
in sight is surely suffering from severely arrested development and is in need of treatment; but in the mindless context of sitcom this is merely a lovable foible. The sharpest
performance came from Liz Gebhardt as a scrawny, thin-
lipped Catholic charmer who at one point addressed a
prayer to God as if she really believed He were there. But
the rest of the cast seemed to be suffering from histrionic
malnutrition, a condition that frequently affects performers
in series starved of something to act. Worth noting, in-
cidentally, that Carol Hawkins who had a half-dozen lines
in the whole episode was given a two-page spread in that
week's *TV Times* and dubbed 'television's most recently
established sex symbol'.

9.0: *Solo* on BBC 2. The one programme on television, as
the title implies, wholly devoted to the art of acting. Each
week a particular performer is matched with a famous
writer and artist and given the freedom to develop as

detailed a portrait as possible within twenty minutes. This week Alec McCowen is playing Van Gogh. McCowen is an actor who has received recognition relatively late in life: for years he showed himself an actor of finesse, precision and bite both in the West End and in a wide range of classical roles at the Old Vic. But, strangely enough, it was only when he played the lead in *Hadrian VII* as the priestly reject envisioning himself as Pope that he received the recognition he deserved. Yet this performance was not inherently better than his fanatical, steely-eyed accountant in John Bowen's allegorical *After The Rain* or his dapper, spring-heeled suitor in Ben Travers's *Thark*. Perhaps the answer is that it takes a virtuoso performance in a mediocre play to make one a star. Anyway in *Solo* McCowen achieves the difficult feat of presenting a mind at the end of its tether without lapsing into self-indulgent rhetoric. And he does this chiefly through stressing Van Gogh's memories of happiness and self-fulfilment. 'Humanity and again humanity—I love this series of bipeds from the smallest baby to Socrates' was the theme; and McCowen, weasel-eyed, trim-bearded and full of sharp, sudden impulsive movements, genuinely gave one the feeling that Van Gogh was a man who ached for close contact with other human beings but who was irrevocably isolated from them both by his temperament and his genius. 'It would be better to create children than to paint pictures,' he rasped at one moment, crouching in a corner like a hunted animal; yet there was a great cry of exultation when he asked his brother Theo if he had received the sketch of his bedroom as though the act of creation relieved the incessant pain. It was a model demonstration of how to present madness— one minute guffawing with delight at Gauguin's portrait of himself and the next enacting the unspeakable loneliness of waking up in the morning without a fellow-creature

beside one—and a remarkably large-scale piece of acting
for a medium in which the gently shrugged eyebrow and the
quivering upper lip are generally expected to convey everything. It proved to me there is room for passion and size
in television acting: just too few actors capable of providing
it and too few writers capable of demanding it.

9.20: *Review*, a weekly arts magazine which happened to
contain a tribute to Daisy Ashford in the form of readings from *The Young Visiters* by Vivian Pickles, with Alan
Bennett supplying Sir James Barrie's introduction in a
Scots tea-room burr. Interesting chiefly because Miss
Pickles's straight, unvarnished reading of the extracts ('My
life will be sour grapes and ashes without you' had the
proper anguish as Mr Salteena realised Ethel was not to be
his) contrasted neatly with the ever-so-faint mockery of
Bennett's approach. A good example of how the professional
player can be teamed with a writer-performer and of how
a careful piece of casting can help give life to literary extracts
(the previous week the same programme had John Wood
of the accosting profile and woodpecker voice reading,
superbly, from the work of Mervyn Peake).

10.30: ATV's *Shirley's World*. Not so much a programme,
more a disaster-area. The great, the incomparable Shirley
MacLaine reduced to playing a famous woman photo-
grapher in a series of almost sublime daftness. In this episode
(the first) our Shirley turns up in London to work for a
magazine called *World Illustrated* which apparently operates
from St James's Palace to judge from the size of the offices.
Assigned to get an interview with a former Lord Chamberlain, Miss MacLaine does so by besieging his club with the
help of a bevy of Soho strippers. Numerous establishing
shots of Miss MacLaine getting in and out of taxis presumably to remind American viewers that the programme
really had been shot in London; John Gregson, as the

magazine editor, forced to snap into a telephone idiot remarks like 'Put a box round that and keep it to 200'; and a lot of excellent character-actors like Charles Lloyd Pack and Arthur Howard left spluttering on the sidelines playing clubbable old gentlemen. That it should come to this: Shirley MacLaine, the girl with legs up to her armpits and a personality that leaps through a camera lens, should be mouthing sitcom dialogue in a sit with absolutely no com.

10.40: BBC 2's *Late Night Line-Up*, which discussed a film conceived by the Transport and General Workers Union and made by a director of Harlech Television. The discussion was splendidly acrimonious with a myopic BBC producer putting the point of view of the beleaguered professional who suddenly sees a danger that part of his empire may be chipped away. But one significant point did emerge: the question of whether or not the trade unionists involved were acting the role of trade unionists knowing there was a camera present. The charge was made and strenuously denied; but this raised the significant question of what is acting for television. Anyone who has appeared on the box will know that one does in fact give a performance when one goes on—whether it be to do a straight-to-camera report or to take part in a discussion. The surroundings are so artificial that one inevitably makes minor adjustments to one's manner, to one's style of speech, even to one's way of listening to other people talk. In that sense everyone who appears on television is a performer; and the man who reads the news differs from the hero of a police series only in that the one is concerned with fact and the other with fiction. We are all actors now.

Picking on one particular evening's television may be regarded as unfair but it does leave one with a number of slightly melancholy conclusions. One is that the literary

standard of many drama series is so low that normally
excellent actors (Laurence Naismith in *The Persuaders*,
John Gregson in *Shirley's World*) are made to look a shadow
of their normal selves simply because they have nothing to
act. A second is that, given sufficient richness in terms of
human content, it is perfectly possible to escape from the
puritan heresy that on television less means more: Alec
McCowen's *Solo* performance proved that vocal variety,
facial animation and the use of the whole body—in other
words, acting in its total sense—is perfectly possible on the
box. And a third point is that the infusion of Hollywood
stars into television series only serves to expose the thread-
bare journeyman quality of so much television writing.

Occasionally, however, the importation of a Hollywood
star can prove enriching. Thus two nights after I staged my
own sit-in in front of the box, I saw Lee Remick on BBC 1
in Tennessee Williams's *Summer and Smoke*, an attractive,
sentimental study of a demure Southern virgin whose
sexual instincts are aroused by a rakehelly doctor at the
same time as she is converting him to a more virtuous and
steadier life: they are like ships that pass in the night making
only the most fleeting and spasmodic contact with each
other. If the play were revived in the theatre, it would be
one's duty to point out that it is interesting minor Williams
somewhat too schematic for its own good and with characters that, as Tynan once noted, are 'too slight to sustain
the consuming emotions which are bestowed on them'.
On television, however, a play like this becomes a major
dramatic event. Indeed a letter to *The Times* after trans-
mission made the point that, with work of this quality
around, the BBC's standards were clearly as high as they
had ever been. It was a not unintelligent letter; but I thought
it proved the point Professor Roy Fuller is always making
—namely that we are living in an age when good middle-

Ken Dodd looking suitably tickled,
a comedian who can transform a bunch of strangers
into a half-crazed and uproarious assembly.

A pair of kings:
Left, Ian McKellen as Marlowe's Edward II
reluctant to yield his crown;
Above, As Shakespeare's Richard II
swathed in pomp and ceremony.

Katharine Hepburn in *The Lion in Winter*.
'A performance that embraced opposites: masculine
and feminine, emotion and irony, aggression and submissiveness.'

brow work is constantly being elevated to the status of high culture.

However this is not to deny the marvellous performance of Lee Remick. At first she was all fluttery hand movements, nervous, sawn-off gestures and vocal mannerisms (drawling the long 'a' sound in 'Baltimore, Maryland' beautifully) in a way that perfectly suggested the minister's daughter with pretensions to gentility. Even the way she sang 'It Breaks My Heart' under the white Victorian-style bandstand on Glorious Hill was just sufficiently off-key to let us know that Alma was not one of nature's sopranos. And the slight pursing of the lips when she discovered one of the town teenage flirts had asked for a sex-book conveyed the woman's spinsterish veneer. What Miss Remick, with a profile of rigorous purity, did so marvellously was to show this surface slowly cracking like dry, parched ground opening up after rain. In the town square she was all decorous formality, even cleaning the rim of a public drinking-cup with a lace handkerchief after use. Within doors, however, she showed the woman's suppressed desires breaking through the shell of politesse. Admittedly the first hint we had of her profound love for the doctor came when, in the square, he gazed up at a firework display while she looked longingly at his back; but indoors she managed to convey, even in the course of a telephone call inviting him to a literary soirée, the profundity of her passion simply through a voluptuous smile when he agreed to attend. And the panickiness of Alma's reiterated cry that she'd never be able to get through the summer became like an early warning signal for the unleashing of a reined-in sexuality.

What Miss Remick did was to present us with a woman in whom a natural beauty of soul could not be completely crushed. She brought real tenderness to the confession of her love for the doctor and a rapturous intensity to the dubious statement that 'we were so close we almost breathed together'. But after Alma has realised that she and the young doctor can never be lovers, the natural tendency is for the actress to show us a woman going steeply and radically into decline (a tendency not always avoided by Geraldine Page in the movie version) as she resorts to picking up commercial travellers in the town square. Miss Remick, however, still took the most alert interest in her pick-up when he confessed to a natural shyness, as if this answered to something inside herself. And when she went off with him to the first of, presumably, many such encounters it was with a certain bruised gaiety rather than the air of one entering a life of degradation. In short, Miss Remick charted the progress of the character most astutely; but she never tried to editorialise about her. It was a memorable and touching performance.

Perhaps the most significant thing about acting on television, however, is that the work that sticks in the memory is usually to be found in long-running series and classic serials: not the mid-Atlantic time-fillers, the sitcoms and the rubbish-shows that are simply an extension of the world shown in commercials but the decently written series that give the actor a chance to develop. Think of some of the best performances in recent years: Eric Porter's Soames and Susan Hampshire's Fleur in *The Forsyte Saga*; Keith Michell's Henry VIII and Glenda Jackson's Queen Elizabeth in the respective series about those two monarchs; Stratford John's Barlow in *Z Cars* and *Softly, Softly*; Alan Badel's Count of Monte Cristo; Freddie Jones's Claudius in *The Caesars*; Margaret Tyzack's venomous Cousin Bette in the adaptation of the Balzac novel; Patrick Wymark's Sir John Wilder, and Edward Woodward's Callan. All these performances had the chance to grow over months or even years. They all relied on a cumulative impact as episode by episode the actor revealed to us further facets of the character. They also emerged from a branch of television drama that is perhaps less dominated by the writer and director.

But the striking thing about that list is that, with one notable exception, all the actors in it came to television with a well-established theatrical reputation. The exception is Stratford Johns who before he played Barlow was virtually unknown. He is a prime example of the actor created by television: an actor whose fame rests on the exploration of a single character over the span of a decade. And if you happen 'to drop in on the programme casually you still find his performance as fresh as ever. The physique has perhaps grown a little fuller over the years: the pointed, diamond-shaped chin is now enclosed in folds of flesh, the short-cropped black hair has receded a little further across the skull, the paunch is perhaps more pronounced. But the essentials of the character remain intact: he is still the hard professional cop who approaches his work with missionary fervour and whose attitude to criminals is one of unmitigated loathing. One could, I suppose, argue that the popularity of such a character is socially unhealthy in that it suggests we still take a punitive attitude to criminals. But the good thing about the performance is that Johns also shows us the smugness, the arrogance, the insensitivity that go with a life of dedicated crime-busting. And, as Barlow has risen in the police hierarchy, Stratford Johns has endowed him with a pomposity that is the other side of his delight in pitching in and personally conducting an interrogation like some massive Andalusian bull charging a matador.

Other performers have come to television with an established stage and screen reputation but have grown markedly in stature through their work on the box. Susan Hampshire

is a case in point. She started out in the theatre at the age
of sixteen as a lowly paid Assistant Stage Manager, got her
first big break with a show-stopping role in *Expresso Bongo*,
graduated (if that is the word) to Slade-Reynolds musicals
and Hugh and Margaret Williams comedies. She even had
a stab at Hollywood which, after a totally fruitless period
of five months, she disenchantedly described as 'the land of
the bottom-pinchers'. But it was as Fleur Forsyte that she
proved she could combine a brittle vivacity with a latent
acidity and that she could capture exactly the iron-butterfly
quality of a spoilt 'Twenties darling. In fact, she herself is a
pretty shrewd cookie. Donald Wilson, the programme's
producer, has recalled that she arranged their first meeting
in a French restaurant in London and that she arrived
early, thus managing to be deep in conversation with the
maître d'hôtel when he turned up. She knew Fleur was half-
French; and he was immediately struck by her intelligence
in demonstrating her knowledge of the language. He was
also attracted by her liveliness and by the fact that 'she
was very much a 'Twenties figure'.

She was involved for nine months in the making of *The
Forsyte Saga* and subsequently went into *Vanity Fair* and
The First Churchills. But I wondered if the idea that classic
series gave the actor more room for manoeuvre was illusory.
I remember being told by David Giles, who directed *Vanity
Fair*, that for one episode they had only four and a half days'
rehearsal and one day in the studio. And on that last day
they had fifty extras and five horses to cope with. So I asked
Susan Hampshire what it was like from the performer's view-
point.

'Well, *Vanity Fair*,' she explained, 'was the first of the
classic serials to be done in colour so they were up against
problems they had never encountered before such as the
risk of the cameras overheating. And I remember some

weeks one was changing one's costume as one dashed from set to set. It was all a bit like weekly rep where you play the parlourmaid in the first act and the vicar's wife in the next. In those circumstances any research you do is purely off your own bat since no one's got much time in the studio for any argument. You can only argue about things that are immediately relevant. But you find it all works provided you come to rehearsals completely prepared and provided you can talk to the other actors on the phone at night. You work out the basics on the floor but any work on the interrelation of character you do on the phone when you get home. This is how a lot of the things Maggie Tyzack and I did in *The Forsyte Saga* were evolved.'

This is a significant comment on television acting. A stage performance is invariably worked out in close contact with a director: time and again, however, one hears actors say that, simply because of pressure of rehearsal time, they have to work out the detail of a television performance for themselves.

Like Susan Hampshire, Eric Porter is another actor whose whole career received a new impetus from *The Forsyte Saga*. Before it, he had always been something of an actor's actor whose technical precision and iron command were much admired by colleagues and by the more discerning members of the public: after the *Saga* he became a household name. Yet hearing him interviewed by Derek Hart on BBC Television one was struck by how much of the remarkable physical transformation seemed to come from his own cumulative observation of the ageing process:

'When one is studying age (and I wouldn't say I was an experienced geriatrician!) one thinks in terms of muscles, bones, tautness, tension, laxity, the whole thing. Now obviously the more upright the carriage, the younger, the more vigorous you are. Then one begins to observe that in middle-age—and let's face it, I've always played middle-aged parts, I was born middle-aged—you begin to see the slow sag in the spine. Then it begins to go at the neck, the head goes forward, but there's still pride so the head has to come up. Then the whole pelvic area is slightly shoved forward because of the tension in the back of the knees, trying to pull the knees back straight, so there's the slight sagging in the knees. You find, of course, that this is why people get shorter when they get older, because of this slight sag. Then you find, as you walk around, you can't help but behave in this particular way. Having once set oneself like that, that's fine. But at the end of a year it took me a hell of a long time to straighten myself out again!'

This not only proves how much in television depends on the actor's own artistry and intelligence: it also shows that basic Stanislavskian principles can be rigorously applied to television as much as to the theatre. In *My Life In Art* Stanislavski explains how he approached at the age of twenty-six the role of a senile general in a play by Pissemsky called *The Usurpers of the Law*. For a start he turned to a real old man he used as a model to see what happened when he removed his upper plate of artificial teeth. He noticed that between the upper teeth and the lower gum there was a crack and so he tried to make a crack between his own upper and lower teeth. This interfered with his speech but having created this obstacle he did not set out to exaggerate it: he simply acquired a very slow rhythm of speech that you often find in old men. Next he paid attention to the character's movements:

'I tried first of all to understand and study the physiological cause of the physical process, that is, why the rhythm of action and speech is slow with old men, why they rise so carefully, why they straighten so slowly, walk so slowly, etc. Becoming aware of these principles and their results, I began to apply them on the stage. Before I would rise I looked for something to rest my hands on, and rose with the help of my hands, slowly straightened myself in order to ease my back, for I knew that without this carefulness old men may be attacked by lumbago. Conscious relation to action that was typical to old age guided me and as a result I tuned my own feelings to the physiological phenomena of senility. This created a kind of method from the outer to the inner, from the body to the soul, based upon an unbreakable bond between physical and psychical nature.'

This progress—from the outer to the inner—was precisely the one used by Porter as Soames and it resulted in a classic piece of television acting in which the minutest gradations took place from episode to episode without the overall sense of design being lost. Soames's caution, temperance, distrust of outward emotional display were carried right through the series and became the key to the character. At the same time the performance left us with a memorable set of images from the upright young solicitor with ramrod-stiff back, sleek patent-leather hair and a dry precision in his manner to the old man on his death-bed staring like a basilisk at the camera and emitting periodic moans like a tormented seal. In contrast the ageing process adopted by Kenneth More as Jolyon and Nyree Dawn Porter as Irene came to seem a matter of alteration and adjustments to wigs and make-up: essentially More's Jolyon still seemed to have a youthful heartiness and briskness even on the verge of death. Porter, however, offered a superb feat of impersonation in which he seemed to get through to the core of the character by close attention to the physical externals.

But, as I suggested earlier, television acting of this calibre is not all that common. What we see most of the time is actors struggling to infuse life and personality into wretchedly pedestrian material; and the sheer economics of television mean that rehearsal time is often insufficient for the actor gradually to elaborate on a performance. In the theatre weekly rep is dead; but one could argue that the conditions of weekly rep have been transferred to television. Even in an age of recorded television, it is amazing to see lines being fluffed, the shadow of the microphone boom stealing over actors' faces, joins in the set becoming apparent if the camera happens to linger too long on one shot.

However, the main charge I would make is that at all levels of the profession acting for television is still not taken seriously as a specialised craft. Drama schools—partly for reasons of finance, partly for obscure reasons of principle—still refuse to teach it as a separate subject. No television company in Britain has made the slightest move to train actors for television in the way that they do directors, cameramen, lighting engineers, sound recordists, commentators and interviewers. And even critics devote a tenth of the space to consideration of performances that they give to writers and directors: for instance, Dennis Potter's sequence of plays on Casanova was scrupulously analysed but there was scarcely any detailed coverage of the way Frank Finlay developed the character over the six weeks.

Furthermore, television drama departments have been curiously slow to catch on to the advantages of ensemble. Their very own series show them that there are distinct advantages to keeping a group of actors working together over a long period of time; yet when it comes to tackling theatrical classics they still adopt the five-stars-for-comfort-but-six-for-absolute-certainty policy that characterised the

West End in the mid-1960s. Thus BBC 1's Play of the Month series, admirable in concept, frequently misfires because ensemble plays are done with *ad hoc* casts: you can no longer hope to do a satisfactory *Cherry Orchard* simply by getting together a host of well-known names, and even a play like *Tartuffe* (given a fatally effeminate production in that same series) gains immeasurably from being presented by a cast of actors familiar with each other's styles and techniques. What I am advocating is that the BBC should assemble a more or less permanent company for the presentation of classic drama*; and that the independent companies should keep actors together for regular seasons of plays. The experiment was tried by London Weekend Television early in its career when John Neville led an ensemble in six plays and the results were conspicuously successful. Similarly Granada set up the Stables Theatre Company in Manchester in a building adjacent to its own and then presented the best of its productions on television. Again the result was artistically successful but, when the theatre closed for financial reasons, that was the end of that.

In short, we shall never get more than a decent mediocrity (with occasional spurts of brilliance) from television acting until the industry, the drama schools, the critics, the public all pay more attention to it as a separate art comparable to stage or movie acting; until the literary standards of scripts dramatically rise; and until actors themselves become slightly more conscious of the dignity of their calling and slightly less ready to exploit their instant fame by doing commercials and comedy shows. Great acting is not impossible on television; but it is about as rare as sunshine in November.

* An experiment that was tried, with great success, with new drama in the BBC 2 *Sextet* series in the summer of 1972.

7

THE ACTOR IN SOCIETY

'I've written for the theatre for many years
and I'd never vote for an actor to represent
me for anything.'
(*Irwin Shaw on 'Late Night Line-up'*)

INTERVIEWING Melina Mercouri in a Paris film studio
some years ago, I had the temerity to ask her whether there
was any danger in actors being heavily involved in politics.
My point was a simple one: that if certain actors could use
their fame to help worthwhile liberal causes, could others
who were equally popular not lend their support to illiberal
and even harmful movements. Fixing me with a stony
stare Miss Mercouri proclaimed (there is no other word):
'For me an actor is first of all a citizen. You can vote if
you're an actor—you don't have a disease. Moreover the
actor is familiar with the greatest poets in the world and
they speak always of freedom and democracy. You may
find some Right-Wing actors but where are the poets and
dramatists to support them, ha?'

'For me an actor is first of all a citizen.' It is a crucial
phrase because in recent years we have seen actors playing
an increasingly important role in public life. And inevitably
this has led to a developing conflict between the actor's
duties as a professional entertainer and his obligations as
an ordinary member of society. When CND protest marches
were at their height in the early 1960s Vanessa Redgrave

ran the risk of missing a matinée performance of *As You Like It* at Stratford by going on a Bank Holiday march that would almost certainly lead to her arrest. Having weighed up the consequences—and having had them weighed up for her by an attentive press—she duly went on the march, also managing to get to Stratford for the matinée. When the Six-Day War broke out in Israel in the summer of 1967, Topol—then playing the lead in *Fiddler on the Roof* at Her Majesty's—left the production to offer his services to the Israeli army. Danny Kaye, due to arrive at Chichester that same summer to play the lead in *The Servant of Two Masters*, at very short notice advised the theatre that he was not coming because of his desire to go and entertain the troops in the aftermath of the Six-Day War. In all these cases conscience triumphed over immediate professional considerations.

Such conflicts inevitably arose long before the 1960s. But what is interesting is that in previous decades the actor's duty to his profession invariably came before anything else. Over the last decade we have seen an entirely new concept of the actor grow up. His role as public figure active in politics and the championing of specific causes has enormously increased; the growth of the television chat-show in Britain has meant that his views have been solicited on everything from contraception to cookery; and in newspapers and magazines the interview-industry has grown to such amazing proportions that every new film and play is accompanied by a stream of exegesis and anecdote which is tied to it like a tin can. The actor is no longer judged solely by his performance but also by his general demeanour off-screen and his capacity to project interesting and controversial views.

This is a complete reversal of the actor's historical role in British life; for until the end of the nineteenth century he was always apart from society rather than a part of it. In 1572 a famous Act of Parliament was passed which designated as 'Roges, Vagabondes and Sturdye Beggars all Fencers, Bearewardes and Common Players in Enterludes and Minstrels'. All these categories were lumped together as 'lewd' and were to be punished unless 'Belonging to an Baron of the Realme or Towardes any other honourable Person of Greater Degree'. And the anonymous T. G. writing in a work called *The Rich Cabinet* in 1616 produced a staggering catalogue of the attributes of the professional actor:

'Players are discredited in the very subject of their profession, which is only scratching the itching humours of scabbed minds with pleasing content and profane jests; and how can he be well reputed that employs all his time in vanity and lies, counterfeiting and practising nothing else.

'Player is afraid of the plague, as much as a coward of a musket: for as death is formidable to one, so is poverty and wants to the other.

'Player is afraid of the statute, for if he have no better supportation than his profession, he is neither admitted in public, nor if he be a roamer dares justify himself in private, being a flat rogue by the statute.

'Player's practices can hardly be warranted in religion: for a man to put on woman's apparel, and a woman a man's, is plain prohibition: I speak not of execrable oaths, artificial lies, discoveries of cozenage, scurrilous words, obscene discourses, corrupt courtings, licentious motions, lascivious actions and lewd gestures: for all these are incident to other men. But here is the difference: in these they come by imperfection, in them by profession.

'Player is a great spender, and indeed many resemble strumpets, who get their money filthily and spend it profusely.'

This is, of course, only part of the story: actors who won the patronage of powerful lords were exempt from prosecution if not from public attack. But if one studies English theatrical and social history from the sixteenth to the nineteenth century one is struck by the extremely volatile nature of the actor's relationship with his public and the way in which he was subjected to insults, abuse and derision that would not now be tolerated. John Philip Kemble had to face three months of sustained public rioting in the Old Price Riots directed against the Covent Garden management for daring to put up the prices to subsidise a foreign opera singer. Edmund Kean was described as 'that obscene little personage' by *The Times* after he had been found guilty of 'criminal conversations' with a London alderman's wife and throughout his career had to face explosively rowdy audiences. William Charles Macready was something of an exception in that he had many friends in London's literary and artistic community (including Dickens and Bulwer Lytton) but he also had a keen distaste for the acting profession and wrote on one occasion: 'I had rather see my children dead than on the stage.' But it was not really until Henry Irving received his knighthood in 1895 that the actor came to be regarded as a more or less acceptable part of British society. As Bernard Shaw wrote in the *Saturday Review* in February of that year:

'Numbers of respectable English people still regard a visit to the theatre as a sin; and numbers more, including most of those who have become accustomed to meeting even rank-and-file actors and actresses in society where thirty years ago they would have as soon expected to meet an acrobat, would receive a proposal from an actor for the hand of their daughter with a sense of mesalliance which they would certainly not have if the suitor were a lawyer, a doctor, a clergyman or a painter.'

When Irving's knighthood was bestowed in May of that year, telegrams of congratulation poured in from all over the world, not least from such renowned figures as Coquelin and Sarah Bernhardt. Bram Stoker, Irving's business manager, wrote that his colleagues felt that 'he had lifted from their shoulders that burden of contumely and prejudice which, to a greater or lesser degree, each one of them had to bear in the exercise of their profession'. William Archer also saw the honour as a decisive slap in the face for English Puritanism. With masterly irony, however, that self-same Puritanism received one of its greatest fillips on the very same day the knighthood was bestowed with the news that Oscar Wilde had been sentenced to a term of imprisonment at the Old Bailey. One thing can be said about the English Puritan instinct: it is never slow to recover from a defeat.

Today, however, the actor has advanced so far towards respectability that his opinion is sought on every conceivable subject. If the knighthood bestowed on Irving symbolised the desire of late-Victorian England to make the theatre rather more socially acceptable, then the life peerage conferred on Laurence Olivier in 1970 symbolises our elevation of the actor to the role of sage and prophet.

Yet, in case this sounds like a sneer, I should say that I regard the modern actor's direct involvement in politics as a welcome step forward. The House of Commons contains one forceful actor-MP in the massive shape of Andrew Faulds, notable for the liberalism of his opinions and his somewhat theatrical exuberance in debate. And, unbeknownst to many people, Shirley Williams, one of the most dynamic members of Mr Wilson's Front Bench until she was dropped because of her radical commitment to the Common Market, had a notable career as an undergraduate actress and at an even earlier age was considered for a lead role in *National Velvet*, though the part ultimately went to a Miss Elizabeth Taylor. And, outside the House, actors have been consistently involved in demonstrations, marches and charity shows waged and staged against the independent nuclear deterrent, apartheid, the Greek Colonels, Vietnam and Rhodesia.

Not everyone, however, regards this as admirable. In November 1966 Richard West wrote a downright, polemical piece in the *New Statesman* attacking the actor's increasing involvement in politics. 'There are many reasons for regret,' he wrote, 'at the news that Ronald Reagan has won the governorship of California. He is a gross reactionary. He is a dullard. He is also an actor. . . . For many years the simple mummer has taken upon himself the role of sage, statesman and leader. Actresses in this country are recognised as leading spokesmen on South Africa, the wage freeze and international liquidity. The Royal Shakespeare Company's pantomime, *US*, is regarded as somehow relevant to the miseries of Vietnam. . . . Surely the theatre is the one thing in England that is treated seriously? It should not be so. In the old days actors were kept in their place.'

I can accept Mr West's condemnation of Ronald Reagan: a man who can tell an interviewer one moment that his favourite character was 'the Prince of Peace, the man of Galilee' and the next that he does not believe in altering the American gun laws 'because the wrong person can always get the gun, so perhaps it's proper that the right person should have them at least available'. But to extend this into a blanket condemnation of all actors is simply stupid. Why is the mummer necessarily simple? Why should the word 'actor' be given an automatically pejorative ring? Why should *US*, an attempt to define the muddled liberalism of the helpless English onlooker, be condemned as a pantomime? And what is this place back to which actors must be driven? The stocks? I deplore the attitude

of a man like West since it is built on the assumption that
the arts are not concerned with politics and since its im-
plication is that the acting profession should be filled with
simpletons deprived of any social conscience. It is itself
a reactionary and trivial attitude.

If one wants to attack actors' involvement in politics, I
think it will have to be on more sophisticated grounds.
One such ground may be that actors and entertainers are
open to possible exploitation and that their unquestioning
trust in the good faith of a specific cause may be abused.
A fascinating example of this arose in 1966 when a number
of well-known figures—including Kenneth Haigh, Sheila
Hancock, Dudley Moore, Larry Adler, Roy Hudd, Miriam
Karlin and Alfred Marks—agreed to take part in a Sunday
charity concert sponsored by Medical Aid for Vietnam.
All the participants understood from the literature they
were sent that the money raised would be distributed
equally to both sides in Vietnam. However one of the
participants was David Frost and in his Rediffusion television programme he unearthed the point that all the money
was to go exclusively to the North Vietnamese or to the
Viet Cong groups in South Vietnam. As soon as this was
revealed, then a number of the performers involved
decided against doing the concert. Kenneth Haigh, for
instance, explained that the material he had been sent made
it clear that the funds would be distributed through the
International Red Cross. Frost explained that this was not
the case: the Red Cross send their funds to North and
South alike whereas on this occasion the funds were going
only to one side. The officials of Medical Aid for Vietnam
present in the studio defended themselves by saying that
they were not a Communist organisation and that they
had made it clear from the start where the money was
going. However none of the performers concerned had

realised this; and one can only conclude that had not someone like Frost, with a vigilant research team at his elbow, elicited the true facts, the other performers would unwittingly have seen their charitable efforts used for purposes they did not fully appreciate.

The other strong argument against the actor's involvement in politics is that it can, in a sense, be too easy to make a liberal gesture purely by standing up on a platform. The actors one really admires are not so much those who appear with great regularity at rallies, demonstrations and concerts but those who are prepared to make personal sacrifices for a cause in which they steadfastly believe. Irving Wardle once reported himself unmoved by the sight of 'John Neville and Glenda Jackson bravely defying the Greek Colonels' from the relative security of the Albert Hall. However, few, I think, could fail to be moved by Melina Mercouri's continuing battle against the Colonels and her genuine suffering at the hands of their regime.

In America the actor's immersion in politics is, of course, a good deal deeper than it is in England. Ronald Reagan is Governor of California and ex-tap dancer George Murphy was, for many years, a Senator for the same state. At election time actors line up publicly behind their chosen candidates and in recent years we have had Paul Newman campaigning on behalf of Eugene McCarthy, Burt Lancaster on behalf of John Tunney (son of the famous heavyweight champion, Gene Tunney) and John Wayne on behalf of a number of prominent Right Wingers. And in the States the election is surrounded by much more showbiz razzamatazz than in any other country in the world. None of this seems to me harmful or damaging in any way. What does sometimes bring the American situation into disrepute is the fact that old showbiz loyalties often seem to transcend political ones. Thus in 1970 both Frank Sinatra and Dean

F

Martin, long-standing rooters for the Democratic cause, sang and entertained at a $125-a-head fund-raiser to support Ronald Reagan's campaign for re-election. Since Sinatra was at the time heavily involved in difficulties with the law, Reagan may have been less than wholeheartedly enthusiastic at having his support, although Bob Hope quipped, 'Ronnie is thrilled to have Frank in his camp but he wishes they'd stop calling him the Godfather'. But for actors to switch their political allegiances to help out old buddies is precisely the kind of thing that lends support to the Richard West argument.

Where America scores over Britain, however, is in the fact that politics has long been regarded there as a natural subject for comedy. Sure enough in Britain every tuppenny-ha'penny comic uses the name of the current political leaders to raise a cheap laugh. Indeed during the Labour Government's term of office from 1964 to 1970 one comic said rightly enough that the Harold Wilson joke had slowly replaced the mother-in-law joke; and it is noticeable that salacious innuendo about the private lives of our leaders which, at the start of the 1960s, would have been considered in poor taste, is now happily publicly acceptable. Danny La Rue, for instance, has a stock joke in which Mr Heath is asked what he intends to do about the Homosexual Bill. His reply is 'Pay it'. That was night-club material in 1962. But by the end of the 1960s Mr La Rue was able to repeat it from the stage of the West End theatre without the roof falling in. But it would be hard to argue that Britain is exactly steeped in political satire. It played a surprisingly small part in *Beyond the Fringe* and was chiefly embodied in Peter Cook's impersonation of Macmillan performing on television like a heavily doped walrus. It flourished briefly during the years of *That Was The Week That Was* before the BBC got cold feet and

killed the programme off. And one British film of the
1970s, *The Rise and Fall of Michael Rimmer*, presented us with
a lightly disguised version of Heath and Wilson as well as
a cynical dismissal of the electorate as totally foolish and
gullible.

But what we have always lacked in Britain is a night-club
or vaudeville performer for whom the events of the day
or the week form the substance of his act: a Mort Sahl or a
Lenny Bruce, for instance. Sahl usually came on brandishing
a rolled-up newspaper (which he referred to as his security
symbol) and began his act by satirising its headlines. A
wisecracking nervous idealist, he would then spend an hour
or so with comment on social mores and lambasting the
politicians of his day. He flopped disastrously on English
television in 1961, partly, I suspect, because this kind of
humour springs from a rooted attachment to a particular
social scene and even in America his influence seems to have
waned. But, especially with a Right Wing government in
power again in England, we desperately need a comic with
a comparable astringency. The trend in English humour
today, particularly in television, is towards a kind of loony
surrealist inconsequentiality best typified by *Monty Python's
Flying Circus*. I have nothing against that; but I wish we
also had a few comics plugged into the present day.

If it is good to see actors involving themselves directly
in politics and using their fame to help promote liberal
causes, charities and appeals (whatever the occasional
dangers), I am equally sure that it is damaging to see actors
treated as oracular figures with views on everything under
the sun, as fodder for chat-shows on British and American
television and as a means of filling the column-inches for
hard-pressed newspapermen. On one occasion, when
Albert Finney was appearing at the Chichester Festival, I
approached a friend of his to see if I could get him to give

one of his rare interviews. Back came the reply that Mr
Finney had decided 'to shut up and let others do the
talking'. Disheartened at the time, I have come to think
ever since that his answer was the shrewdest imaginable.

If anyone still doubts that the doings of the acting profession and its members are hot news, let him but consider
a not untypical issue of *The Times*. The date is April 27,
1970. On Page 1 there is a story about a well-known
American film-star arriving at Heathrow Airport and being
charged with possessing cannabis. On Page 2 there is a very
full account of Equity's Annual General Meeting calling
for an actor's charter to give them sick pay, holiday pay
'and all those twentieth-century amenities so far denied to
performers'. On Page 3 there is a picture of Miss Melina
Mercouri reading a message from Mikis Theodorakis to an
audience of more than 5,000 at a performance of Greek
drama and music at the Albert Hall. In the Diary there is a
story about a party given for the actress Yvonne Mitchell,
to celebrate the publication of her latest novel. And on the
Woman's Page there is an interview with Mary Holland,
the television commercial's Katie, for ever despatching
meat cubes into her husband's lunch and dinner. This one
issue crams in just about every aspect of Fleet Street's
fascination with actors: with their industrial activities,
with their private misdemeanours, with their political
activities, with their writing skills and with their everyday
suburban existence. The only thing not mentioned was how
they actually went about the business of acting.

What is surprising, of course, is that actors themselves
(and their advisers) often fail to appreciate the boomerang
effect of excess publicity. Richard Burton and Elizabeth
Taylor are two film-stars who could be said to have suffered
a good deal from journalistic intrusion over the years: at
the time of their romance, during the making of *Cleopatra*,

they were endlessly pursued by the world's press and photographers who often earned small fortunes by capturing pictures of private beach parties and the like. Yet in the spring of 1972 we find the Burtons inviting the attention of the world's press by holding a series of slap-up parties in Budapest to celebrate Mrs Burton's fortieth birthday. We hear of the lemon-coloured diamond, cut for a Mogul Emperor, that Mr Burton gives to Mrs Burton; of the arrival of world celebrities from Princess Grace of Monaco to Stephen Spender; of the cost of the whole thrash, said to be at least £30,000. But we also hear of Hungarian resentment that no guests from that country should have been invited to such a lavish rout; of an ugly incident at a night-club party when Mr Alan Williams, an expert on Budapest, asked a number of preoccupied guests if the Hungarian revolution meant anything to them; and of widespread criticism of the whole spectacular in other countries. And indeed it does seem a mark of extraordinary political insensitivity to hold such a party in a country suffering from Communist oppression; and it seems even more extraordinary that no one in the Burtons' entourage was capable of realising that the coverage of such an event would necessarily be counter-productive.

But perhaps the greatest single danger any actor faces these days is over-exposure via the television chat-show and the newspaper and magazine interview. In England, curiously enough, the television chat-show has had a somewhat chequered history. Eamonn Andrews, Dave Allen, David Jacobs, Simon Dee and Derek Nimmo have all been lumbered with this kind of programme in which actors trip on one after the other to puff their latest film or play, discuss their views on sex and marriage and possibly commit some minor indiscretion to satisfy the embarrassment-perverts. Indeed, after many wasted hours spent watching this kind of show, the only things that stay in the mind are the awkward and hot-flush-inducing moments. Laurence Harvey telling blatantly dirty stories in front of the correct Mr Andrews, Diana Dors getting angry with a saucily intrusive Freddie Trueman, Simon Dee making it all too clear to his guests that he did not know the difference between Carol Reed and Oliver Reed, Derek Nimmo confusing Gene Kelly and Grace Kelly, Peter Cook being rude (not that I hold this against him) to Zsa Zsa Gabor, Michael Parkinson being ingratiatingly deferential to Orson Welles, Kenneth Williams madly overdoing the campery on occasions too humourless to mention. One can argue that such shows are harmless enough, providing a few hours every week of drip television. My contention is, however, that they devalue actors and that they make it difficult to distinguish between one's reaction to the performer and one's reaction to the private personality. One well-known actor has, for instance, appeared numerous times on television chat-shows and has emerged as a loose-tongued, boorish egomaniac. The result is that whenever, as a critic, I go to see his films I have to do my damnedest to wipe his personal appearances from my mind and concentrate on his acting. And since many actors are now better known for their chat-show appearances than for their films, the problem grows regularly more acute.

Perhaps the most poignant and intelligent articulation of the hazards of personal appearances, however, came recently from Robert Shaw. He is not only a distinguished actor but also a very good novelist and a more-than-capable playwright. And BBC 1's *Omnibus* presented a film showing him at different stages of his working year (writing and relaxing at his Buckinghamshire home, filming *Figures in a Landscape* in Spain and rehearsing a musical on Broadway) and talking about the connection between his work as an

actor and his career as a writer. To put it in a nutshell his
thesis was that acting was relatively easy and grossly over-
paid whereas writing was extremely difficult and under-
rated. Fair enough. But by the end Shaw began to have
doubts about the wisdom of a programme such as this.
'Even as I am talking I know half the people watching
will think what an egocentric, aggressive, charmless, loud-
mouthed man that is. . . .' The trouble is that almost anyone
who spends an hour talking about themselves on television
is bound to appear somewhat arrogant and self-absorbed
and I would say that, on balance, Shaw was right: the programme did not do him any good. It is worth recalling that
the same week also saw the première of *Figures in a Landscape*
in which Shaw not only played one of the two principal
parts but also wrote the script. More than one critic
suggested that Shaw the writer had provided a fat, juicy
part for Shaw the actor and scaled down the other character
accordingly; and it is interesting to speculate on whether
or not such an unwarranted charge would have been made
if Shaw had not, unwittingly, given the appearance on television of being a trifle self-centred.

In America, of course, the problem is even more acute
than in Britain: the talk-show is there a staple product of
light entertainment and indeed occupies peak-time and
late-night viewing spots. One must not be hypocritical
about this. For the visitor it is extremely refreshing, after
a hard day in Manhattan, to come back late at night and
watch a chat-show. Johnny Carson, above all, seems a
master of his craft in that he can soothe a nervy guest,
squash an uppish one and wordlessly converse with the
camera in a way that even David Frost has not yet mastered.
On one show I recall a bumptious young actor, having
boasted a good deal about his sexual prowess, saying that
one of the pleasures of working with Joan Collins was that

she was a real pro. Carson simply looked at the camera blankly and with the shrug of an eyebrow got an enormous laugh. But even with such an urbane host, many showbiz guests seem to come on the programme hell-bent on self-destruction. On one occasion I can recall Jerry Lewis hogging the camera, drowning the other guests with a carafe of water and even kicking over the drinks table apparently in an endeavour to see that the attention never strayed too far from himself.

Talk-shows can obviously be enjoyable; but, on the whole, I think they harm rather than help the art of acting. They can be death for professional comics since they prove that, without their scriptwriters or the opportunity to control their timing, they are not the funniest men in the world. They can be harmful for straight actors in that they milk their showbiz anecdotes but rarely give them the chance to talk about their art with any depth or seriousness. They exploit their star glitter without giving anything back in return except free publicity. I can see why agents, producers and other entrepreneurs are glad to have their clients and products puffed in this way. But, if I were a serious and intelligent actor, I would keep well away from the tele-talk shows, and the world of what Jill Tweedie once called 'chatty people stuck like boiled eggs in cup-shaped chairs poaching quietly away under studio lights'.

As far as the newspaper interview goes, it is hard to attack this without appearing hopelessly two-faced since a portion of my own livelihood has been earned by talking to actors at length about their work. My only defence would be this: that as long as one does talk to actors about their work (and many are agreeably surprised when they find that is all you are really interested in) then one may just occasionally come up with something of value. But as soon as an interview becomes a generalised piece about the actor's emotional problems, his views on the institution of marriage or Women's Lib, it tends to become rather valueless.

There has, in fact, grown up over the years an interview industry, carefully organised, insidiously efficient and ultimately destructive. It ensures maximum exposure for everyone connected with the arts. But it also means that artists are increasingly judged by their ability to cope with the press and that minimal or unhatched talent is treated with an exaggerated respect. What usually happens is that before the opening of any new film or play, the press agent concerned rings round the papers, the magazines, the radio and television producers (in the more sophisticated establishments there are separate people to handle the worlds of journalism and broadcasting), offering Miss X or Mr Y for interview. The press agents (usually dedicated and extremely likeable people) of course take good care to offer the right subjects to the right people: in the case of movies, an intellectual foreign director for the 'heavies' and a busty female star for the populars. But with a truly big cinematic name the situation slightly resembles a French farce. Appointments are arranged at hourly intervals throughout the day in a room at, say, the Dorchester or the Connaught, and as one journalist exits through the back door another is admitted through the front. Many is the time I have caught a glimpse of a rapidly disappearing pair of silk stockings or disembodied trousers as I have come in through the main door but, playing the rules of the game, I have never dared to ask which of my colleagues it is I have so narrowly missed. The inevitable result is, of course, that one often tends to get interviews of remarkable similarity appearing in the same papers at roughly the same time.

Any star who refuses to join in the game is regarded as

'difficult'. I saw Julie Christie criticised in print for refusing to give any press interviews while she was making *The Go-Between* in Norfolk for Joseph Losey: presumably this was because the good lady simply wanted to concentrate on a tricky and testing role but her seclusion was regarded as bad form in Fleet Street. I have also heard the charming Maggie Smith described as 'difficult' by film executives because she confines interviews to the post-shooting period and will not talk to journalists on the set. We have, in fact, reached the stage where visiting journalists tend to regard films as something made for their benefit (would they like to be interviewed in the midst of writing a piece for the next edition?) and where press agents are so worried where their next job is coming from that they sometimes make unreasonable demands of the stars. Acting in the end is what suffers.

I am not, of course, decrying all interviews or saying that actors should never open their mouths to discuss their work. The BBC's series of interviews on *Great Acting* and *Modern Acting* were both thorough and revealing; the kind of lengthy interviews carried by papers like *The Guardian* and *The Times* can be similarly informative; and the specialist magazines, where space is no object, can also probe rivetingly into the actor's approach to particular roles. But I still think we have reached the point where the interview business has got out of hand and where it is sometimes enough to have written just one play or appeared in just one film to get yourself widespread coverage. Sometimes one does not even have to appear in anything at all: the delectable Raquel Welch, for instance, was interviewed on British television long before we had seen her in any film. In short, the image, in true advertising style, was sold before the product. It says a lot for the product that it has out-lived and survived the zealous promotion.

To sum up: I welcome the actor's intervention in politics partly because it cements his relationship with the community and may even lead to improvements within his own profession; I applaud, more cautiously, his furtherance of good causes though I think he needs to be on his guard against the exploitation of his goodwill; and I am thoroughly alarmed by the extent to which newspapers, magazines and television exploit the willingness of nearly all actors to talk about themselves in public. More analysis, less gossip is what we need.

8

THE ACTOR AS WRITER

SCRATCH an actor these days and you find a dramatist:
an exaggeration perhaps but a pardonable one. For even if
the acting business is in a terrible muddle, even if the profession is desperately overcrowded, even if there is too
much gossipy publicity about private lives, one fact is very
much to the industry's credit: that many of the best new
dramatists started their career as actors. John Osborne,
Harold Pinter, Peter Nichols, Charles Wood, Henry Livings,
Alun Owen, Charles Dyer all began as actors and many of
them can still be seen performing from time to time. John
Osborne, with his cawing voice, high cheekbones and look
of sullen fury was very impressive as the doomed aristocrat
in David Mercer's television study of post-war Germany,
The Parachute. Harold Pinter crops up periodically in his
own plays: he played Lenny in *The Homecoming* at Watford,
for instance, and according to Martin Esslin was even better
than Ian Holm in the original production because his
particular brand of East End sharpness fitted the role
beautifully. And Henry Livings tends to do a good bit of
radio, television and theatre work north of the Trent
peddling a nice line in amiable gormlessness.

But although attention has been drawn to our almost
unparalleled list of actor-dramatists, not enough notice has
been given to the effect the acting has had upon the
writing. Which, I would argue, is considerable. Looking

back over the career of our most famous actor-dramatist, Sir Noël Coward, it is possible, with the benefit of hind-sight, to see his plays as an extension of his acting career and of the theatrical milieu. He has often admitted that in many cases his principal aim was 'to write a whacking great part for myself'. But, more interestingly, one finds in his work a glorification of the middle-aged female wreathed in spotlit, actressy charm, a delight in Bohemian eccentricity provided it is kept within reasonable bounds, and an affectionate re-creation of the theatre's peculiar combina-tion of savage bitchery and warm-hearted sentimentality. Throughout his career Coward repeatedly returned in his plays to the world of the theatre (*Present Laughter*, *Hay Fever*, *Tonight at 8.30* for instance) but even when portraying characters from the ostensibly normal world (as in *Blithe Spirit* and *Private Lives*) he never got too far away from the smell of the greasepaint.

Our new generation of dramatists is much less stage-struck than Coward or Pinero (whose *Trelawny of the Wells* shows a deep affection for a barnstorming tradition that he helped to extirpate): when our modern dramatists write directly about the theatre it is usually to expose its grub-biness and tattiness. At the same time a large number of them have been deeply influenced by the English music-hall tradition which lingered on well into the 1950s; and many of their characters, although pursuing non-theatrical pro-fessions, still retain values and mannerisms one associates with the green room. Peter Nichols once told me in the course of an interview that he thought all of them (and he very much included himself) were still over-dependent on their actor origins, that they still tended to think in terms of big scenes and 'effective' dialogue: he reserved his admira-tion for a writer like David Storey whose work had a low-key realism and truthfulness with few theatrical flourishes.

I think this is an over-harsh judgement. Much of the vitality of the new English drama stems from its actor-writers; at the same time it is worth noting that over the years their repertory origins have exerted less influence and that their work has broadened in scope.

This is certainly true of John Osborne; yet his early work reveals a more direct theatrical influence than anyone else's. His first hero, George Dillon, was of course an actor-writer by profession; Jimmy Porter may have run a sweet-stall but he was certainly an actor-manqué and his mistress, Helena Charles, was on tour when she tumbled into his bed; Archie Rice definitively embodies the decaying tradition of the English music-hall; and even Luther could be described as a formidable public performer. More recently, the heroine of *Time Present*, Pamela, was a loquacious and acidulous actress, and *The Hotel in Amsterdam* had a showbiz background in that the characters were nearly all fugitive film people. But although Osborne often endows his characters, whatever their profession, with a soaring actorish eloquence, no one could say that his themes are narrowly theatrical: his speciality is indeed taking, at regular intervals, the moral temperature of the nation. And the theme of his most recent work, *West of Suez*, was nothing less than the whole fate of Western civilisation.

Osborne's own theatrical career was not in its early days especially distinguished. He drifted into the theatre by acting as tutor to a group of juveniles in a touring company. He himself acted for the first time in a touring production of that hardy low-life perennial, *No Room at the Inn*. He then became an actor-manager running rep companies in minor seaside resorts like Sidmouth and Ilfracombe. And he had a stint in rep at Derby Playhouse which may have acquired a new prestige in recent years but which in the '50s was hardly one of the key outposts of the theatrical empire. In other words, it was a background of low pay, poor digs, Sunday trains and cold theatres on a Monday morning. With the establishment of so many comfortable, well-subsidised reps and the virtual disappearance of the touring network, it is hard to remember that such an era ever existed. But the meticulous observer will find much of it recaptured in early Osborne.

Take first of all *Epitaph for George Dillon*, written in collaboration with Anthony Creighton. Most critics see it simply as an interesting precursor to *Look Back In Anger* in that its hero is self-pitying, frustrated and ferociously articulate. But what is revealing is that, in its form, it harks back to the dominance in weekly rep of the conventional, three-act lower-middle-class play in that it employs the same kind of outrageous coincidence, the same kind of calculated conversational clichés, the same kind of rather artificial neatness. It uses all the devices of the type of play Osborne must have appeared in as a rep actor in the early '50s. Yet it has something more: a central character endowed with rhetorical fury. And in a curious way George Dillon's description of his embattled, complex, turbulent relationship with an audience seems to foreshadow Osborne's own equally turbulent relationship with his public:

'I attract hostility. I seem to be on heat for it. Whenever I step out on to those boards—immediately from the very first moment I show my face—I know that I've got to fight every one of those people in the auditorium. Right from the stalls to the gallery to the Vestal Virgins in the boxes. My God, it's a gladiatorial combat. Me against Them. Me and mighty Them.'

This comes very believably from a writer who has said that he is more than happy if he can make a few seats tip up in protest. Not only does the central character seem to embody some of Osborne's own personal qualities; but the play also understandably exploits Osborne's intimate knowledge of the theatre's seedier fringes—not least in the character of Barney Evans, the tatty provincial impresario who persuades George to dirty up his material and who argues that if you can get someone in the family way in the Third Act you're half-way there.

Look Back In Anger, however, utilises much more of Osborne's theatrical background. The play has been discussed from every possible angle—as a social document for the '50s, as a Strindbergian analysis of modern marriage, as a starting-point for a new theatrical movement—but not much attention has been paid to its relationship to the career of a struggling young actor. At the centre of the play is the notion of a lone, martyred hero who has an energy, passion and concern that find no response either in his environment or in the people who surround him. Obviously this struck a chord in the heart of any number of young people at the time and has a perennial relevance as long as emotional frustration exists. But, to alter the focus slightly, the play very plausibly reflects the problems of an actor buried in the rut of a Midlands weekly rep in the '50s, knowing that he has a talent and energy that have so far gone unrecognised. In its detail, also, the play suggests Jimmy belongs more to the theatre than he does to the sweet-stall business.

Take the point where Jimmy launches into an excoriating fantasy in which his wife beomes a fleshy Roman matron, Lady Pusillanimous, married to the weedy Sextus. 'If he were put into a Hollywood film,' says Jimmy, 'he's so unimpressive they'd make some poor British actor play the part.' That sounds more like the sour comment of an Equity member than of a licensed Midlands stall-holder. Then there is the preoccupation with homosexuality which punctuates nearly all Osborne's early work and which comes naturally to a member of a profession that spends a lot of its time asking 'Is he or isn't he?'. There is the delineation of Helena Charles, a very recognisable type of actress, who combines a predatory sexual instinct with a display of religious zeal. There is the use of the bears and squirrels game between Jimmy and Alison which at least one critic has noted contains perceptible echoes of a similar game in *The Doll's House*. There's the inclusion of a complete double act between Jimmy and Cliff with which they half-seriously propose to tour the halls: they think of calling themselves T. S. Eliot and Pam (based, of course, on Freddie Bamberger and Pam), but when it comes to the content it proves to be a combination of standard music-hall cross-talk and Flanagan and Allen pastiche. There is the fact that the idolised Ma Tanner was married to an actor. And there are touches like the camp imitation of lower middle-class banality— 'Well I mean it gives you something to do, doesn't it? After all, it would be a funny world if we was all the same, that's what I always say' *à propos* attendance at a black mass—revealing a decidedly actorish flourish.

I am not trying to suggest the play is simply the auto-biography of a struggling young actor. But I would suggest Jimmy is less like a university graduate and stall-holder than he is like a typical young man in rep; and even his style of conversation is more reminiscent of green room than junior common-room, more evocative of the music-hall than the market-place:

Jimmy: . . . Do the Sunday papers make *you* feel ignorant?
Cliff: Not 'arf.
Jimmy: Well, you *are* ignorant. You're just a peasant. (*To Alison.*) What about you? You're not a peasant, are you?
Alison: What's that?

Jimmy: I said do the papers make you feel you're not so
          brilliant after all?
Alison: Oh, I haven't read them yet.
Jimmy: I didn't ask you that. I said. . . .
Cliff: Leave the poor girlie alone. She's busy.
Jimmy: Well, she can talk, can't she? You can talk,
          can't you? You can express an opinion. Or does
          the White Woman's Burden make it impossible
          to think?

Jimmy's reiteration of certain phrases, his communication
through interrogation, his slight alteration of emphasis to
give a new meaning to a repeated sentence are all devices
common enough on the halls. Jimmy's soaring tirades also
embody an actor's delight in anecdote and wild meta-
phorical exaggeration. Amongst themselves theatre people
frequently colour and heighten reality as if to absorb it
into their own theatrical ambiance, to make the outside
world match the drama of their professional world. Thus
when Jimmy talks about Alison's mum ('Mummy and I
took one quick look at each other and from then on the
age of chivalry was dead. I knew that to protect her innocent
young she wouldn't hesitate to cheat, lie, bully and black-
mail. Threatened with me, a young man without money,
background or even looks, she'd bellow like a rhinoceros
in labour—enough to make every male rhino for miles
turn white and pledge himself to celibacy'), Mum becomes
a deliberate and grotesque exaggeration, a caricature of the
upper-class mother with a tribal loyalty to her class.

Its crypto-theatrical content aside, *Look Back In Anger*
also relies heavily on traditional dramatic structure. The
act endings are perfectly arranged, new characters are
introduced at precisely appropriate moments; there is even
a use of a stock device, like the loss of a child, to heighten

tension and bring about a reconciliation between the principal characters. As Simon Trussler notes in his admirable study of Osborne, *Look Back In Anger* adapts all the familiar mechanics of the problem play comfortably enough. But in its formal conventionality, its scalding rhetoric, its constant reference to the world of the theatre and its use of a precise music-hall idiom, it seems to me every inch an actor's play.

In *The Entertainer*, of course, Osborne makes more explicit and obvious use of his first-hand knowledge of the theatrical scene. In fact, what gives the play its extraordinary tone is its juxtaposition of a grimy, peeling showbiz world with the realities of Suez, Trafalgar Square demonstrations and the disastrous Premiership of Sir Anthony Eden. The decay of the music-hall mirrors, the decline of England itself; and when Archie Rice warns us— 'Don't clap too hard, it's an old building'—he is clearly talking about something more than the fading world of vaudeville.

But the more minutely one examines the text, the more one realises that Osborne has done something infinitely subtler than simply use the tatty world of Archie Rice as a metaphor for a declining land. The bantering music-hall idiom is built so securely into the fabric of the play that even the domestic family scenes retain something of the tone of Archie's front-cloth numbers. Thus the relationship between Archie and his son, Frank, is exactly that between a comic and his feed. Archie's own father is there to be affectionately mocked and insulted like some ageing stooge. And in his long speeches Archie uses all the rhythms of his act as if the performer persona has become an irremovable part of his own self: it is like that chilling sketch of Marceau's in which a party-goer finds that a carnival mask has stuck obstinately to his face. Frank, for instance, explains to his newly returned sister that every night is party night. 'And do you know why?' retorts Archie. 'Do you know why? Because we're dead beat and down and outs. We're drunks, maniacs, we're crazy, we're bonkers, the whole flaming bunch of us. Why, we have problems that nobody's ever heard of, we're characters out of something that nobody believes in. We're something that people make jokes about because we're so remote from the rest of ordinary everyday human experience.' The repetition of specific phrases, the trick of starting each sentence with the same pronoun, the hectoring tone that dares anyone else to interrupt, all stems from the act.

Looking beyond the general subject and tone of the piece, however, one finds evidence of the actor's hand in several small, significant details: particularly in a genuine understanding of what it is like to be up on a stage neither revelling in the experience nor pouring out one's love for an audience but simply going through a lifeless, mechanical routine.

'You see this face,' says Archie, 'you see this face. This face can split open with warmth and humanity. It can sing and tell the worst, unfunniest stories in the world to a great mob of dead, drab erks and it doesn't matter, it doesn't matter. It doesn't matter because—look at my eyes. I'm dead behind these eyes. I'm dead, just like the whole inert shoddy lot out there.'

Just as George Dillon makes one realise what it is like to be up there before an audience that hates you, so Archie Rice tells you what it is like to be performing out of habit. And like *Look Back In Anger*, *The Entertainer* also incorporates the outcast's fear that some zealous missionary is going to come along and improve him. Just as Jimmy Porter was worried that Helena might turn him into an unrecognisably pure parody of himself, so Archie is worried lest his daughter

try and divert his attention from 'that little animal something' that is the motive-force of his existence. I do not
think it is too fanciful to see in this an actor's identification
with the social pariah, fearful of being got at by some do-
gooding reformer.

In the last analysis, *The Entertainer* is a play with the
defects of its qualities. Its use of the music-hall as a metaphor
for a seedy, run-down England is a potent and striking one;
and it provides one performer at least with a gorgeous
mouthful of acting. But by seeing English life in the late
1950s in purely theatrical terms Osborne necessarily limits
his discussion of contemporary themes. A genuinely strange
and complex figure like Eden is treated purely as a caricature
to be equated with the landlady's dog; society is divided
up into goodies and baddies; and the growth of organised
protest via Trafalgar Square demonstrations is never taken
seriously enough. The theatrical apparatus gives the play
much of its vitality and energy; but in the end I think it
also cramps Osborne's analysis of what was really wrong
with the England of the time.

What is fascinating about Osborne's subsequent work is
seeing how the actor-hero manages to survive changing
backgrounds and in detecting how often Osborne falls back
on theatrical imagery and metaphor. Thus in *Luther* the
Protestant hero is endowed with many of the actor's
instincts ('I'm never sure of the words till I hear them out
loud,' he says at one point) and before his gruelling first
Communion his father talks to him as if he were making his
stage début—'Men like you just don't forget their words,'
he reassures him. Even Martin's desire for unmediated
contact with God is given a theatrical turn of phrase:
'When I entered the monastery, I wanted to speak to God
directly, you see. Without any embarrassment, I wanted
to speak to him myself, but when it came to it, I dried up

as I always have.' One can even detect the old vaudevillian use of the repeated phrase which brings an unwonted touch of Max Miller into the Middle Ages. The weakness of the play, however, lies not in its use of residual theatrical imagery but in Osborne's inability to give due weight to the opposition to Luther. For instance Eck, the spokesman for the Church Establishment, simply denies Luther's right to question official edicts without in any way intellectually justifying his position. As with Bolt's More in *A Man For All Seasons*, we are simply being asked to admire Luther because he is a rebel defying an authoritarian organisation: there is no quickening dramatic excitement, because Osborne fails, as Shaw never did in parallel circumstances, to take the opposition seriously.

In subsequent work Osborne's preoccupation with theatre has been more successfully absorbed into the texture of the material. In both *The Hotel in Amsterdam* and *West of Suez* the heroes are writers but they are both deliberate and self-acknowledged performers who demand an audience; indeed the most moving moment in *West of Suez* was Sir Ralph Richardson's look of utter dread and desperation as he was left alone on stage for the first time in that strange and frightening Caribbean island. In *A Patriot for Me* the theme is the assimilation of the homosexual into his society (in this case that of the Austro-Hungarian empire), but the most striking scene is a drag ball beginning with an operatic duet which Osborne directs should at the beginning 'be accepted as the indifferent effort of a court opera house cast with amateurs'. In *Time Present* the heroine is an actress with a strong allegiance to a dying way of life symbolised by her old matinée-idol father; but again the fact that she is an actress is in no way arbitrary—it illumines her attachment to the past. Perhaps Osborne's only wanton acting cross-reference comes in his television play, *The Right*

Prospectus, where he has a character demolish a whole
school house by saying—'They'd all like Vanessa Redgrave
to be their mother and visit them on Speech Day.' But that
is a forgivable lapse.

What has Osborne's career as an actor lent to his writing?
Firstly, an obsession with displaying on stage an emotional
freedom and ebullience that shocks the audience into some
kind of new awareness. Osborne's heroes are the theatrical
equivalent of sexual exhibitionists flashing their inadequacies,
their fears, their private neuroses at us with unabashed
delight and tremendous verbal vigour. The actor is a man
who, by definition, exposes his own self to the public night
by night, and Osborne is a writer who exposes fragments
of his own self to the public play by play. Secondly, his
early grounding in rep manifests itself in an initial belief
in three-act naturalistic drama as the dominant theatrical
form. This obviously clashes with his determination to
whittle away at a single character until he has reached the
poor, bare, forked animal underneath, and with time one
sees him suiting the structure to the material: thus by the
time he reaches *The Hotel in Amsterdam* and *West of Suez*
he is exploring the possibilities of the Chekhovian conversation piece. Thirdly, I would say his training as an actor
provided him with a fund of experience and a chain of
imagery on which he was able to draw in his early plays.
With time this has been more successfully assimilated into
the texture of the work, but with the first four plays (up
to *Luther*) one feels it gave him some sense of internal
security. With his latest work, *West of Suez*, I think he now
stands on the threshold of greatness: blessed with an actor's
understanding for what works in theatrical terms and with
an ungovernable concern for the fate of our whole civilisation, I believe he is now about to enter on his richest
period as a dramatist.

With Harold Pinter the theatrical influence is never, predictably enough, quite so explicit or direct as it is with Osborne. But it is there nevertheless. Unlike Osborne, Pinter was fortunate in working for a time with two great actors (Anew MacMaster in Ireland and Donald Wolfit in London) as well as doing the usual stint in rep, including Colchester, Bournemouth, Torquay, Worthing and Richmond. If Pinter's early work shows strong traces of the actor's hand, it is less in terms of specific imagery than in a feeling that he is using his knowledge of the Gorkiesque world of impoverishment, hardship and hunger. We know that he faked a nervous breakdown to get out of RADA and spent a year subsequently 'roaming about a bit'; that when his first child was born, he and his wife had nowhere to go on her departure from hospital; that much of his repertory career was spent by the seaside and in the tattiest of digs.

This would seem to have left its mark very clearly on his first full-length play, *The Birthday Party*. The seaside lodging-house with its sour milk on the cornflakes, its disgusting fried bread, its smothering, mothering landlady are all typical of theatrical digs. And the victimised hero, Stanley, also has pretensions to being a performer in that he claims to have been a celebrated pianist. However, his blatantly fictitious account of being offered a job in a Berlin night-club smacks of actorish self-delusion and fantasy; and his sad account of his spectacular decline after arriving one night in Lower Edmonton to find the hall locked up reminds one instantly of actors' tales about arriving at a deserted theatre on a Sunday during a tour. As for the central image—the invasion of Stanley's seedy world by menacing strangers—it would obviously be crass and silly to pin too precise a meaning on this or to apply it too single-mindedly. Its very potency lies in the fact that it can reach out to all of us. As Harold Hobson said in his original, historic review, 'Though you go to the uttermost parts of the earth and hide yourself in the most obscure lodgings in the least popular of towns, one day there is a possibility that two men will appear. They will be looking for you and you cannot get away. And someone will be looking for them too. There is terror everywhere.' But looking for the origin of that image in terms of Pinter's own life, one can relate it to his upbringing in the East End of London in the 1930s when Mosleyites were on the rampage; or even, possibly, to the actor's natural fear and suspicion of a world of administration and organisation that is far removed from his own environment. Remember Archie Rice performing out front while in the wings 'they' are waiting to take him away for unpaid income tax? Can Stanley not also stand for the struggling artist harried by landladies, income-tax men, debt collectors and all the bureaucratic pressures that bear down on the poor players? To anyone who has never worked in the theatre this may sound exaggerated and implausible: others will know that actors often love to perpetuate their image of social outcasts by turning organised authority (the police, the Inland Revenue) into fearsome bogy-men.

In both *The Birthday Party* and *The Caretaker* Pinter also uses the needling bantering repetition that, in Osborne's case, I suggested seemed to derive from the halls. With the virtual extinction of the nationwide network, one forgets how dominant a part of the theatrical scene music-halls were in the '40s and '50s and how understandable it is that the rhythms of the stand-up comic should have implanted themselves in any writer's mind. The only way to prove the point is by extensive quotation. Take, for instance, this colloquy between Davies (the tramp) and Aston (the house-owner) from the first act of *The Caretaker*:

Aston: I'm in charge.

Davies: You the landlord, are you? Yes, I noticed them heavy curtains pulled across next door as we came along. I noticed them heavy big curtains right across the window down there. I thought there must be someone living there.

Aston: Family of Indians live there.

Davies: Blacks?

Aston: I don't see much of them.

Davies: Blacks, eh? Well, you've got some knick-knacks here all right, I'll say that. I don't like a bare room. I'll tell you what, mate, you haven't got a spare pair of shoes?

Aston: Shoes?

Davies: Them bastards in the monastery let me down again.

Aston: Where?

Davies: Down at Luton. Monastery down at Luton. . . . I got a mate at Shepherd's Bush, you see. . . .

Aston: I might have a pair.

Davies: I got this mate at Shepherd's Bush. In the convenience. Well, he was in the convenience. Run about the best convenience they had. Run about the best one. Always slipped me a bit of soap, any time I went in there. Very good soap. They have to have the best soap. I was never without a piece of soap, whenever I happened to be knocking about the Shepherd's Bush area.

This is music-hall cross-talk elevated to the level of art. Notice how that whole dialogue-sequence is built around the repetition of key nouns: 'Curtains . . . curtains . . . blacks . . . blacks . . . shoes . . . shoes . . . monastery . . . Luton . . . monastery . . . Luton . . . mate at Shepherd's Bush

... mate at Shepherd's Bush ... convenience ... convenience ... convenience ... soap ... soap ... soap ... soap ... Shepherd's Bush.' Repeat this sequence out loud and you will find the words convey an almost musical sense of form with the repetition of a single word giving way to the repetition of two words and the reiteration of a word three or four times. Evidence of Pinter's accurate tape-recorder ear for dialogue? Perhaps. Myself, I see it also as a reflection of the music-hall trick of nagging away at phrases until they have been soaked of meaning and of carefully patterning speech so that it, subconsciously, works on the spectator like a piece of music. Ken Dodd once told me that he regarded the comedian as a solo singer. And if you take a typical stretch of Max Miller patter you can see what he means: 'Women? Now I shouldn't talk like that about the women because I'm very fond of the women. I like them very much. I should do, I'm a married man myself and I'm proud. It's no good being otherwise, it's too late. I have fifteen children. I know fifteen children's a lot of children. I took them to the zoo many years ago. I was living in Brixton at the time. It cost me one and fourpence in bus fares. And when we got to the zoo the man at the gate said, "Come inside and have a look at the baby Boojah". I said, "No thanks, there are too many of us". He said, "They're not all yours, are they?" I said, "Yes, they are". He said, "Stop where you are and I'll bring the baby Boojah out to have a look at you".' Not only have rhythms like that crept into Pinter's work: even some of the physical business, such as a sequence where Aston, Davies and Mick pass a bag from hand to hand, reach back beyond *Waiting for Godot*, to silent screen comedy and to the archetypal routines of vaudeville.

What one sees in Pinter's work, however, is a steady process of refinement in which some of the coarse theatrical influences are weeded out and in which more and more of the author's viewpoint is omitted. In *The Birthday Party* we can sense the author's pity for the persecuted pianist and his detestation of the mysteriously brutal intruders. In *The Caretaker* we are delighted to see the defective, Aston, turning the tables on the aggressive intruder, Davies. But by the time we come to *The Homecoming* Pinter has withdrawn from the action any frame of moral reference: the action shows an academic returning from America to his North London home and seeing his wife snatched from his clutches by his rapacious relatives. But, as Harold Hobson pointed out, we have no idea what Mr Pinter thinks of Ruth and Teddy (the returning couple) or what value their existence has. Moreover, such is the ambiguity of the action we do not even know whether they are telling the truth about their background or their own relationship; what interests Mr Pinter is the fact their presence exacerbates conflicts that already exist within this riven proletarian household.

In his more recent works Pinter goes even further. In *Landscape* and *Silence* he not only removes any moral framework: he dispenses with such familiar props as narrative and naturalistic characterisation. *Landscape* presents us with two parallel monologues that never interlock or coincide but that lead us to assume we are in the presence of two people who are or have been married; that the woman's lover was their joint employer; and that the woman found in him a gentleness and sensitivity lacking in her earthy, coarse-grained husband. The play works on one like a prose-poem and leaves its reverberations in one's head long after one has left the theatre. Its weakness is that it gains little from being seen rather than heard. The same applies to *Silence*, a much more cryptic and obscure piece in which we see the distorting effects of memory at play as two middle-aged men and a woman look back over aspects of their past life. In the Aldwych production John Bury's set with its shimmering opalescent surfaces lent a strange mysterious glow to the proceedings. But on radio the play seemed even better because, in a medium that is primarily a talk-box, the silences registered even more pronouncedly. But these two plays hark back to Pinter's first published work in the realm of prose-poetry rather than to his years floating around the seaside reps. As with Osborne, when Pinter touches now on the entertainment industry it is at a rather more exalted level than in the past: just as *The Hotel in Amsterdam* deals with a blandly affluent crew of movie-makers, so Pinter's *Old Times* is set in the comfortable rural retreat of a successful documentary-director, though admittedly there is a good deal of specu-lation about who went with whom to see the movie of *Odd Man Out* back in the 1940s. This very speculation, in fact, gives one a clue as to the work's main themes: the ambiguity of memory, the conflicting claims of personal ownership, the elusiveness of most people's private persona, the hunger for possession. What is heartening is that, after the rather anti-theatrical nature of *Landscape* and *Silence* Pinter has come up with a play that could only work, fully and satisfyingly, in the theatre. To understand the battle that is going on for private ownership, you need to *see* the three characters in their physical and spatial relationships. On radio, many of the lines would become meaningless if you could not witness the effect they were having on other people; and in the cinema, the almost inevitable need to open up the action would rob the work of its haunting, claustrophobic power. *Old Times* proves that Pinter is irrevocably a man of the theatre.

So too is Peter Nichols who owes even more than Osborne and Pinter to the popular theatrical styles of the 1940s.

His father was a zestful amateur performer who treated the living-room as his stage and who, in Nichols's own words, invariably made half a dozen exits from any room he was in; the bulk of Nichols's own theatre-going as a child was done at the Bristol Hippodrome where he saw people like George Robey, Harry Tate, Norman Evans, as well as Vic Oliver and Beatrice Lillie in *Tonight at 8.30*; and his own acting career began in Service revues in the distinguished company of people like John Schlesinger and Kenneth Williams. Unlike Osborne and Pinter, he has not pursued his acting career while writing; and he says that, as a professional actor, he worked on 'the lowest level'; by which he means policemen in telly series, walk-ons at Covent Garden, and weekly rep, though he proudly records that his performance as Count Dracula won him a local newspaper headline—COUNT DRACULA NEVER SO FEARSOME.

But, of all modern dramatists, he is the one who has most successfully integrated music-hall into the very fabric of his work. *A Day in the Death of Joe Egg* started off apparently as a naturalistic study of a young married couple trying to cope with the desperate problem of rearing a spastic child; but the more he wrote, the more Nichols found the naturalistic material kept bursting at the seams and so he introduced the technique of direct address to the audience. It is a device that works brilliantly because it saves an enormous amount of time in the communication of narrative fact and because it also reflects the parents' technique of learning to live with the problem by adopting a tone of manic levity. Significantly, the more the director heightens the music-hall element, the more moving and powerful the play becomes. Thus Michael Blakemore's original West End production exploited it to the full by casting a magnificent comic actor, Joe Melia, as the hero and by putting a small-sized band into the theatre boxes. But when Peter Nichols himself directed a production at Greenwich Theatre in 1971 he tried to keep the action more within naturalistic bounds: as a result it seemed a less audacious and affecting play.

Nichols has, however, used the music-hall idioms to consistently good effect. In *The National Health*, where a dowdy hospital ward becomes a microcosm of modern Britain, he transforms a cynical ward orderly into the equivalent of a lewd stand-up comic: while the staff are saving human life in the background, he is downstage peddling to the audience his warped view of the healing arts as inherently bent. Many people seemed to think he was the spokesman for the author but nothing could be further from the truth. He is, in fact, an exuberant National Health Thersites whose warped view of medical activity is more a comment on his own diseased nature than an accurate reflection of the truth. In *Forget-Me-Not-Lane* the music-hall influence is even more ubiquitous: the hero chats freely to the audience as he surveys his past life, a wartime concert party complete with Union Jack tableaux is put on stage and there is even a re-creation of an incident from Nichols's own youth in which his father interrupted a smutty comic in the middle of his act.

Nichols thus has the actor's fascination with the mechanics of theatre. He himself now talks of this somewhat as if it were a limitation. But is it? First of all the technique of direct frontal address, though associated by us with stand-up comedy, has a respectable theatrical ancestry going back to the Elizabethans: it is both a very simple way of imparting information and of punching a hole in the artificial fourth wall created by naturalistic drama. Secondly, Nichols never allows his use of vaudeville devices to take precedence over his preoccupation with the state of modern Britain: like Osborne and Alan Bennett, he has an ambivalent attitude towards social progress, obviously welcoming raised standards of living but deploring the kind of shoddy tat that affluence has brought in its wake. Clearly he loves Britain: at the same time he loathes the internal combustion engine, unearned luxury and the cult of youth. Thirdly, I believe his passion for an exuberant theatricality and for boisterous comedy enables him to popularise subjects generally considered unpalatable on the modern stage: sickness, decay, the awfulness of seeing people die. 'To move wild laughter in the throat of death. It cannot be: it is impossible,' says Berowne in *Love's Labour's Lost*. Mr Nichols's three stage plays happily show this to be otherwise.

Charles Wood is another dramatist who has exploited his first-hand knowledge of the entertainment industry—in *Fill the Stage with Happy Hours* and *Veterans*—but who is never sentimental about his background and who never allows his theatrical interests to dominate his exploration of wider themes. In fact if you talk to him about the theatre, you discover the same kind of love-hate relationship towards it that he has towards the army. His parents and grandparents were both in the business. He himself worked as a stage manager and scenic artist as well as an actor. 'But,' he once told me, 'I hated the fact that my parents were in the theatre. It meant there was no security; we had to live in digs and, if we did manage to raise a mortgage for a house, we were never there long enough to take it up.' And working in the theatre is exactly like being in the army. There is the same sort of discipline: being in before the half* is exactly like being ready before a parade.'

And something of this comes out in *Fill the Stage with Happy Hours* which gives a bitter-sweet picture of life in a seedy provincial theatre where Father dreams hopefully

* The half-hour before the curtain rises.

of next week putting on Ibsen and Shakespeare instead of
the usual commercial rubbish, where Mother serves behind
the bar and where the son is seduced by a visiting actress.
Wood describes it all with a certain humour but you are
left in no doubt about his gratitude that this kind of
theatre is now a thing of the past. And, like Osborne and
Pinter, when he now writes about the world of entertainment it is at a much more exalted level reflecting his own
graduation (or declension?) to the role of screen-writer.
Veterans, staged at the Royal Court in 1972, is a witty,
slightly in-jokish account of a script-writer's experiences
on location shooting for a big-budget movie; and clearly it
derives a good deal from Wood's experiences as a writer
on *The Charge of the Light Brigade*. But what is fascinating
is that Wood feels it necessary, like Osborne, to set down
something of his disenchantment with the film industry
where the writer is dependent on increasingly unreachable
tycoons, where people are thrown arbitrarily together in
a kind of restless camaraderie and where money is the
only compensation for all the boredom and humiliation.
It is as if they both felt the need to purge themselves of
particular, discomforting experiences.

Wood's work is, as I have suggested, founded on a series
of paradoxes. He loathes military life yet feels a compulsion
to write about it—*Cockade*, *Drill Pig*, *Dingo*. He proclaims a
detestation of the stage yet he is drawn to recording his
impressions of theatrical life. And, though he once decried
the ladies who love the drama and let themselves be bathed
in beautiful words, he is one of the foremost stage poets of
the time. Take this short extract from his play about the
Indian Mutiny, *H*:

I have swept the badmashery
from the city of Benares

G

with gun
with sword
with grape and with Enfield
bullets.
I swept them up.
I found them in holes,
rooted them out from their
holes.
I Am the Arm of the Lord.

Cocteau once said that theatrical poetry should be not tenuous like gossamer but thick like the rigging of a ship and visible at a distance. And Wood's poetry falls exactly into that category. Notice in that brief extract the repeated alliteration, the use of hard, tough consonants, the echoing employment of the first person singular to give rhythm to the piece, the use of strong, sharp proper names. Compared to Christopher Fry, whose theatrical poetry seems increasingly tenuous and literary, Wood seems to me like a genuine theatrical poet knowing how to give words an almost gestural and brutal force. I only hope Wood can conquer some of his alleged distaste for the medium.

Charles Dyer (*Rattle of a Simple Man*, *Staircase*, *Mother Adam*) meanwhile clearly has pretensions to being the Flaubert of Shaftesbury Avenue. He writes for three or four hours a day and at the end of that time has usually produced one usable sentence. This is partly because he cannot bear to see any crossing-out and so always goes back to the beginning of a page if he makes a mistake, and partly because of his own sensitivity to the different shades of meaning a line can carry. 'As an actor-writer,' he says, 'I think one's greatest asset is audience-control. This is something that has to be worked for, though. In all, it took me seven years to write *Staircase* and five to do *Rattle*.

I first of all create a book so that I know the characters inside out; then, during the second stage, I juggle with the individual lines. As an actor, I can use my theatrical experience to take my characters, write their histories, imagine what they would do in each and every one of their moods. The important thing is to combine a feeling for the way a character really speaks with the job of interesting an audience. The two things never come into conflict if one has the proper audience-control.'

Dyer's meticulous approach pays dividends in that *Staircase* at least has extraordinary density of texture. The price one pays for such an approach is a certain monotony of tone. However what is interesting about the play is the way Dyer incorporates his knowledge of camp actorish argot into his study of two homosexual hairdressers, one of whom might have stepped right off the back pages of a yellowing edition of *The Stage*: he was last seen on the stage as a broker's man just before the war, has done one television commercial in the last decade and yet dreams constantly of a glorious comeback. Through him Dyer gives us authentic dressing-room camp ('I'll stick a skewer in my ear and go to hell as a kebab') heightened, polished and veneered. But after a time the lack of tonal contrast becomes wearing and one longs (or at least I do) for the sound of a third, unaffected, heterosexual voice.

But, looking at the actor-dramatists as a whole, is there anything to differentiate their work from that of men like Storey, Stoppard, Shaffer, Arden, Wesker, Bolt who have never been professional performers? It is difficult to lay down hard and fast rules. Inevitably the actor-dramatists deal, directly or indirectly, with their own theatrical background. But this is perfectly proper since autobiography is a necessary ingredient of drama. I was astonished a while back to hear a colleague say that he thought it was 'cheating' for the writer simply to exploit his own private experience. But if Ibsen had thought thus there would have been no *Master Builder*; if Strindberg had not been prepared to cannibalise his own marital experience there would have been no *Dance of Death*; if O'Neill had shared similar reservations, he would never have given us *Long Day's Journey into Night*. All writers are on safe ground to start with by writing about the world they know best: the type of first play I really distrust is the one that is set in the year 3002 or the one that offers a hazy re-creation of life at the court of Gustavus Adolphus.

The actor-dramatists also have a slight advantage over their colleagues in that they have an immediate instinct for what will work in purely theatrical terms and for the natural rhythms of drama. This does not mean that dramatists who have not worked in the theatre are technically helpless: ironically enough the most mature first play by any writer since 1956 is almost certainly Peter Shaffer's *Five Finger Exercise*, yet Mr Shaffer came into the theatre from teaching. But the fact remains that, although a writer like John Arden exploits the varied resources of theatre with the enthusiasm of a water-colourist suddenly let loose in oils, one sometimes feels his material is not perfectly related to his form. Storey too in his first play, *The Restoration of Arnold Middleton*, provided a powerful study of the divided self but handled the actual mechanics of the story-telling rather nervously and uncertainly: in fact, before writing the play he had scarcely been to the theatre more than a dozen times in his life. David Mercer's first full-length stage play, *Ride a Cock Horse*, similarly had great gut-power and strength; but the fact is it kept going over the same ground like a lost wayfarer constantly retracing his steps in a circuitous wood. But with Osborne, Pinter, Nichols, you find a fairly quick apprehension of how to organise a play, of where to place one's theatrical climaxes, of the best moment to introduce a new character. Indeed Osborne and Pinter began by writing plays that were deeply traditional in form and original only in content.

I am not arguing that writers who have been actors are inherently superior to those who have not. I am simply suggesting that in their first few plays they may be more surefooted in their handling of the actual mechanics of play-writing. But, as David Storey has dazzlingly proved, the ground-rules are very quickly absorbed. For the future one can only assume (and hope) the acting profession will continue to provide the theatre with new writing talent. Actors naturally write theatrically workable dialogue. The touring and repertory systems give them access to a wider segment of English life than most people ever gain in a life-time. And there is always a large pool of unemployed actors, many of whom pass the time between jobs by putting their ideas down on paper. Obviously being an actor does not automatically make one a good writer. But knowing something about audience reactions, actor-psychology and traditional theatrical forms cannot be any great hindrance when it comes to compressing one's experience of life into the two-hour traffic of the stage.

9

THEORIES OF ACTING

> 'It is easy to dream and create theories
> in art but it is hard to practise them.'
> (*Constantin Stanislavski*)

IF it is hard to practise theories, it is even harder to write about them. The moment one tries in any way to define the principles governing the various approaches to acting, one finds oneself in a terrible linguistic impasse in which words like truth, realism, style, technique get bandied around to the point where they gradually lose all meaning. Even a close reading of Stanislavski's works leaves one with a slight headache with words like 'inner content' buzzing around one's confused, fatigued brain. So although in this chapter I shall attempt to deal with the two main approaches to acting current today, I shall, wherever possible, relate what I am talking about to concrete and specific examples.

The modern actor is, of course, subject to many more stylistic influences and pressures than his counterpart in simpler days. As Richard Findlater writes in *The Player Kings*, a young actor's style today may be made up of 'acting in rep in Restoration Comedy and Strindberg, acting in a film spectacular about the Napoleonic Wars and a television soap-opera, acting in the West End run of a Neil Simon hit and a Sunday-night happening. He will probably keep an open mind about Grotowski and Brecht, Stanislavski and Artaud, Simon and Garfunkel, Morecambe

and Wise.' True enough: the modern actor has to be a kind
of histrionic chameleon capable of fitting in to all sections
of the entertainment spectrum. Yet although the English
theatre is currently a kind of anthology of acting styles—
in which you can find strong residual traces of both Gerald
du Maurier and Mick Jagger—I still believe there is a
definite, discernible shift to a cooler, more detached style
than was apparent in the '50s and early '60s.

The two great modern theorists for actors are, of course,
Stanislavski and Brecht. Between them they provide the
most fully-documented and completely articulated studies
of acting-styles written this century. Both, I think, are
often misunderstood; both also need to be looked at
critically since neither provides the answer to every style
of play ever written. I do not think the Stanislavski approach
is much help to an actor playing Genet; and I can live
contentedly without seeing the Brechtian style applied to
The Importance of Being Earnest. And significantly I think
both of them were slightly less doctrinaire than some of
their more devout followers. As Stanislavski once wrote:
'A formal approach to our complicated creative work and
a narrow elementary understanding of it is the greatest
danger to my method, my whole system . . . there is
nothing more harmful or stupid so far as art is concerned
than a system for the sake of a system. You cannot make it
an aim in itself; you cannot transform a means into an end.
That would be the greatest lie of all.' Words that should
perhaps be engraven above the entrance to the Actors'
Studio.

Let us look, however, at the theories of Brecht and
Stanislavski and see what influence they have on contemporary practice. The first and most obvious thing to be
said about Stanislavski is that his approach was revolution-
ary and his achievement massive. He began his career in the

1880s during the period of the Russian producer-autocrat yet it is clear that although he shared some of their characteristics he also had a questing, probing intelligence: 'I treated my actors as mannequins. I showed them what I saw in my imagination and they copied me. Whenever I was successful in getting the right feeling, the play came to life, but where I did not go beyond external invention it was dead. The merit of my work at that time consisted in my endeavours to be sincere and to search for truth. I hated all falsehood on the stage and especially theatrical falsehood. I began to hate the theatre in the theatre and I was beginning to look for genuine life in it: not ordinary life, of course, but artistic life.'

To read *My Life in Art* is to become aware of Stanislavski's relentless desire for self-improvement as an actor and producer and his never-ceasing search for essential theatrical truth. It is also fascinating to see him put his finger on a number of defects in the Russian theatre of his time that are still alarmingly relevant today. For instance, in a chapter on Russian dramatic schools he categorically states that many schools take far too many pupils in order to meet the cost of their overheads—and that is as applicable to the London of the 1970s as it was to the Moscow of the 1880s. And again when talking of the businessman, Morozov's, contribution to the erection of a new building for the Moscow Art Theatre, Stanislavski writes: 'All for art and the actor—that was the motto that controlled his actions. In this manner he did exactly the opposite of what is usually done when a theatre is built. Usually three-quarters of the money is expended on the foyer and the various rooms used by the audience and only one quarter on art and the actors.' He might almost be talking of new British theatres.

And when one comes to the evolution of the famous

Stanislavski system in the course of that momentous holiday he took in Finland in 1906, one realises it is the product of cumulative experience rather than deductive reasoning. Many years of trial and error both as actor and director went into the formulation of the ground-rules of the system: it would be wrong to attack them, as some have done, because they are too cerebral. Having said that, let me attempt to summarise them briefly.

Stanislavski's first point was that the actor's immediate priority on stage is to get himself into the right creative state of mind. This could only be achieved through a complete freedom of the body and a total relaxation of the muscles. The body must be at the beck and call of the will. But how to achieve this desired state? Through exercises riveting the actor's attention on the sensations of the body and distracting him from what was happening in the auditorium. It follows from this that the actor must stop consciously trying to amuse the spectator. 'If nobody amuses the spectator there is nothing left for him to do in the theatre but to seek himself for an object of attention. Where can that object be found? On the stage, of course, in the actor himself. The concentration of the creating actor calls out the concentration of the spectator and in this manner forces him to enter into what is passing on the stage, exciting his attention, his imagination, his thinking processes and his emotion.' Thus the actor concentrates on the role; the audience concentrates on the actor. The actor identifies with the character; and the audience identifies with the actor.

But Stanislavski's most crucial point was that the actor must believe in everything that is taking place on stage and, above all, he must believe in himself. The work of the actor begins the moment what Stanislavski calls 'the creative if' appears in his soul and imagination. 'Just as a little girl believes in the existence of her doll and in the life in and around her, so the actor the moment the creative *if* appears is transported from the plane of real life to the plane of a different kind of life which he himself has created in his imagination. Believing in this life, the actor can begin to create.' Endowed with a highly-developed imagination, a child-like naïveté and trustfulness and an artistic sensitivity to truth, the actor can then transform the most crude stage lie into the most delicate truth. If the actor believes convincingly enough in the reality of what he sees around him, then so will we.

It would be absurd to underestimate the historical importance of Stanislavski's discoveries. At the same time we have reached a stage today where we can afford to view them critically. For the weakness of the Stanislavski approach is that it assumes the actor's overriding purpose is to convince the audience that he is watching a slice of reality; that he must make the audience believe they are watching Ibsen's Doctor Stockman rather than an actor playing Ibsen's Doctor Stockman. Yet the theatre is not reality and it seems to me a mark of aesthetic failure if the spectator is so carried away that he forgets he is in a theatre. A drama lecturer I know once quoted to me the example of a spectator in Paris crying out in warning as Marcel Marceau mimed a man crossing a high-wire in a circus. And he evinced this as an example of Marceau's supreme theatrical art. Doubtless Stanislavski would have approved also since it vindicates his point about the actor's concentration. Yet to me it seems a mark of aesthetic weakness. Only the very innocent or the totally insane believe that what they are witnessing on a stage is the literal truth; and the moment you leave an audience confused as to whether they are watching life or art, then you have in fact failed. The American lady who cried out 'You big black fool' as she saw Othello being ensnared by Iago may have been transported by the actor's belief in the creative *if*; but she was hardly the ideal theatrical spectator.

Stanislavski also underestimates the actor's own critical and intellectual response to the work he is playing. Personally, I do not want a stage filled with actors of child-like trustfulness and naïveté. I want actors of a resonant and questioning intelligence who are capable of approaching a character not through the creative *if* but through their own first-hand observation of life, their own knowledge and wide reading and their own speculative intelligence. I want informed actors more than I want highly imaginative actors. And I believe actors of this type are not so hard to find as all that. Jonathan Miller once told me that when directing at the National Theatre he suggested a course of lectures for the company on the social, historical, pictorial and intellectual background to the work in production. The actors themselves were delighted at the prospect and indeed hungry for information. Only the inevitable lack of rehearsal time prevented the execution of the plan.

The other great flaw in the Stanislavski approach can be discerned from reading *An Actor Prepares* and *Building a Character*. I would not deny for a moment that these are key works in any actor's training and that they should be read and absorbed by anyone intending to take up the stage. And it is worth noting that an accident of publishing led to a certain distortion of Stanislavski's intentions. *An Actor Prepares*, which deals mainly with the internal aspects of acting, was published in 1936. And *Building a Character*, which deals chiefly with the external side, was not published till 1949. The two volumes were intended by Stanislavski to be thought of together; yet the gap in publishing dates meant that for a long period Stanislavski was thought of primarily as a man concerned with the actor's inner states.

As Robert Lewis pointed out in *Method - or Madness?* Stanislavski would have abhorred a lot of the 'mumbling but
with feeling' that goes on in his name. In fact he quite
specifically said in *Building a Character*: 'Letters, syllables,
words—these are the musical notes of speech out of which
to fashion measures, arias, whole symphonies. There is good
reason to describe beautiful speech as musical. Many actors
who are careless of speech, inattentive to words, pronounce
them in such thoughtless, slipshod speed without putting
any endings on them that they end up with completely
mutilated, half-spoken phrases.'

Where the Stanislavski system now seems slightly out of
date is in the emphasis it puts on the achievement of a
single super-objective in acting and the reduction of all
the actor's drives and energies to what he called 'through-
action'. But for the 'through-action', all the pieces and
problems, the given circumstances, moments of truth and
belief and so forth would remain quiescent, separated from
each other and without hope of coming to life. The
through-action, however, welds them together, threading
all the elements like beads on a string and directing them
towards the ruling idea of the play. The graph of through-
action represents a straight-line made up of the different
lines of the actor's part, some short and some long, but all
moving in one direction thus:

$$\longrightarrow \quad \longrightarrow \quad \longrightarrow \quad \rightarrow \ \rightarrow \ \longrightarrow \quad \longrightarrow \quad \longrightarrow \ \text{Ruling Idea}$$

Stanislavski's spokesman in *An Actor Prepares* explains
that all the lines are headed towards the same goal and fuse
into one main current. 'We have agreed, have we not, that
the main line of action and the main theme are organically
part of the play and they cannot be disregarded without
detriment to the play itself. But suppose we were to introduce an extraneous theme or put what you might call a

tendency into the play. The other elements will remain the same but they will be turned aside by this new addition. It can be expressed this way:

$$\longrightarrow \searrow \longrightarrow \searrow \underset{\text{Tendency}}{\longrightarrow} \searrow \longrightarrow \text{Ruling Idea}$$

A play with that kind of deformed broken backbone cannot live.'

But the point is that modern drama has proved that it can. A whole school of drama now exists in which it is impossible to boil down the whole drive of a play into a single sentence or to find one single ruling idea which governs all the wishes in a character. As long ago as 1888 Strindberg was attacking the one-sided manner of looking at things that prevailed in most drama and that enabled a character to be summed up by a single trait. In the preface to *Miss Julie* he wrote: 'An author's summary judgement upon men (this man is a fool; that one brutal; that one is jealous; that one stingy, etc.) ought to be challenged and rejected by the Naturalists who are aware of the richness of the human soul and who know that vice has another side to it that is very like virtue. I have depicted my characters as modern characters, living in an age of transition at least more breathlessly hysterical than the period immediately preceding it. Thus I have made them more vacillating, disjointed; a blending of the old and the new.'

And, since Strindberg, the Theatre of the Absurd has shown that drama can cope perfectly well with inconsequentiality of action, fragmentation of experience, the many-sidedness of human character. How, for instance, can one talk in terms of through-action with a play like Arrabal's *The Architect and the Emperor of Assyria* where two characters marooned on a desert island act out a series of sado-masochistic, master-slave fantasy relationships? What relevance has super-objective to a play like Peter Weiss's *Marat-Sade* which reproduces with great fidelity the externals of madness and which boils the action down to a series of separated slabs? What does integration of personality count for in a play like Genet's *The Balcony* which relates man's sexual drives to his authoritarian ones and which is again concerned with men's fantasy natures? One cannot blame Stanislavski for failing to anticipate the Theatre of the Absurd. But one can argue that while his system provides the actor with a codified and organised working method, it by no means meets all the demands the actor faces in twentieth-century drama.

The area, of course, where Stanislavski is still intensely applicable is in naturalistic drama. Take, for instance, a play like E. A. Whitehead's *Alpha Beta* which explored an ailing marriage—or perhaps one that had already ailed— over a ten-year period. Ultimately I think the play was dealing with the restrictive pressures of a rigid working-class and Catholic morality on a pair of modern unfortunates. But its surface was intensely naturalistic and ideally suited to the traditional Stanislavskian approach. By that I mean the actors were called upon to convince us of the reality of the background through the intensity of their concentration; and to force us to identify with the characters in the situation through their own total absorption. And the two performers in question, Albert Finney and Rachel Roberts, gave perfect Stanislavskian performances. Finney, for instance, got the externals absolutely right as the boozy, randy adolescent Peter Pan of a husband. Everything was authentic: the cutting, grating Liverpool accent that sounded as if it had been transmitted through a clogged sewer-pipe, the exuberant drunkenness which meant that when aiming a puff at a cigarette he actually missed, the tell-tale narcissism that entailed a slight duck when he passed a mirror (something Olivier did also in *Uncle Vanya*). At the same time through conscious application to outer detail, he gave one a complete chart of the man's inner life. It was a superlative vindication of the creative *if*—the approach that says 'If everything around me were real, what would I do next?' Yet without denying Finney's genius or the validity of the Stanislavskian approach for a certain type of play, I would still come down on the side of Eric Bentley who wrote in *In Search of Theatre*: 'Acting may be called fresh, vital and modern when it leaves behind what may be called the Ibsen-Chekhov-Stanislavski period during which actors learn to embody a mood and sustain it during the whole evening and attempt a freer, cooler manner in which a wider range of quickly changing moods is achievable.' It is time in short to get beyond Stanislavski.

Towards Brecht? Where else? The cornerstone of the Brechtian approach is that the old idea of an enthralling theatrical illusion is degrading to the audience who stare at the stage as if spellbound—'which is an expression from the Middle Ages, an age of witches and obscurantists'. Brecht specifically does not want us to identify with the characters on the stage: 'How long are our souls going to have to leave our gross bodies under cover of darkness to penetrate into those dream figures up there on the rostrum in order to share their transports that would otherwise be denied to us?' The essence of the Brechtian approach to acting is that the actor should regard himself not as impersonating the character but rather as narrating the actions of another person at a specific time in the past. It should be like the director demonstrating his intentions to the cast. Or another illustrative instance Brecht always liked to quote was a street accident in which a solitary eye-witness recounted the events to bystanders. The eye-witness wants to indicate that the old man who has been run over walked slowly so he will imitate his gait to show precisely what he means. He, in fact, quotes the old man's walk. He never impersonates the victim. 'He never forgets, nor does he allow anyone to forget, that he is not the one whose action is being demonstrated but the one who demonstrates it.'

The actor admittedly has to feel his way, Stanislavski-wise, into the character in the early stages of rehearsal; but he also has to make some implied comment on the character's actions so that the audience can see his approval or disapproval. In addition, the actor must be able to suggest, 'apart from what he does, something else he does not do, i.e. he acts in such a manner that one can see the alternative course of action, so that the acting allows the audience to detect other possibilities, so that any given action can be seen as only one among a number of variants'. As Martin Esslin wisely points out in his book on Brecht, the description always sounds more complicated than it is in fact. As he says, the villain in a Victorian melodrama is a perfect example of a style of acting without identification between the actor and the character he portrays. And this applies to villains in other periods of drama. Why, asked Brecht, is the principal negative character in drama so much more interesting than the positive hero? 'Because he is performed in a spirit of criticism.'

Where, however, in the modern theatre does one find any evidence of the acceptability of the Brechtian approach? The first and most obvious place to look is the world of the music-hall. Eric Bentley once wrote that Maurice Chevalier's skits were all Brechtian 'in that Chevalier always stands outside the role, carefully showing the audience his attitude towards it'. The same is true of a British vaudevillian like Frankie Howerd who constantly steps outside the frame of the action to show us what he

George C. Scott as Patton:
a pygmy when seen against the broad horizon of
history, a Titan when seen against his contemporaries.

The three faces of Walter Matthau in *Plaza Suite*:
as a middle-class philanderer (*above*), a Hollywood
Lothario (*below left*) and an apoplectic father (*below right*).

The three faces of Eric Porter in the BBC television production of *The Forsyte Saga*: as the young, eagerly acquisitive Soames, fingers delicately poised over an objet d'art (*left*); as the middle-aged Soames, rich, befurred and cuckolded (*below left*); and as the aged, disappointed Soames, all lines in the face now pointing glumly downwards.

Lee Remick in the BBC television production of
Tennessee Williams' *Summer and Smoke*: a performance that showed a demure Southern virgin's
spinsterish veneer slowly cracking like dry, parched
ground opening up after rain.

thinks of the script, the director and even his fellow-actors. He also builds up an instantly recognisable Howerd persona: an amiable, gossipy simpleton who's a bit of an old woman and who's driven into a state of panic and fluster by the prospect of sex. At its very crudest, you see this working in something like *Up the Chastity Belt* where Howerd plays a humble medieval crusader who happens to be the dead spit of Richard the Lion Heart: in one scene, for instance, as he is dragged half-protestingly on to a couch by a heavy-breasted Teutonic maiden crying '*Ich liebe dich, Ich liebe dich*', Howerd simply turns to the camera and observes—'You can say that again'. But his distancing technique goes beyond mere asides. In any given situation Howerd never asks you to identify with the character: he simply presents you with a buffoonish entertainer all the while deploring the dirty-mindedness of the audience and the incompetence of his colleagues. He is arguably the most Brechtian actor in Britain.

Joan Littlewood's work over the years at the Theatre Royal, Stratford, although varying in quality, has always seemed to me to embody the basic Brechtian belief that the actor should not so much impersonate the character as present him. Miss Littlewood is much too sentimental to be regarded as an out-and-out Brechtian: the show, for instance, with which she returned to the Theatre Royal in 1972, *The Londoners*, was pure Cockney pastoral in that it portrayed a kind of jovial working-class togetherness that never really existed even before the rise of East End tower-blocks and the onset of the dreaded civic improvement scheme. But Miss Littlewood (who was, as far as I can trace, the first person to play Mother Courage in Britain) adheres to Brechtian principles not only in the use of alienation but in her dedication to the cause of *spass* (roughly translatable as 'fun'). The perfect apotheosis of this was *Oh What a*

Lovely War: the performers were, of course, clad in silky pierrot costumes to which were added various appurtenances indicative of the 1914-18 situation. Not only did this enable the actors to switch roles in an instant: it also provided some memorable images such as that of George Sewell in leather boots, pierrot pantaloons and military top-coat exhorting the troops into battle. You knew all the time you were not watching someone trying to incarnate Haig before your eyes: you were watching George Sewell in a pierrot costume *presenting* Haig. Compare the brilliant effectiveness of this technique with the attempt by the Canadian actor, John Colicos, in *Soldiers* to re-create Churchill. Mr Colicos, a good and conscientious actor, left no stone unturned in his attempt to bring Churchill before our eyes: the body assumed the same defiant slouch, the shoulders were aggressively rounded and the face, due to hours spent on make-up, assumed a heavy-jowled Churchillian quality. No actor could have worked harder. Yet in the end what was it all for? One knew this was not Churchill in front of one. One knew one was seeing only a piece of Tussaud-like re-creation. Far, far better to adopt the Littlewood-Brecht technique and *indicate* a historical character, at the same time letting us see the actor's comment upon him.

Proof positive, however, of Littlewood's affinity with Brecht came in a production that she herself did not direct: the recent West End revival of *The Threepenny Opera*. I must admit I found it a lack-lustre affair deficient precisely in that quality of lightness and gaiety you often find in the best Berliner Ensemble productions. But significantly the one totally successful performance came from a former member of the Joan Littlewood company, Barbara Windsor. While the rest of the company were giving us heavy and doggedly Teutonic performances, Miss Windsor simply brought her own natural vitality and ebullience on to the stage, always making it abundantly clear that it was Miss Windsor *as* a vengeful, lustful Soho tart and not Miss Windsor trying to *be* a vengeful, lustful Soho tart. Hugh Leonard put it well when he said in *Plays and Players* that she had a touch of 'rumbustiousness' appropriate for Brecht and missing elsewhere in the production.

Olivier is another actor I would call a perfect Brechtian performer. 'But you're always very conscious it's Olivier' is the standard charge levelled against him by people who fail to understand the basic principles of acting. But the answer is much of one's pleasure lies in the fact one *is* so conscious of Olivier's sharp ironic presence—and, I would say, of his critical interpretative intelligence. His Coriolanus, for example, was a classic example of a Brechtian performance in that he indicated to us through myriad detail that the martial hero was emotionally flawed by his attachment to his mother's apron-strings: that the great man was, in terms of his personal development, still in fact a boy. Or take his most recent performance: as James Tyrone in *Long Day's Journey into Night*. On one level I suppose one could describe it as a brilliant piece of physical impersonation: the thinning, slicked-back hair, the solid four-square build, the light, glancing irony all accorded perfectly with biographer's descriptions of James O'Neill. Yet at the same time Olivier went far beyond impersonation and expressed a clearly defined attitude towards the character. The perfect embodiment of this came in a piece of business that was widely interpreted as gratuitous, applause-begging showing-off on Olivier's part.* I refer to the moment when in the last traumatic act the father lights the lamps as dusk descends. Olivier mounted the table to accomplish the

* In fact when I saw the production a second time, in September 1972, Olivier had removed this action altogether.

task; and once it was completed he stepped backwards off the table in a single, graceful parabolic movement landing lightly and easily on the balls of his feet. It was not only an athletic and exciting piece of business in itself: it also told us a lot about Olivier's attitude to the character and that this man—no mean actor—retained all his delight in external flourishes and slightly empty, grandiose gestures. This was exactly the kind of thing one might expect from a man who had played *The Count of Monte Cristo* four thousand times in a quarter of a century. Again one could hardly imagine a more Brechtian performance than Olivier's Archie Rice in *The Entertainer* in which the ear-to-ear grin, the flat centre parting, the deadness behind the eyes all seemed like a comment on the utter spiritual bankruptcy of this fading front-cloth comedian. Interestingly enough, one of the best descriptions I have seen of the quintessential Olivier is provided by Cecil Beaton in *The Happy Years: Diaries 1944-48*. He describes how one evening in Paris Olivier outlined the look of his prospective *Hamlet* film through a series of pops, bangs, explosions, farts and other coarse noises. 'It was a most gymnastic performance that we were treated to', says Beaton. 'Larry's imitations have about them something of the original clown or, at least, the essential entertainer who can be found in some remote music-hall or performing in the street outside a pub. This was the real Larry—the mummer, the ale-drinking Thespian—not the rather overwhelmed and shy cipher with wrinkled forehead that goes out into society.' To me this says a lot about the peculiar nature of Olivier's talent; for, as I suggested earlier, what figure is more Brechtian in the theatre than the clown and essential entertainer?

But as a symptom of the change that has come over the English acting profession in a decade I would pick out two particular performances of one role: Davies, the tramp, in

Harold Pinter's *The Caretaker*. In the very first production of the play at the Arts Theatre and the Duchess in 1960 Donald Pleasence was Davies: a man who is charitably taken into another's house, exploits his position to his own advantage and is then brutally expelled. Pleasence played the character as a blustering, belligerent, selfish impostor. It was a remarkable performance in that he seemed to inhabit the role completely. The voice was strident and cawing; the constant pounding of the left palm with the right fist suggested all the suppressed violence in the man; and yet the perennial stoop, as if he was all the time expecting someone to give him a deft blow between the shoulder-blades, evoked a lifetime of subservience and oppression. There was a complete blending of actor and role. Pleasence did not play Davies: he *was* Davies. And it came as no surprise to learn that, when the play was being filmed by Clive Donner in Hackney, Pleasence went out on to the streets during breaks in the action and sold matches to passers-by.

Twelve years later Leonard Rossiter played the same role, no less brilliantly, in a revival of the play at the Mermaid. It would be impossible, however, to imagine Mr Rossiter standing out in Puddle Dock and selling matches; or at least, if he had done so, he would not have fooled many of the customers. For on this occasion the role was *presented* to us and the actor's identification was somewhat less than total. From the first one was acutely conscious of Mr Rossiter's assumption of mock-gentility and refinement ('I've had dinner with the best', he announced in terms suggesting many a nosh-up in Belgrave Square); of the way the mouth formed a repulsive rectangle rather like the aperture in a letter-box with the tongue protruding against the lower-lip; and of the deferential gestures with two fingers raised to the brow in mock-salute. Above all

Rossiter indicated to us that this was a man for whom work was the dirtiest four-letter word in the English language. Whenever an item of furniture needed moving he would station himself in the vicinity of the action making ineffectual traffic-cop gestures without actually coming into contact with the dust-covered objects themselves. This man was, above all, a skiver, a work-shy drop-out, a born malingerer. But whereas Pleasence seemed to be working from the inside out, Rossiter worked from the outside in presenting the character to us through an accumulation of external detail. One may, of course, see this as no more than the product of the stylistic differences of two separate actors. But to me it was a perfect symbol of the way actors have, over the last decade, slowly moved away from a total Stanislavskian realism towards a greater degree of Brechtian presentation.

Why should this be? Partly, it is the result of our increased knowledge of Brecht. I would not say English productions of Brecht have been conspicuously successful; but there have at least been plenty of them. In addition the visits of the Berliner Ensemble in 1956 and 1965 proved to sceptical English spectators that the apparently forbidding Brechtian theories worked marvellously in practice and did indeed lead to a cooler, less intense style of playing. Admittedly Sam Wanamaker wrote of Helene Weigel's Mother Courage that her performance was indistinguishable from that of 'a superb Stanislavski-trained actress'. But the moment you compare her performance with that of English-trained actresses, you can see the difference: they sentimentalise the character, making her triumphantly plucky, whereas Weigel was sardonic, hard-edged, unsentimental. I also remember seeing the Ensemble stage a Sunday afternoon production of *The Little Mahagonny* for members of the acting profession; and here precisely was that disciplined gaiety and sense of fun that Brecht was after. In a word, *'Spass'*.

I also think the changing physical shape of our play-houses has altered the course of English acting. As long as we retain the picture-frame stage and set actors firmly behind the proscenium arch in a naturalistically accurate set, we are obviously going to get performances aiming at a total representation of truth. The open stage—or even one without a conventional arch—however breeds a different kind of actor and a different kind of audience response. The moment, for instance, you see an actor against a back-ground of human faces rather than a stage-set your attitude towards him changes. You become aware that he is only an actor presenting a character. Similarly if he is within spitting distance of the front row of spectators it seems absurd for him to feign ignorance of their presence. The more theatres we get like Sheffield, Leeds, Chichester, Greenwich that do away with the old peep-hole, pro-scenium-arch approach the further we are going to move from Stanislavski.

But on top of this there is the slowly changing nature of the whole theatrical experience. Television has, I think, helped to destroy the idea of close emotional identification with a piece of fiction. People are less ready to be enthralled by a narrative: they find it more acceptable to sit in front of it and criticise it as it goes along. On a very simple level this is, I am sure, one reason for the increased amount of chattering that goes on in theatres and cinemas these days. But, more positively, it can also be an encouragement to a different kind of drama in which music plays a crucial role, in which the atmosphere in the auditorium can be closer to that inside a café or a pub and in which the actor is not obliged to identify with the character he is playing. Brecht, it will be remembered, advocated the kind of theatre in which one could smoke; and he contrasted the 'elegance, lightness, dryness and objectivity' to be found in sporting events with the theatre's exaggerated passions and lack of fun. Significantly, in recent years, there have been a handful of theatrical events produced in the conditions he asked for and they have vindicated his attitude. For instance there was Luca Ronconi's memorable production of *Orlando Furioso* in which the action went on in, around and amongst the spectators and from which one could periodically withdraw to talk to one's neighbours and discuss what one had seen. The Royal Court's Theatre Upstairs has also staged a number of productions which it has been possible to sit and watch with a drink in front of one. I am not saying that this is the only kind of drama one wants or that there is no pleasure to be got out of immersion in a strange, make-believe world. All the same I think the theatre has to recognise that audiences are these days conditioned by television; and that they are perhaps less ready than they once were to abandon their critical awareness and self-consciousness the moment they are seated in an auditorium.

As I said at the beginning of this chapter, English acting is open to a number of influences; and it would be foolish to pin any one label on a profession that can contain performers as diverse as Fred Emney and Edith Evans, Denise Coffey and Constance Cummings, Gerald Harper and Alan Howard, Wolfe Morris and Brian Murphy. And even our most illustrious of drama schools, RADA, proudly boasts that it teaches no one system. The English theatre is—and always has been—a bundle of contradictions made up of ensemble dedication and *ad hoc* casting, method and madness, profound hope and blind faith. Yet, picking one's way gingerly through the acting styles that confront one, I still think it possible for the discerning eye to see Brechtian principles percolating through, aided by inspiring example, restructured playhouses, regional documentary and more detached audiences. And if I had to make any prediction for the rest of the theatrical '70s it is that we shall see many more plays like Peter Nichols's *Forget-Me-Not-Lane* in which Brechtian methods are absorbed into old-style English vaudeville. I hope so, anyway.

10

SEX AND ACTING

'The actor must have the soul of a
fairy and the hide of a walrus.'
(*William Redfield: 'Letters from an Actor'*)

I COME now to a relatively little-charted area of the
acting business: its relation to man's sexual drives. For
there is, I believe, an umbilical connection between acting
and sex. This takes many forms. There is the androgynous,
bisexual quality that invariably underpins great acting.
There is the element of sexual equivocation that runs like
an electric current through most comedy acting. There is
the audience's own instinctive response to a performer's
sex appeal and their indulgence of private fantasy and
wish-fulfilment in the voyeuristic act of watching a play
or film. There is the element of exhibitionism that exists,
to a greater or lesser degree, inside most actors. And there
is the acting profession's awareness of sexual freedom, due
mainly to the rather special, privileged position it occupies
in society. Wherever you turn in acting, you come up
against the dark, mysterious power of sex.

The bisexual element in great acting has, of course, often
been remarked upon; but I think it needs to be examined in
some detail. And where better to begin than with that
most captivating and mysterious of all actresses, Greta
Garbo. The American writer-director, Garson Kanin, tells
a splendid story of how he once said to Ernst Lubitsch

that whenever he saw Gary Cooper on the screen he
thought of Greta Garbo and whenever he saw Greta Garbo
he always thought immediately of Gary Cooper. Why, he
asked, should this be? Simple, said Lubitsch. They're one
and the same person. But they can't be, protested a mock-
innocent Kanin. I can prove it, said Lubitsch with clinching
fervour. Have you noticed how they've *never* appeared in
the same picture?

An idiotic story; but it does make the point that Garbo's
astonishing sexual ambiguity was one of her most magnetic
features. To me three other things made her a great screen
actress: a remarkable physical equipment, a superlative
technical control and an ability to convey thought. Many
actresses have one or other of these qualities: in very few
do they smoothly coalesce.

The body itself is extraordinary. The shoulders are
square, broad and resolute and such as no discus-thrower
would be ashamed of: indeed there are shots in *Ninotchka*
which remind one of Sid Field at his most outrageously
padded. The bosom is small and delicate: when, for instance,
in the temple dance in *Mata Hari* Garbo appears androgyn-
ously in the scantiest of rigs one wonders if the trouble with
this particular Hari is not a lack of feminine voluptuous-
ness. But it is the legs that are most fascinating of all. As
Alexander Walker has pointed out, 'Garbo has a great
length of leg between knee-cap and pelvis and it gives her
movements a piston-like quality'. It also reinforces the impression one frequently has of watching a big outdoor girl
trapped in a life of wearisome sophistication.

As for the technical control, what is fascinating is the
use of two specific muscles: those controlling the left
eyebrow and the left-hand side of the upper lip. Observe
the way she repeatedly arches the former and lets the latter
quiver with sensitivity and you have one clue, I think, to

her unique power in front of a camera: her muscular control. Thus in *Anna Karenina*, Clarence Brown's potted 1935 version of Tolstoy's novel, she registers the deepening conflict between her love for Vronsky and her feeling for her son in a series of tiny, often scarcely noticeable gestures. Rebuked by her husband for her public indiscretions, her mouth tightens as if the slack corners were being pulled taut by invisible threads. When he talks of the inviolability of the marriage tie, she subconsciously puts her hand to her neck as if it were something one wore. And when she is emphatically told she must give up her son, she moves her head a barely perceptible inch or two to the left as if thrown physically and morally off balance. It is also quintessential Garbo that, when welcoming her lover, she should dig her nails into his back rather like an eagle securing its perch on a rock.

And this in itself provides an index to the strong masculine streak you find in all her work. The role, of course, that allows it fullest play is Queen Christina. Before her encounter with John Gilbert's Spanish Ambassador she parades happily round the court in male attire, surrounds herself with nocuous-looking hounds and, in a famous and resonant line, tells her Chancellor, 'I shall die a bachelor'. Her relationship with a darkly beautiful lady-in-waiting whom she greets in the morning with a resounding smack on the lips is also forthright and unequivocal. But not only is this display of masculinity fascinating in itself: it also marvellously heightens her surrender to feminine impulse when circumstances force her to share a bed with the roving Ambassador. And the famous morning-after scene in which she wanders round the room caressing the furniture in dreamily erotic fashion is not just a vivid portrayal of a girl's sexual awakening: it also shows the ultimate defeat of her crypto- (or perhaps not so crypto-) lesbianism. In other circumstances Garbo could be voraciously feminine. For instance, most of the time she never kissed men: she devoured them. Or, to borrow a phrase from *Othello*, she plucked up kisses by the root. Even in a straightforward embrace she usually managed to assume the dominant position, often by the crafty expedient of tilting her head back at an angle of forty-five degrees to her body. And nothing in *Grand Hotel* is more watchable than her manoeuvre to achieve a crucial up-screen position during her frenzied kissing-bouts on a quilted divan with John Barrymore. Within the same film—sometimes even within the same shot—Garbo was capable of embodying both the masculine and feminine principle; and in that simple fact lies much of her fascination.

Amongst male performers I can think of no one who makes more positive and creative use of his femininity than Laurence Olivier. I remember once hearing Peter Hall asked what he thought Olivier's great quality was, the one that made him such an astonishing actor to watch. And he replied, 'His sheer sexiness'. But the charm of this sexiness is that it is equivocal, shifting, sometimes a bit camp. Long ago when he played Richard III, Tynan noted 'the deep concern as of a bustling spinster with which Olivier grips his brother George and says with sardonic effeminate intentness, "We are not safe, Clarence; we are *not* safe", while even as he speaks the plot is laid which will kill the man'. And thinking through a long line of Olivier performances one always remembers their AC/DC elements. His Malvolio, for instance, was a social upstart with tell-tale vowel sounds, a nerve-racking uncertainty as to how to pronounce certain words and a dandy-mincing refinement. His Macbeth was flecked with a delicate feline irony and was even on occasions audaciously funny: his treatment of the two murderers, for instance, was supercilious and feminine so that when they assured him they were but men, he replied, 'Aye, in the *catalogue* ye go for men', as though he personally was of a very different opinion. Two years later his Archie Rice was, of course, shamelessly, rightly, necessarily camp with his wicked eyes flashing from underneath those thick-lined eyebrows as he teased audiences with the prospect of his queerness: 'You think I'm like that, don't you? You think I am. Well I'm not. But *he* is' (pointing vigorously to the conductor). In *Coriolanus* one recalls his shy girlish embarrassment at the public acclaim he received for his military valour, the rolling of those great calf-like eyes as he heard his nothings monstered. And one might argue that even that famous first entrance in *Othello* with the rose held gently between thumb and forefinger and the hips rolling slightly was the sexiest thing since Dorothy Dandridge in *Carmen Jones*. Olivier is a great actor partly because he shows us so much of himself in all his performances, partly because he is unafraid to reveal those elements in his personality that most of us are trained to keep hidden. Men are taught from childhood to be ashamed of their femininity: Olivier exploits his brilliantly and therefore enables all of us to come to terms with a part of ourselves.

Olivier's technique is an impressionist one: he will bring out the feminine element in a character through the heightening of a key phrase or gesture. But there are other ways in which the actor can translate the battle of the sexes into personal terms. One of the most effective is to establish a total contrast between appearance and manner: the rugged appearance with the giveaway effeminacy or the effeminate appearance camouflaging the rugged reality. The latter is harder; and in recent years was exemplified most brilliantly by Donald Sinden in Dion Boucicault's *London Assurance*. In this rambling but genial nineteenth-century comedy he played Sir William Harcourt Courtly,

a superannuated narcissist with a son in his early twenties
and with vain hopes of taking to himself a young bride.
Sinden came on looking like some ruined Regency Apollo
Belvedere. The hair was a mass of jet-black curls with
strands coiling down on either side of his head giving him
a vaguely satanic look; two splashes of rouge whimsically
decorated either cheek; the waist was tightly wasped; and
the trim, shapely legs looked as if they belonged as much
to a Brighton belle as to a Regency beau. Everything about
the appearance, in fact, suggested a radiant femininity:
the removal of his hat was the equivalent of a lobotomy
operation, the titfer being corkscrewed off the head with
an infinite patience and care; any reflection on his looks
('Whose head grew your hair?' someone cruelly remarked)
was greeted by him with an aghast, withering stare; and the
brocaded silk dressing-gown in which he first appeared
was of a kind that made Noël Coward in *Private Lives*
look positively under-dressed. But what made the performance memorable was that while, on the outside, Sinden
looked like some florid Greek god or berouged and
bedizened male tart, yet the personality underneath was
indisputably masculine. At the first sight of the equestrian
Lady Gay Spanker ('A rural Venus'), he twitched with
lechery; and when kneeling importunately at her side, he
was still capable of clambering on top of her with a single
gazelle-like leap. English actors always tend to assume that
the long line of fops in seventeenth- and eighteenth-
century drama—the Foppingtons, Flutters and Oglebys—
are necessarily effeminate because they pay enormous
attention to their toilette and because they are preoccupied
with style and manner. But Sinden's achievement—both
in *London Assurance* and in Vanbrugh's *The Relapse*—was
to show that a concern with bravery of apparel and verbal
elegance is not automatically a sign of queerness.

The fascinating thing about Sinden's technique (highly decorated exterior concealing a rugged interior) is that it is the official public explanation for the tumultuous success of a very different performer: Danny La Rue. Mr La Rue, so the edict runs, always manages, however dazzlingly begowned, to remind us that underneath all the expensive trimmings lies a good old-fashioned male with good old-fashioned masculine impulses. And indeed his act is full of hidden persuaders carefully inserted to remind us that he's really a fella. 'Wotcher mates' is his standard opening line delivered in a gruff, unequivocal baritone. And in his phenomenally popular show at the Palace there were gags specially emphasising his possession of all the usual appurtenances. In one sketch he played a beauty queen being asked her measurements. The answer was, '40, 26 and I couldn't half make you jump'. And he played heavily on the audience's worries about how he managed to contain his penis within his array of tight-fitting costumes. 'I just whistle and it goes away on its own', he cheerfully remarked.

Yet, having said all this, I think one has only scratched the surface of his extraordinary appeal; and extraordinary it is because he has managed to take a form of entertainment that until recently was associated with covert homosexual minorities and that flourished chiefly in gay bars and turn it into something that brings the coach party trade rolling down the motorways. My own theory is that La Rue's act is a perfect example of the alienation technique at work. 'Look, I am a man,' he says in effect, 'but now I am going to dress up as a woman and show you that man can be twice as much a woman as the real thing.' At the same time he is constantly on his guard against over-identification and is jolting us into recognition of the fact that it's only a chap doing an act. It is fascinating that he scarcely ever allows himself to be touched on stage which again prevents us ever taking him too seriously as a real woman. But, ultimately, his act also has a lot to do with the shock that comes from hearing a string of *double-entendres* emerging from the mouth of an attractive, expensive female: socially we would be shocked by such a phenomenon but on stage it generates a certain frisson. There is a parallel, I think, in the fact that Max Miller, the most risqué of comics, was always immaculately attired in white hat and highly decorated suits as if to counterpoint the essential vulgarity of his material: if a really dirty, seedy old man came on and unleashed a string of filthy gags, I suspect we should not be amused. But finally I suppose what La Rue is offering is a vague, harmless sexual fantasy in which everyone in the audience can consciously partake. Women can aspire to achieve this kind of slender shimmering elegance: men dimly would like to possess a girl who looked like that. When La Rue comes on stage, he helps us to fulfil our dreams; and that is as much as one can ever ask of an entertainer.

Mr La Rue is, of course, a somewhat specialised form of comedian; but what is significant is the extent to which even the trousered comic relies on sex—and particularly the revelation of feminine attributes. In a sense all comedy can be said to be an attack on human pretension—and on the roles we adopt in public; and there is no role we play more strenuously than that of the manly male or the ultra-feminine female. Society teaches us to disguise the ambiguities and contradictions within our personality: comedy exposes them to us. Instances abound. One has only to think of the balletic grace and manual delicacy with which Chaplin, say, fends off a policeman about to arrest him in *Modern Times*: no Victorian maiden defending her impregnable virginity against a stage-villain could exercise more grace and it is true to say that at times, Chaplin looks even more feminine than his delectable co-star, Paulette Goddard. The

H

quality that shone through the work of Sid Field was, as Kenneth Tynan once noted, 'a certain girlishness that seeps through the silly male bulk of the man, a certain feminine intensity on the emphatic words'. He illustrates this with a moment from the famous golfing sketch when the instructor would tell him to make the tee with sand. 'Mr Field, mistaking him, would make a slightly hurt, recoiling movement and then venture defensively: "I'm not drinking that *sterf*": his voice climbing to a pained shrillness and then, after a moment's consideration, "More like *co-coa*".' Again, Frankie Howerd is a comic who adopts the buttonholing manner of some ageing gossip full of secrets forever to be indiscreetly imparted. I love particularly those moments when he leans into the camera as if about to embrace it and spills some ludicrously improbable beans, glancing nervously to left and right in case anyone might be listening: I remember for instance seeing him enliven some stuffed-shirt, TV Awards-dinner audience with the news that a suitable partner had at last been found for Edward Heath. Risking *lèse-majesté*, he lunged towards the camera and hissed, with sibilant intensity, '*Dorothy Squires*'. Without extending the list indefinitely, one can also say that those two great masters of American comedy, Bob Hope and Jack Benny, rely heavily on a display of unguarded femininity. Hope likes to pose as an elegant and accomplished lady-killer, tugging dandyishly at the back of his suit before setting off for a romantic assignation or gratuitously smoothing down the remnants of his slicked-down hair. But he will leap into a girl's arms at the first suspicion of a mouse or set those teeth rattling like beads at the faintest whiff of danger. Again with Benny one finds a serene, calm, blandly ageing figure whose cool masculine omniscience is belied only by his limply flapping wrist and by the worries about his toupee.

But if solo comedians trade heavily on sexual ambiguity and shamelessly reveal to us the impulses we keep hidden, then double acts have an even stronger sexual quality. I once heard a Hollywood script-writer say that in the 1940s studios were always thinking in terms of teams and were always looking for what they called 'he-she chemistry'. But where, he asked, is the he-she chemistry in Laurel and Hardy? A naïve, imperceptive question, I felt, since Laurel and Hardy (like Abbott and Costello, Morecambe and Wise, Jewel and Warriss and any other comedy team you care to mention) depended heavily on a male-female relationship: the imposer and the imposed upon, the bully and the victim, the doer and the person unto whom it is done. Obviously the relationship is capable of infinite variations: the gentler spirit may end up winning all the battles. Yet the he-she principle always underlies the routines. Think but of Laurel and Hardy, with Ollie grand, bulky and formidable yet with ludicrous pretensions to elegant lady-killing: Stan meanwhile wiry, crushed, miniscule and devoid of *amour-propre*. There is a sequence in one of their old two-reelers in which a rapacious female in smooth satin is trying to wrest from Stan a pile of dollar-bills secreted about his person. It is an incredibly erotic scene as a matter of fact; but only because, even rolling around on a bed with an attractive girl, Stan still seems submissive and totally dominated. And even in a film like *The Music Box* where they are jointly trying to get a piano up a perilously steep flight of steps it is Stan who manages to reserve a shred or two of feminine dignity while it is Ollie who sees his stage-managing masculine pretensions dashed to the ground—though, in the cause of truth, it is only fair to point out that when a giggling nurse forces them to retreat with the piano to the foot of the steps, so that she can get past with her pram, it is

Stan and not Ollie who gives her a resounding boot up the butt.

I have tried to show so far that there is a strong degree of bisexuality in all great acting and that a good deal of comedy is dependent on the exposure of man's feminine frailties. But of course actors have in recent years been asked to do rather more than reveal their complex sexual natures: they have also been asked to strip. In what is loosely termed 'fringe' theatre it is quite common these days to see people capering naked about the stage; a show like *Pajama Tops* exploits nudity for tired businessmen, of which these days, such are the pressures of London commercial life, there seems to be an inexhaustible supply; and both *The Dirtiest Show in Town* and *Oh Calcutta* are devoted more or less entirely to sex, though one should add that the latter contains a good deal less nudity than many people seem to think. In theory, I have nothing against this concentration on sex. An actor's body is a vital part of his equipment; and it seems to me no more sinful to delight in physical beauty than it is to delight in vocal beauty. Likewise there are plenty of occasions when stripping makes good dramatic sense. There is something patently absurd about the spectacle of two people clambering into bed on stage with the man impregnably fortified in trousers and the woman chastely clutching her Freudian slip—rather like those '40s British movies in which one foot had to be kept securely anchored to the floor.

My only doubts about stage nudity spring from the fact that it is widely assumed to be synonymous with eroticism; and that it can lead to serious exploitation of individual performers. The fact is, of course, that genuine eroticism on stage is a very mysterious force often springing from some strange tension between the overwhelming physical urges of the character and their limited means of fulfilment.

One of the most intensely erotic performances I have ever seen was by the Spanish actress, Nuria Espert, in Victor Garcia's stunning production of *Yerma* which came to the World Theatre Season in 1972. She never appeared naked; though admittedly at one point she bared her voluminous and attractive breasts. The reason it was so erotic was, I suspect, that Yerma herself was filled with an overpowering desire to bear children and that she found herself in a society where fertility is equated with moral virtue; on the other hand her husband's refusal to give her children consigned her to a life of barrenness. Out of the tension between her desire and its fulfilment, Señorita Espert—with her dark, flashing eyes, sturdy peasant legs and seductive frame—wove a performance full of brooding sexual power. She was helped of course by Garcia's stunning set: a malleable trampoline that took on whatever shape was necessary and that gave to even the most earthbound of actors a marvellous spring-heeled quality. But at the opposite end of the erotic spectrum is the kind of show where the cast strip to the buff and then give every impression of being visibly unexcited by each other's physical presence: you can fake almost anything in acting but you can't fake an erection. And that simple biological fact deprives a lot of stage nudity of its power.

As for the exploitation of the performer, this of course is something that is carefully guarded against by Equity. Indeed they have drawn up a necessary and fascinating agreement with management representatives. Its provisions include:

'No performer may be required to disrobe in whole or in part until after he or she has been auditioned as an actor, singer or dancer, etc.

'No sex acts shall be required of any performer at any audition.

'Nudity or semi-nudity at auditions may be permitted only if:

(*a*) an official Equity observer or an observer agreeable to Equity is present.

(*b*) the direct professional and artistic interest of all persons present has been agreed between Equity and the Management.

'Managers auditioning for plays involving nudity or simulated sex acts must make it clear in their preliminary advertisements the nature of the production for which they are casting.'

Sensible enough rules; but not insuperable. As a rather cynical British film, *Nobody Ordered Love*, suggested recently, all that a producer or director need do when auditioning a girl who has to appear naked is call in a secretary to give the proceedings a spurious respectability. And I have direct knowledge of one scandalous case where an actress accepted a West End part only on condition that she did not have to strip, as her predecessor in the role had done: if she was required to do so, then she was not interested. Okay, said the management, we'll respect your wishes. But as the opening date grew near, the pressure was put on her by the management concerned, the director, the author, to strip in this allegedly vital scene: she was bullied, cajoled and browbeaten. But, loyally, she stuck to her guns and she spent almost a year in the play without ever removing her clothes. Virtue, I suppose, could be said to have triumphed; but not before being given a pretty severe going-over.

When one turns from the finished product to the drives that make up an actor's personality, then I think one is again brought up against the sexual element. Obviously there are many reasons why people turn to acting in the first place: fame, money, a genuine love of drama and literature, a desire to channel their own emotional turbulence into a succession of roles, a feeling that by becoming other people they may more honestly fulfil themselves. But underneath all this there has to be a fundamental delight in self-display, an urge to parade oneself before a public akin to the urge of the sexual exhibitionist. In *The Playmakers*, an acute analysis of the workings of Broadway theatre by Stuart W. Little and Arthur Cantor, a Manhattan psychiatrist, Dr Daniel Casriel, says quite clearly that the actor's desire for public approval transcends the normal desire for public acceptance: 'Actors don't trust the approval they get from one significant person. Going before an audience becomes in effect an addiction. It doesn't solve their neurosis: it feeds it. Each time they go before an audience it is like throwing another log on the fire of their anxiety. It fuels their anxiety: it doesn't cure it. Success never makes most actors secure.'

Going before an audience also becomes an equivalent to the sexual act. One actress I know in one of the twin national ensembles told me that after a performance she usually feels much as she does after she has, in fact, made love: exhausted, satisfied and complete. She also observed that she usually finds it difficult to make love after a performance: her sexual appetite is much sharper on the days when she does not have to perform. An actor, in a sense, makes love to his audience: he woos them, courts them, teases them, plays with them, entices them, rejects them and finally has them. It is something you find in all acting, but the process itself is most visible with solo performers: singers and comedians who stand in front of a curtain and respond directly to an audience. A Ken Dodd performance is, as I have said, like a great fertility rite and it usually ends with an orgasmic explosion of joy in which the most absurd props are wheeled on stage and the man himself whirls about the field singing sawn-off snatches of dirty lyrics before ending it all with a rendering of 'Happiness, Happiness, the greatest gift that I possess'. Sending an audience away happy is exactly akin to sending a lover away satisfied.

What of the audience's part in the equation? They too, I believe, get a sexual excitement out of play- and movie-going that is not often admitted. Because the performance is live, the theatre particularly has a strong element of voyeurism about it. We go to the theatre to see other people baring their breasts morally, spiritually and (nowadays) even physically. Exactly like voyeurs, we sit in darkness watching other people living out their lives apparently totally oblivious to our unseen presence. And we cannot, unless we are made of stone, remain for long indifferent to the physical appeal of men and women alike. In judging a new Hamlet, for instance, we are partly making an assessment of the actor's physical suitability for the role and of his physical impact upon us. I think it is also significant that throughout the long history of the theatre the element of impersonation of members of the opposite sex has been enormously popular, long after the period when it was a necessity imposed by the absence of girl players. The theatre, I believe, is a place where inhibitions can be released by both the performer and the spectator. It is a place where we can all admit that our natures are a compound of masculine and feminine and where we can watch other people's sexual behaviour in the comfort and sanctity of a darkened auditorium. The theatre is rooted in sex; and sex has certainly taken pretty firm root in the theatre.

Finally, one comes to the question of what part sex plays in the structure and organisation of the theatre. I think it would be foolish to deny that there is, if not a greater promiscuity, at least a greater tolerance and freedom in the acting profession than in most others. I have never heard anyone condemned for his sexual irregularities in the theatre, even when these might be regarded as socially undesirable. There is a well-known theatre story, for instance, about a Shakespearean actor playing in New York and getting arrested for soliciting small boys. The case hit the headlines in all the New York papers (this was in the days when there were several of them). And the next night, while the actor was making up, the leading man popped his head round the door of the dressing-room and observed, 'Loved your notices'.

But is there any connection between sexual gratification and professional advancement in the theatre? Is the casting couch—of either the homo- or heterosexual variety—entirely a discarded instrument? I must admit I have never heard of any actor who achieved fame solely because of a capacity to grant sexual favours; on the other hand I have heard plenty of stories to suggest it can oil a few wheels. Managers often expect girls playing small parts in their productions to oblige them sexually. Directors, the bulk of whom at any one time seem to be homosexual, have an often-observed capacity to select one boy in a company to be either whipping-boy or teacher's pet—and sometimes both. And I know of one specific instance where the two male stars of a show actually got a girl the sack because she refused to sleep with them on tour. Indeed if there is any exploitation of sex, it probably takes place outside London rather than in it. There was the famous old story of the actor who was asked if he thought Hamlet slept with Ophelia. His reply was: 'Only on the tour, laddie'. And what more natural than that a company, free from the domestic restraints of London, should form temporary alliances while on tour? It is exactly the same in other fields. A girl television reporter said recently that she had never been on an assignment out of London without being propositioned by some member of the crew. And I have no doubt that if the staff of my bank went on a twelve-week tour of the provinces, there would be plenty of sexual attachments formed in the course of it.

My feeling then about the connection between sex and acting is that it explains a large part of the mesmeric effect that great actors have upon us; that it is at the root of all comedy; that the sexual nature of acting allows the audience to indulge in wish-fufilment and healthy fantasy; and that the acting profession is probably more conscious of sexual freedom than the rest of us because of the rather special position it occupies in our society. Sex and acting are, in fact, both here to stay—and so is the umbilical connection between them.

11

ACTRESSES' LIB

'In London no young actress can be brought to the footlights
unless she is pretty. The public does not want to see plain
actresses, however great may be their talent.'

(*Max Beerbohm*)

As I have tried to make clear throughout this book,
acting is not something that can be discussed in isolation
either from the structure of the entertainment industry or
the society surrounding it. In Britain today it may be
influenced by any number of things: the anti-heroic
tendencies within society itself; the constant journalistic
pressure on artists to explain their work in public; the
muddle and chaos that prevails within the acting profession; the post-war rise of the young graduate director.
If Laurence Olivier had played Shylock in his New Theatre
seasons at the end of the war, his interpretation would
obviously have been different from that offered in Jonathan
Miller's production at the National Theatre in 1970:
following hard on pogroms and persecutions it would
inevitably have shown Shylock in a mellower, more
sympathetic light. Likewise I cannot imagine that any
previous age can have boasted a Coriolanus quite so
deliberately and calculatedly unheroic as Ian Hogg's in the
Royal Shakespeare Company's 1972 Stratford production;
but this again reflected a period of deepening cynicism about
military exploits and about the dependence of nation-states

on 'great men'. In a sense, we get the performances we deserve. If we live in a society suspicious (with good reason) of the dictatorial political leader, then we must not expect to find an abundance of actors who believe in the primacy or the virtue of the individual will. One does not have to accept the absurdities of a Dr Timothy Leary (who writes in *The Politics of Ecstasy* of 'pitiful Shakespeare' with all those 'grim, suffering, ham-actor heroes') to realise that in a world like ours heroic acting is inevitably going to be in short supply.

If one believes there is a direct connection between the acting profession and the world at large, then it becomes relatively easy to see why actresses have traditionally enjoyed a subordinate role in drama. Any society that treats women as under-privileged citizens is inevitably going to produce plays—and now films—that reflect this fact; and this in turn is going to mean that actresses have limited opportunities. But how, one might ask, does this account for the fact that over the last century a number of dramatists have written nourishing and substantial roles for women? Mother Courage, Yerma, Hedda Gabler, Saint Joan for instance. The answer is that most of the great female roles since the 1870s have been written by radical political figures who firmly rejected bourgeois society and the conventions attached to it and, more often than not, in periods when the subject of women's rights was under active discussion.

The traditional male chauvinist dramatist will, of course, incorporate women into his plays but he will invariably show them as totally sympathetic and/or highly decorative. Beerbohm's saw that the public does not want to see plain actresses is only half-true: the fact is dramatists do not usually write parts for plain girls. It takes a true radical, like Brecht, to create a devastatingly, rigorously unsentimental heroine such as Mother Courage who makes a profit out of death and who battens on war like some vicious carrion-crow hovering about a rotting corpse. Of course, the anti-Brechtians argue that Brecht never really followed his conception through and that in practice we come to sympathise with this woman doggedly hauling her cart round the battlefields of Europe. But I suspect this is largely the result of coming into contact with the play's rare English productions when great stress is laid on the heroine's stamina and pluck: a performance like Helene Weigel's allowed no room for false sentiment.

Like Brecht, Lorca is also a writer whose rejection of bourgeois society enabled him to write generous and expansive parts for women. In his great trio of folk-dramas (*Blood Wedding, Yerma, The House of Bernada Alba*) Lorca deals constantly with the sexual freedom of the individual and specifically with the socio-sexual subordination of women in Spanish society. In *Yerma* for instance (as Ian Gibson pointed out in a *Guardian* article) he 'explores the misery of a childless and desperately frustrated wife in a society which prohibits divorce, exalts motherhood and castigates female infidelity'. In other words, he launches a full-scale attack on the Spanish bourgeois ethic—sufficient to guarantee a violent reaction from the Right-Wing press when the play was first staged in 1934; and in so doing he creates one of the greatest acting roles for a woman over the last fifty years. Ibsen and Shaw lend substance to the idea that it is usually dramatists prepared to challenge the assumptions of bourgeois society who write best for women. Ibsen wrote in his notes for *A Doll's House* in 1878: 'A woman cannot be herself in today's society, which is an exclusively male society, with laws written by men and with prosecutor and judge who judge women's conduct from a male point of view'. It was Ibsen who sent a shiver down the spine of the Scandinavian Society in Rome by suggesting a year later that women be admitted as full members; and it was Ibsen whose passion for women's rights was so extreme that he delivered a scathing denunciation at the Society's gala night of those renegade females who had actively sought to defeat his proposal. Only a dramatist who believed women enjoyed precisely the same rights as men could, it seems to me, have created a Nora, a Hedda, a Mrs Alving. Shaw also travelled much of the same ground as Ibsen in actively campaigning for women's rights; and, rather like Ibsen, he met shocked opposition when suggesting, as a vestryman in the St Pancras borough, that public lavatories should be provided for women and that women should sit on the committee concerned. He was totally opposed to the subordinate role women were forced to play in society; and this was the fuel that gave us many of his greatest heroines.

Am I suggesting, then, that only Left-Wing or radical-thinking dramatists are capable of writing great parts for women? Not entirely; for I would argue that homosexual writers too frequently have the capacity to penetrate deeply inside the female sensibility. Partly this is a matter of self-projection in that the homosexual can more easily imagine than the heterosexual the plight of the ageing female whose crows-feet and wrinkles limit her sexual opportunities: partly it is the fact that the homosexual, having no wish to lay every other woman he meets, usually finds it easier to form lasting friendships with females and thereby achieve a greater imaginative understanding of their problems. It would be absurd to be dogmatic about this. Right-Wing heterosexuals may be able sometimes to write about women with dazzling perception and understanding; but in the field of drama I just cannot think of many outstanding examples.

When one comes to the present, it is sad to think how few opportunities have been created for actresses since the alleged theatrical breakthrough of 1956. Indeed one can count on the fingers of two badly maimed hands the number of dramatists who have, over the last sixteen years, explored either the role of women in society or the intricacies of the female temperament. John Osborne has created a gallery of incomparable modern heroes: few notable heroines. Indeed from his early work one might deduce that he had a touch of the male chauvinist about him; and it is not insignificant that in a marvellously impassioned review of a collection of Tennessee Williams's plays for the *Observer* (January 20, 1957) he exulted in the defilement of the dramatist's heroines, most especially Baby Doll and Blanche Dubois.

'Make no mistake about it—this Baby Doll kid is a killer. She would eat a couple of guys and spit them out before breakfast. When Archie Lee says, "You'll get your birthday present all right," every male from Houston to Boston must want to throw his hat in the air and cheer. "You and me have had this date right from the beginning", says Stanley. The female must come toppling down to where she should be—on her back. The American male must get his revenge sometime.'

Over the years Osborne's portraits of women have admittedly deepened and improved; but even the heroine of *Time Present* frequently talks like a chip off the old Osborne. Arnold Wesker has perhaps ventured further into the female interior. In fact in *Roots* he did something rare and remarkable: created an entirely believable female character and yet one who was confronted with a recognis-able, even universal, dilemma. Beatie Bryant was, on one level, a tough Norfolk girl still heavily under the influence of her London boy friend; on another she was a symbol of all the half-educated everywhere struggling to find their own voice. No one else in Britain in the last sixteen years has come up with a female role half as good as this, though there have been some significant gestures towards our neglected actresses. Robert Bolt in *Vivat! Vivat Regina!* may not vastly have increased our historical understanding of either Mary, Queen of Scots or Elizabeth I but he did at least provide two well-contrasted roles that should keep actresses in a variety of countries happy for the next decade. Again, David Hare's *Slag*, though in the last resort somewhat anti-feminist, is at least set in a girls' school and explores very wittily the way women behave when removed from male society.

But I know of only one dramatist in recent years who has consistently built his plays around women; and that is Frank Marcus. His speciality is the comedy with the tragic ending; and he claims that he finds it easier to write a comedy about women since the form requires that the author distance himself from the characters. That may be one reason. But I suspect that for Mr Marcus, a very sharp observer of the contemporary social scene, the study of women also gives him access to relatively uncharted waters. In *The Formation Dancers* the pivotal character is a vivacious young poetess and through her Marcus explores very wittily a segment of society many of us know intimately: the literary-critical fraternity where every experience must be evaluated, weighed and rolled-round-the-tongue even if it be something as mundane as the worth of a plate of sandwiches. In *The Killing of Sister George*, although lesbianism is ostensibly the subject, he is also dealing with that slightly clannish, all-girls-together atmosphere that surrounds Broadcasting House. In *Mrs Mouse Are You Within?* he takes us into West London bed-sit land where people gather for bonfires in the square, where men come to visit their girl friends every Tuesday and Friday, where girls have problems with their roving, sleep-around sisters. And even though I do not care vastly for his latest play, *Notes on a Love Affair*, he again creates an instantly recognisable character (expertly realised by Julia Foster) in the drab little dental hygienist who ultimately turns out to have far more intelligence and character than the people who try to manipulate her.

Marcus, however, is an exception. If, in the British theatre, an actress wishes to establish any sort of reputation for herself, she must inevitably turn to the classics. But even here it is interesting to note that opportunities are severely rationed and that, having established one's promise with a Juliet or a Rosalind, an actress may have to wait some time to consolidate her early achievement. Most likely she will turn to the movies. One would, for instance, expect the Royal Shakespeare Company and the National Theatre to be places where actresses can quietly mature and develop. But are they? At the time of writing the Royal Shakespeare Company is immersed in its season devoted to the Roman plays at Stratford-upon-Avon. And in a company of fifty-one there are but seven actresses: not, of course, due to any male chauvinism on the part of the directorate but simply because the cycle demands no more. But at the National Theatre things are not appreciably better: out of a company of thirty-eight in May 1972 only eight are actresses. Again this is a recognition of simple fact: out of the three plays in the repertoire at that time, *Richard II* is about as exclusively masculine as the Athenaeum, Tom Stoppard's *Jumpers* contains only one good female role and only Sheridan's *The School for Scandal* (dating from 1777) makes any great demands upon actresses' talents. Of course, statistical accusations are unfair: situations change. And over the years the RSC has brought on a number of striking female talents—most recently, Helen Mirren,

Frances de la Tour, Sara Kestelman and Heather Canning. But the fact is that even in our civilised twin ensembles actresses have to be even more desperately competitive for the few pickings available than do their male counterparts.

Actresses have, on the whole, a desperately hard time of it in the British theatre. Along and around Shaftesbury Avenue their role is all too often a purely decorative one: stripping to bra and panties for a bed-hopping farce, showing off costume in a period revival, indulging in mild adultery to fuel some evanescent comedy. And even in the classical ensembles they have to cultivate a serene, optimistic patience if they want to get anywhere. Significantly the one area where they have made any significant breakthrough is in Fringe theatre. Obviously it is a crucial tenet of the Alternative Society and the Underground in all its manifestations that women should play as important a role as men; and in the Fringe theatre you can see this working in practice. The most highly praised performance by a British actress in 1971-2 was not to be found in any major theatre but in the back room of a remote Islington pub called the King's Head. Here a totally unknown actress named Doreen Mantle gave a staggering performance in William Trevor's *Going Home* as a middle-aged woman recalling the one moment of true affection she had known in her grey and sombre life. Another remarkable performance turned up at the Bush Theatre in a pub on Shepherd's Bush Green where an actress called Annette André played the abducted heroine of John Fowles's *The Collector*, very skilfully combining a wanton intellectual snobbishness with a breath-taking beauty: she made clear that the central point of the play is that it is really the girl who has the man enchained and imprisoned. One could multiply instances; but the point is that if women want to get a fair crack of the whip these days they usually have to go on or beyond the Fringe to find it. Though admittedly with the number of plays about cruelty to be found in Fringe theatre a fair crack of the whip is often precisely what they will get.

If women play a subordinate role in drama, it is all too often because they play a subordinate role in life: indeed, despite the fruitful agitation of Women's Lib, it is still as much of a disadvantage in Britain to be a woman as it is to be black. But there is another reason why actresses get a raw deal and that is because so few women write plays. To me this is something of a mystery. It is hard, for instance, to imagine the English novel without Jane Austen, George Eliot, the Brontës, Mrs Gaskell; or, in modern terms, without Margaret Drabble, Elizabeth Bowen, Iris Murdoch, Edna O'Brien, Elizabeth Jane Howard. But where are their theatrical equivalents? Women's Lib supporters might argue that since the theatre has always been as male-dominated as other forms of entertainment, then it is hardly surprising that women have been actively deterred from writing plays. Yet even this argument does not really hold up since many women have run companies with great success and in the twentieth century have been active as pioneers: one has only to think of personalities as diverse as Lilian Baylis, Joan Littlewood, Helene Weigel, Nuria Espert, Ellen Stewart (founder of La Mama), Caryl Jenner. If women have the combination of energy, pluck and audacity required to establish their own projects, why is it that so few of them actually write plays?

One reason is again tied up with the role women play in society. If we deny women many of the best job opportunities and the most exciting careers, then obviously they are rarely going to find themselves involved in the kind of moral dilemmas and public conflicts that make for exciting drama. There is a limit to the amount of dramatic mileage

you can get out of the agonies of life behind the ironing-
board or the joys of procreation. Plays about politics, the
law, trade unions, the media, advertising are therefore
inevitably going to be plays about masculine worlds with
masculine protagonists; and even when dramatists turn to
the subject of marriage, like E. A. Whitehead in *Alpha Beta*,
they perhaps unconsciously still reflect a world in which
man does and woman is; in which the man goes out and
earns the bacon and the woman stays behind and cooks it.
But on top of the temporary social reasons why women
rarely write plays, I wonder if there may not be something
in the nature of drama that also acts as a deterrent. In a
novel a writer may choose just how much of himself he
chooses to expose: in a play the author exposes himself
totally. This is a paradox because the novelist can always
declare his presence through editorialising comments on the
characters, the narrative, the state of the world in general:
the dramatist only expresses himself through his characters.
Yet just as actors, in the process of impersonating other
human beings, always reveal more of themselves than they
realise, so also dramatists give themselves away completely
through any number of things: choice of period and setting, the social status of the characters, the organisation of
incident, the actual language they use. A novelist like
Fielding may apparently tell you everything going through
his mind in the course of a book like *Tom Jones*; but I would
still argue that by the end of a play by, for instance,
Chekhov, you know much more about the man's real
preoccupations, his hopes and his despairs. I suspect that
women (to judge from the fact that there has hardly been
a successful woman dramatist since the Abbess of Hroswitha
in the tenth century) may prefer the conscious almost
diary-like opportunities for revelation provided by the novel
to the rather brutal self-exposure demanded by the stage.

Not only the theatre is short on rich opportunities for actresses: the cinema too (in Britain, anyway) hardly makes the best use of the talent available. And the point was never better put than by Penelope Gilliatt writing in the *Observer* a decade ago:

'As we know all too well, the British cinema industry is not adept at reflecting the reality of this country. One of the lies is the picture of British women that it gives through its young stars. I defy anyone to hold a candle to us in casting nurses, tremulous sixteen-year-olds or put-upon wives; our films are full of actresses with the moderate Victorian virtues, English beauties with mouths like grapes and a faintly managing air-hostess basis to their lyric frailty. But if one is looking for someone capable of creating a feminine equal of the young heroes who now fill the arts in England, one has to look to life.

'It is typical of the range of actresses used in British films that, to cast the big female part in *Room at the Top* we had to go to France for Simone Signoret; the persistent little dingy role, of course, was easily filled at home. Contrary to the evidence of the society we live in, and with a few treasured exceptions like Billie Whitelaw and Joan Plowright, English film actresses give the impression that their sex as a whole was reared at a Harrods' authors' tea. They could never play Lady Macbeth or Tennessee Williams's Cat; Moll Flanders would be still harder and Fanny Hill out of the question. Of irony, recklessness, humour, tenacity, sensual abundance or moral candour of the exacting sort that many women possess, there is hardly a trace on our screen. Some of what we lack can be summed up in two words: Sophia Loren.'

This was written in September 1961. But much of the charge is still true today. Admittedly there are now a handful of actresses on the screen capable of suggesting a sexy contemporaneity. Ever since Julie Christie came swinging nonchalantly down that damp Northern High Street in *Billy Liar* she has been a symbol of the new woman: cool, unattached and frankly randy. Interestingly she has spent most of her time over the last few years playing not in contemporary situations but in costume (*Far from the Madding Crowd*, *The Go-Between*, *McCabe and Mrs Miller*); and, although she never got the measure of the Hardy heroine, she has proved herself to be an actress of considerable versatility. Amongst her younger rivals I would single out Susan George who has a similar effortless sensuality and inviting self-possession. Unfortunately she seems to have spent rather a lot of her cinematic career getting harassed, assaulted and raped (In *Straw Dogs* she was ravaged on the sofa by a Cornish peasant and in *Fright* pursued round a darkened house by a wild-eyed Ian Bannen), but then this in itself is a commentary on the role of women in contemporary British cinema: once required to maintain stiff upper lips while their husbands went off to war or to pop out and put a cuppa on when the men came home from work, they are now required to spend a lot of their time with vampires' fangs biting deeply into their neck, getting attacked by madmen in the Surrey woods or impersonating waxwork-like figures from British history.

Perhaps the worst thing one can say about the British cinema, though, is that it has completely failed to exploit the remarkable range of female acting talent available in Britain. Penelope Gilliatt mentioned Billie Whitelaw (who has yet to have the leading role in a film) and Joan Plowright. And to that list I would add the names of Eileen Atkins, Jill Bennett, Judi Dench, Geraldine McEwan, Dorothy Tutin,* Gemma Jones, Julia Foster, Irene Worth,

* Since writing this Miss Tutin has starred, brilliantly, in Ken Russell's grossly under-rated *Savage Messiah*.

Diana Rigg, Sian Phillips. In any other country, I suspect, a grateful film industry would have snapped them up; but here they have either had the odd lead role in mediocre films (like that superb comedienne, Miss Rigg, in *The Assassination Bureau*) or they have been consigned to providing valuable but modest support. It is small consolation to think that even the theatre has not used them quite as well as it might.

There are, however, exceptions to these strictures. A small handful of stage-trained British actresses have managed to make the breakthrough into movies with some success: Vanessa Redgrave, Glenda Jackson, Maggie Smith and Janet Suzman. All in their different ways are remarkable. Vanessa Redgrave's chief quality, first manifested in her stage Rosalind, is still a breathless ecstasy and a heady physical rapture, suggestive of the night before rather than the morning after. At her best, she also has that invaluable quality of seeming to exist in several dimensions at once: you could see this in her Isadora which combined a rooted concern with everyday detail with the madness of an inspired visionary. It is a quality inherited, I suspect, from her father who is also at his best in roles, like Uncle Vanya, fuelled by a driving neurosis. Glenda Jackson, however, could hardly be more different. Speaking subjectively, she lacks sensuality and sex appeal: what she has in its stead is a glittering irony and steely masculine drive. She is also completely free from that cursed English vice of genteel and ladylike restraint. In Ken Russell's *The Music Lovers* she triumphantly brought off a scene in which, as Tchaikovsky's wife, she was obliged in the course of a violent quarrel to claw the carpet: along with the noise of arrows being released from their bows in Olivier's *Henry V*, the grating of her finger-nails against the cloth is one of the ineradicable sounds of modern cinema. Even more audacious

was a moment in *Mary, Queen of Scots*, where, displeased
with her lover, Robert Dudley, she delivered a crippling
blow to the solar plexus that would have felled Mohammed
Ali. Here, I felt, was the Lady Macbeth of her generation if
only she had not virtually forsworn stage acting in favour
of the movies. Maggie Smith is a superb welterweight
compared with Miss Jackson's heavyweight. Which does
not mean she is any the lesser an actress: merely different.
Her forte, as her work with the National proved, is a wry
astringency. Comedy acting, she once told me, is not simply
a question of technique but of seeing the world itself in a
slightly distorted and peculiar light, of always being aware
of the absurd other side to any serious or tragic event.
Given the right material, one feels she could be a latter-day
Katharine Hepburn, capable of imparting a sense of challenge and ironic verve to the encounters of the sex war:
significantly much the best scenes in *The Prime of Miss Jean
Brodie* were those where she was fending off the amorous art
master (Robert Stephens) rather than those in which she
was imparting a mild dose of Fascism to her willing pupils.
As for Janet Suzman, what she brings to the screen is a
strong suggestion of intellect. Even in the doughy and
ponderous *Nicholas and Alexandra* she managed to convey
the impression that the Czarina was a woman who had
read a few books and who was the possessor of an implacable
iron will. She also has the kind face—slightly hollow cheekbones, firm chin, strong contours—that always looks good
on the screen. Whether, however, she will receive the range
of scripts worthy of her talent still remains to be seen.

So far I have dwelt chiefly on the problems facing the
younger generation of actresses: the contrast between the
phenomenal quantity of talent and the paucity of roles
worth playing. Fortunately however the first lady of the
British stage (now that Dame Edith Evans and Dame

Sybil Thorndike are in virtual retirement) still finds herself confronted by plenty of challenges. I refer, of course, to Dame Peggy Ashcroft who, like Lord Olivier and Sir Ralph Richardson, found herself entering on one of the richest periods of her career during the 1960s and '70s. The question of age and acting is one worth pursuing for a moment, for in our youth-oriented society the assumption is that anyone over fifty is nothing but an empty shell pretty well ready for the scrap-heap. Yet in the arts there seems no necessary connection between age and qualitative deterioration. Picasso goes on painting with the same god-like fertility into his eighties and nineties; Shaw's late plays, conventionally dismissed, have in recent years been shown to be both eminently actable and intellectually lively; and Stravinsky was no slouch even in his seventies. In acting, however, where there is so much dependence on physical skill, one might expect some evidence of deterioration when performers reach their sixties: not a bit of it. Olivier, Gielgud, Richardson, Ashcroft, Guinness have all done superlative work in the last decade and still continue to dominate the British stage, not least because they act more *often* than their talented younger contemporaries. Sören Kierkegaard once wrote a memorable essay, *Crisis in the Life of a Young Actress*, about the transformation that often takes place in an actress's career between the ages of seventeen and thirty-one. Time, he argued, may take away from an actress her immediate, direct, fortuitous youthfulness but it also cultivates, refines and develops her, giving her command over her essential powers so that the execution may match the concept. And the process, he suggests, is a continuing one throughout her career. 'The youthfulness of the seventeenth year is indeed fragile,' he wrote, 'but perfectibility and potentiation are absolutely dependable.'

I was never fortunate enough to see Dame Peggy when she was seventeen; but I *can* vouch for the fact that since the mid-1950s her art has seemed to grow ever richer. When I saw her first, she was playing, with enormous grace and beauty, the great line of Shakespearean comic heroines: Portia, Rosalind, Imogen. I can recall even now in *As You Like It* her sudden fling of rapture on 'But what talk we of fathers when there is such a man as Orlando?'; her incarnation of goodness and simple faith as Imogen and her wild ecstatic cry of 'Oh for a horse with wings!'; the wit and steel of her Portia far removed from the usual mooing moppet who does not look as if she could impose on a group of superannuated country magistrates, let alone the court of Venice. As W. A. Darlington gallantly enquired in his notice of *As You Like It*: 'When is Dame Peggy going to lose that miraculous gift of youth? Probably never. One can see her, like Ellen Terry, continuing to deny, rather than defy, the years until she is an old lady. Even now she makes nonsense of arithmetic. Who could believe to see her boyish bearing in the part that she had been old enough to play Rosalind twenty odd years ago? Yet there the fact stands in the records.' Even in 1960 Dame Peggy was a spirited Kate in *The Taming of the Shrew* and in 1964 in *The Wars of the Roses* she showed us Margaret of Anjou passing plausibly from youth to middle age to crabbed senility. It was exactly as Kierkegaard said: an actress in her middle years playing the *idea* of feminine youthfulness is far more moving and aesthetically pleasing than a seventeen-year-old presenting the same thing. But one reason for Dame Peggy's success in recent years has been her willingness to align herself with new authors. For the Royal Shakespeare Company she has appeared in works by Duras, Grass, Pinter and Albee. While many of the older generation of actors waited a long time before dipping a reluctant toe in the new movement, Dame Peggy plunged in head first and as a result showed us new facets of her remarkable personality. But, for my money, her performance as the wife of the dying paterfamilias in Albee's *All Over* was one of the most triumphant of all: hard to eradicate the image of this poker-backed, grey-haired, stiff-jointed figure stoically enduring her husband's demise, waspishly and vigorously insulting her loathed daughter and at the end, when asked why she is crying, releasing thirty years of pent-up emotion with a despairing howl of 'BECAUSE . . . I'M . . . UNHAPPY. . . .' English actresses have many great gifts but rarely do they have an Olivier-like ability to send a shiver down one's spine with the utterance of a single phrase. Yet with Dame Peggy one was truly and genuinely thrilled.

If I dwell on the achievements of Dame Peggy, this is not to deny my original thesis: that English actresses are brimful of talent but in most cases are prevented from exercising that talent completely because there are so few parts in modern drama that really stretch and test them. Where are the female equivalents of Jimmy Porter, Archie Rice, Bill Maitland? Where is the play that gives us a girl's-eye-view of growing up in the Britain of the 1940s comparable to Peter Nichols's *Forget-Me-Not-Lane*? Where is the play that does for enclosed female societies what David Storey's *The Changing Room* did for sealed-off masculine environments? The answer, of course, is that until women play as vigorous a part as men in the media, in politics, in law, in business and finance, we cannot really expect to see them playing a particularly vital role in drama. As long as most of the crucial decisions in our society are in men's hands, then they will inevitably be the most fitting heroes for drama; and as long as women are content to sit back on their bottoms and watch men writing plays about their world, then we will have very little notion of what it is like to be a woman in British society in the '70s. Given the existence of pressure groups whose sole purpose is to improve women's status, then there is hope we may see important changes in the role of women over the next decade or so. But until that happens we cannot really expect to find women becoming protagonists of modern drama. Liberate women first and then you will liberate our actresses.

CONCLUSION

I HAVE in the course of this switchback ride through the modern acting profession tried to pick out some of its splendours and miseries: to highlight the wealth of talent we possess in Britain and yet to emphasise how we squander it, to welcome the great heroic performances of the past decade and yet to deplore the flatness of so much film and television acting, to acclaim any serious analysis of the actor's art and yet to deride the false shiny publicity that surrounds the modern mummer.

I hope I neither over- nor underestimate the power of the actor. I do not really accept the argument advanced in William Redfield's brilliant book, *Letters from an Actor* (which covers the Gielgud-Burton *Hamlet* of 1964), that 'without the actor and without assuring the final supremacy of the actor, there is no truly great theatre'. Great theatre (Chichester's *Uncle Vanya*, the National's *Long Day's Journey into Night*, Peter Brook's *Midsummer Night's Dream*, the Czech Theatre Behind The Gate's production of *Three Sisters*) comes when there is a perfect fusion of acting, writing and directorial talent, when there is a seamless blend of all the arts of the theatre. You can have great performances in mediocre productions (Wolfit proved this constantly). You can even have great productions containing mediocre performances. But to talk of the final supremacy of the actor in the theatre seems to me a piece of meaningless rhetoric since an actor with nothing to perform is a sad creature. Indeed in *avant-garde* theatre we have in recent years seen a number of attempts to dispense with the services of the author and to let productions arise through a spontaneous combustion of acting and directorial talent: the results have almost invariably been disastrous.

But having said that the actor is only a part of the creative mechanism of the theatre, I should still be happy to see him having a greater stake than he does at present in the entertainment industry. I welcome the decision of a number of British actors (including Ian McKellen, Robert Eddison, Moira Redmond) to form a company in which the players will enjoy equal status and will select the works to be performed.* I applaud the fact that some directors (like Peter Cheeseman at Stoke-on-Trent) encourage actors to play a part in the decision-making process. And I wholeheartedly support those actors who at Equity Annual General Meetings batter away at the concentration of so much power in the entertainment industry in so few hands and suggest that some element of worker-participation would be a good thing. Actors are born grumblers; but a lot of energy is still wasted in both the theatrical and film business because actors are so rarely consulted about important decisions and because they so often have to turn to the press for information about companies or productions with which they are involved. Tiny advances are being made in this direction: Trevor Nunn, for instance, at the start of his Roman season at Stratford-on-Avon held a company meeting to discuss whether the press should be invited to the productions. Overwhelmingly, the vote was in favour of the critics coming despite managerial doubts; which seems to me a good example of democracy at work.

The actor is not the be-all and end-all of the theatre; at the same time he deserves a say in its operation by virtue

* The Actors' Company which had a resounding success at the 1972 Edinburgh Festival with revivals of Feydeau and Ford.

of his personal commitment and instinctive intelligence.
And intelligence is a word I come back to again and again
in thinking about actors. Actors are often thought of as
stupid, narcissistic creatures; but stupid they are emphatically not. As Jonathan Miller once said to me, he has often
encountered far more idiocy in the academic world than
he has in the theatrical; and indeed people who devote
their lives to the exploration of human character and who
are required to assume a new identity at very short notice
are hardly likely to be dense or dim. Indeed I believe the
better the actor, the greater the intelligence; and the more
this is manifested in his work. Instances abound. Redgrave's
Hamlet at Stratford in 1958 was one of the greatest pieces
of acting I have ever seen (late in the season, not on the
first night) because of the abundance of insights the actor
offered us into the character and because intensity of
feeling was combined with intellectual volatility: this
Hamlet was anxious to probe the nature of everyone around
him until he had found what he wanted. The irony was
that, by the time he committed himself to action, he was
caught in the trap of events. Scofield's crabbed, un-Titanic
Lear was more remarkable than any other I have seen, not
because it was technically more proficient but because it
offered great interpretative originality; because it showed
that, even though the punishment was disproportionate
to the offence, Lear himself was profoundly culpable.
Beyond the Fringe was the funniest entertainment I have
ever seen, not because its performers combined the timing
of Benny with the frenzy of Kaye and the grace of Chaplin
(they didn't) but simply because they applied their intelligence to the world around them and pinpointed its
absurdities.

If this book proves anything, I hope it is that Britain has
at the moment many of the finest actors in the world but

that the muddle and chaos surrounding the acting profession often leads to criminal waste. In his invaluable book,
The Deadly Theatre, Peter Brook asks: 'How does the average
actor spend his days? Of course, it's a wide range: from lying
in bed, drinking, going to the hairdresser, to the agent,
filming, recording, reading, sometimes studying; even,
latterly, toying a bit with politics. But whether his use of
time is frivolous or earnest is beside the point: little that
he does relates to his main preoccupation—not to stand
still as an actor—which means not to stand still as a human
being, which means work aimed at his artistic growth—
and where can such work take place? . . . The tragedy is
that the professional status of actors over the age of thirty
is seldom a true reflection of their talents. There are countless actors who never have the chance to develop their
inborn potential to its proper fruition.'

Of course there is waste in other systems than our own.
Brook recounts the story of an actor he met in Russia who
rehearsed Hamlet for seven years and never played it because
the director died before it was finished. And Michael Redgrave, also after visiting Russia, pointed out that although
there was no theatrical unemployment in their system,
'there are many artists who are allotted only a few roles
throughout their lives, according to their size, shape and
aptitude'. I doubt, in fact, whether the perfect system
exists anywhere. But in Britain we train actors well and
then turn them out into a profession two-thirds of whose
members are at any one time unemployed. If such a situation
existed in the Civil Service, the Law, the manufacturing
industries, the roof would very properly be raised. But
because people seem to expect the arts to conduct themselves like Fred Karno's Army relatively few objections are
aired.

I also have other qualms about the modern actor:

The fact that he is required by economic circumstance, to be a man for all media, a quick-change artist who can turn in a moment from theatre to cinema to television to radio without necessarily having time to cultivate his art in any one of them;

The fact that successful young actors are often promoted too quickly to lead parts before their technique has sufficiently matured;

The fact that, in an age of communications overkill, too much emphasis is placed on the actor as an off-stage entertainer and celebrity rather than as a skilled performer;

The fact that the modern actor is beset by such a bewildering range of stylistic influences that he needs exceptional judgement to sort out the good from the bad;

The fact that the young actor is too often ignorant of tradition and impatient with the past;

The fact that he too often tends to accommodate the great heroic parts to the limitations of his own temperament instead of trying to extend his own personality in order to make it match that of the character he is playing.

Am I then pessimistic about the actor and his future? Not entirely. For one thing, there is something in the English genius that makes this a country that regularly throws up actors of outstanding talent despite the waste and muddle inherent in our system; for another there are signs that a number of key organisations—Equity, the Arts Council, the drama schools themselves—are beginning to realise that the present system is far from ideal and that the best use is not being made of our acting resources. As I stressed at the beginning, this book is in the nature of things an interim report on the state of British acting: perhaps by the time the next survey of this kind comes to be written some of the reorganisation I advocate will have taken place. We have the talent. We have the buildings.

I

All we need now is the will-power to transform the modern British actor from a casual labourer constantly grubbing for work into someone whose energies can be devoted entirely to the furtherance of his art. Is that really too much to ask?

SELECT BIBLIOGRAPHY

JAMES AGATE: *Ego 1-9*. Hamish Hamilton, Gollancz, Harrap, 1932-48.
These Were Actors. Hutchinson, 1943.
The Contemporary Theatre 1944 and 1945. Harrap, 1946.
JAMES AGEE: *Agee on Film*. Peter Owen, 1963.
W. H. AUDEN: *The Dyer's Hand*. Faber and Faber, 1963.
FELIX BARKER: *The Oliviers*. Hamish Hamilton, 1953.
MAX BEERBOHM: *Around Theatres*. Hart-Davis, 1953.
ERIC BENTLEY: *In Search of Theatre*. Dennis Dobson, 1954.
What is Theatre? Methuen, 1969.
The Theory of The Modern Stage. Penguin, 1968.
PETER BROOK: *The Empty Space*. MacGibbon and Kee, 1968.
KEVIN BROWNLOW: *The Parade's Gone By*. Secker & Warburg, 1968.
HAROLD CLURMAN: *The Fervent Years*. Hill and Wang Dramabook, 1957.
Lies Like Truth. Grove Press, 1958.
DENIS DIDEROT and WILLIAM ARCHER: *The Paradox of Acting* and *Masks and Faces*. Hill and Wang, Dramabook, 1957.
MARTIN ESSLIN: *Brecht: A Choice of Evils*. Eyre and Spottiswoode, 1959.
The Peopled Wound. Methuen, 1970.
RICHARD FINDLATER: *Michael Redgrave—Actor*. Heinemann, 1956.
The Player Kings. Weidenfeld and Nicolson, 1971.
WILLIAM GOLDMAN: *The Season*. Harcourt, Brace and World Inc., 1969.

RONALD HAYMAN: *Techniques of Acting*. Methuen, 1969.

LAURENCE KITCHIN: *Mid-Century Drama*. Faber and Faber, 1960.

SHERIDAN MORLEY: *A Talent to Amuse*. Heinemann, 1969.

WILLIAM REDFIELD: *Letters from an Actor*. Cassell, 1967.

BERNARD SHAW: *Our Theatres in the Nineties*. Constable, 1932.

DAVID SHIPMAN: *The Great Movie Stars*. Hamlyn, 1970.

CONSTANTIN STANISLAVSKI: *My Life in Art*. Geoffrey Bles, 1924.

JOHN RUSSELL TAYLOR: *Anger and After*. Methuen, 1962.

J. C. TREWIN: *We'll Hear a Play*. Carroll and Nicholson, 1949.

Dramatists of Today. Staples, 1953.

SIMON TRUSSLER: *The Plays of John Osborne*. Gollancz, 1969.

KENNETH TYNAN: *He That Plays the King*. Longmans, 1950.

Curtains. Longmans, 1961.

Tynan Right and Left. Longmans, 1967.

ALEXANDER WALKER: *Stardom*. Michael Joseph, 1970.

JOHN WILLETT: *The Theatre of Bertolt Brecht*. Methuen, 1959.

MICHAEL BLAKEMORE: *Next Season*. Weidenfeld and Nicolson, 1968.

HAL BURTON (ed.): *Great Acting*. BBC, 1967.

Acting in the Sixties. BBC, 1970.

DOUGLAS HAYES: *A Player's Hide*. Macmillan, 1972.

MICHAEL REDGRAVE: *The Mountebank's Tale*. Heinemann, 1959.

INDEX